DECIPHERING
END-TIME
PROPHETIC
CODES

DECIPHERING
END-TIME
PROPHETIC
CODES

PERRY STONE

CHARISMA
HOUSE

Most CHARISMA HOUSE BOOK GROUP products are available at special quantity discounts for bulk purchase for sales promotions, premiums, fund-raising, and educational needs. For details, write Charisma House Book Group, 600 Rinehart Road, Lake Mary, Florida 32746, or telephone (407) 333-0600.

DECIPHERING END-TIME PROPHETIC CODES by Perry Stone
Published by Charisma House
Charisma Media/Charisma House Book Group
600 Rinehart Road
Lake Mary, Florida 32746
www.charismahouse.com

Unless otherwise noted, all Scripture quotations are taken from the New King James Version®. Copyright © 1982 by Thomas Nelson. Used by permission. All rights reserved.

Scripture quotations marked AMP are from the Amplified Bible. Copyright © 1954, 1958, 1962, 1964, 1965, 1987 by The Lockman Foundation. Used by permission.

Scripture quotations marked KJV are from the King James Version of the Bible.

Italics in Scripture quotations reflect the author's added emphasis.

Cover design by Michael Dutton
Design Director: Justin Evans

Visit the author's website at www.voe.org.

Library of Congress Cataloging-in-Publication Data:
An application to register this book for cataloging has been submitted to the Library of Congress.
International Standard Book Number: 978-1-62998-233-5
E-book ISBN: 978-1-62998-234-2

15 16 17 18 19 — 9 8 7 6 5 4 3 2
Printed in the United States of America

Our weekly *Manna-Fest* telecast is transmitted to millions of viewers through cable networks, satellite, and over the Internet into 249 nations and provinces of the world. One of my greatest joys is to hear from our men and women serving this nation in the military, and discover how our program is making an impact in their lives. I wish therefore to dedicate this book, dealing with America and prophecy, to our troops both at home and abroad. You will always have a friend in me.

With greatest regards,
Perry Stone

CONTENTS

AN IMPORTANT INTRODUCTION: BIBLICAL TYPES, SHADOWS, PATTERNS, AND CYCLES

Then He said to them, "Therefore every scribe instructed concerning the kingdom of heaven is like a householder who brings out of his treasure things new and old."
—MATTHEW 13:52

URING MY FIRST trip to Israel I discovered how spiritually ignorant I was. I grew up in church and attended services three times a week. Adding revivals, conventions, and special events to the list of spiritual enrichment one would think I had a full understanding of the Bible—that is, until 1985. That's when I heard my Jewish tour guides explain the Bible from a Hebraic perspective, adding details I had never heard preached. At the time I was twenty-six, but I had never heard one minister in my denomination speak about the seven festivals of Israel and their prophetic fulfillments. Classified as "New Testament believers" while growing up, we considered the Old Testament as primarily a collection of powerful, ancient stories.

The Bible itself has various layers of wisdom and understanding; this had not been taught in my denomination. "There is the plain simple meaning of Scripture, and when the plain sense of the Scripture makes sense, seek no other sense!" This is the level of casual reading—applying a particular passage to your situation or building faith through the promises of God. This is the main application taught from most pulpits in North America, and

1

Christians learn at this limited level. Regrettably most believers are uninterested in digging deeper into the other spiritual and prophetic applications. This requires time, effort, and understanding Hebraic levels of hermeneutics (methods of interpreting the Scriptures).

For example, there is the level of types and shadows (Col. 2:17). A type is a person, event, or thing designed to represent or picture something else. A shadow is something concealed in the story or narrative that connects the future with past events. A good example is Genesis 22, where Abraham is taking his "only son" with Sarah, Isaac, and offering him on a mountain (in Jerusalem) called Moriah. Abraham's binding of Isaac was a shadow of the coming redemptive process revealed in Christ.

Abraham Offering Isaac as a Sacrifice	God Offering Christ as a Sacrifice for Sin
Abraham was the Father of Isaac.	God was the Father of Christ.
Isaac was the "only son" (Gen. 22:2, 12).	Christ was the only begotten Son (John 3:16).
Isaac was taken to the land of Moriah (Gen. 22:2).	Christ was crucified near Mount Moriah (Mark 15:22).
Two unnamed men are with Isaac (Gen. 22:3)	Two unnamed men are with Christ (Mark 15:27).
Wood was cut to lay Isaac on the altar (Gen. 22:3).	Wood was cut to make the cross (Luke 23:26).
The third day Abraham saw the place (Gen. 22:4).	Christ was raised the third day (Luke 24:46).
Abraham considered this worship (Gen. 22:5).	Christ's death was a spiritual act (Acts 3:26).
The wood was laid on Isaac (Gen. 22:6).	The cross was laid upon Christ (John 19:17).
God would provide a "lamb" (Gen. 22:8).	Christ was the Lamb of God (John 1:29).
Isaac got up from the altar (Gen. 22:13).	Christ rose from the dead (Matt. 20:19).

Many shadows in the Torah reveal details about the future plan of redemption unknown during the Old Testament events. The redemption plan was revealed and understood when the set time of Christ's suffering occurred. These shadows include the rituals during Passover (Exodus 2) and the sacrifice of the red heifer (Numbers 19). Both examples hide numerous and precise details of what would occur during the crucifixion of Christ!

After my initial Israel tour in the late 1980s, many more tours would follow. To the dismay of my more traditional colleagues in ministry, who felt I was slipping off a cliff to plunge into a river of heresy, I began researching and teaching the Hebraic roots of Christianity. I began adding to my prophetic emphasis the prophecies being fulfilled inside Israel, including a unique message: "The Ashes of the Red Heifer." This message taught the future rebuilding of a Jewish temple. Mixing prophetic messages with an emphasis on our Jewish roots packed out churches with curious listeners; however, it also threw the doors open to critics who distanced themselves from me as if I had a contagious plague. They did not understand teaching on biblical types, shadows, patterns, or cycles. To prevent exposing their ignorance on the subject, they found it easier to say, "Perry has gone off the deep end."

Despite the verbal attacks and slander, I continued to dig deeper. I discovered the Bible is a divinely layered book; too often it is read and not *studied.* It is viewed as a storybook—a nice story here, an interesting narrative there. However, the words of the Bible are more than ancient stories; they are divinely inspired writings that can have many practical applications. You will discover that some conceal prophetic codes—events from the past whose details will repeat at some point in the future. To tap into these hidden truths requires knowledge of the Bible in its entirety, historical context and details of parallel events, and an understanding of biblical prophecies. It demands insight to prophecy predicting the signs and circumstances prior to the return of Christ. One of my most amazing discoveries is how God moves world events in a circular motion. These events are repeated sometimes hundreds or thousands of years apart, yet using parallel dates, the same names often mirror the same type of event or place. It is God Himself who said:

Declaring the end from the beginning, and from ancient times things that are not yet done, saying, "My counsel shall stand, and I will do all My pleasure."

—Isaiah 46:10

I have declared the former things from the beginning; they went forth from My mouth, and I caused them to hear it. Suddenly I did them, and they came to pass.

—Isaiah 48:3

That is what this book is about—how the past can repeat in the future and how what has been is what will be. Through divine wisdom we can see what is coming based on what has occurred. It is not a theological thesis on doctrine, but an explanation on how prophetic revelation is continually in motion—not so much in a vertical line as Westerners think, but in a circular motion to repeat over time. This repetitive cycle, when properly understood, can allow us to imagine the future and at times predict outcomes before they occur.

I will share with you some very important and at times sensitive stories. I have purposely chosen not to give the names of some individuals. My desire is to protect their privacy in the same manner you often hear the secular media say, "an inside source," "a source in the administration," or "a source asking not to be identified." We hear this every day on the news. When I do this, please understand these are people I personally know and their stories are true.

There will also be a strong emphasis on America's link with former empires and what the past can reveal about our future—including how past patterns of presidents may reflect a warning for future presidents and leaders. Because we have new friends, partners, and television viewers who have not read or researched some of our past insights, I have placed in this book material that our partners and longtime friends may have heard. Bear with me, as we will use numerous links to tie some previous points together with new insights.

—Perry Stone

Chapter 1

UNLOCKING CYCLICAL PROPHETIC CODES

DID YOU KNOW the following?

» The second governor of the Plymouth Colony was Sir William Bradford. In the book *History of the Plymouth Colony* he said the Hebrew language was the language in which "God, and the angels, spoke to the holy patriarchs of old time."[1] Bradford used the Hebrew language at the beginning of his books, and the Founding Fathers discussed making the Hebrew language the official language of the colonies.[2] The early Ivy League universities often taught Hebrew, and the seal of Yale University has Hebrew words meaning "light and perfection."[3]

» America's founding documents are based on instruction and laws in the Torah, Israel's divine revelation from God. The Constitution, Bill of Rights, and Declaration of Independence all have laws and rights that are based on the Torah, the Psalms and the four Gospels.

» In England the Pilgrims were called "separatists." The earliest Jews from Abraham's time were called *Ibriy*, translated from Hebrew, this means "one from beyond." This word holds the concept of one who separates himself, just as Abraham separated himself from his land and family to journey to Canaan land.

» Both Abraham and the Pilgrims came into a land already occupied by other tribes. Both possessed the land and tried to teach the tribes within their new nation about God and His Word.

» Both nations were formed with thirteen distinct groups: Israel was founded with thirteen tribes, and America was founded with thirteen colonies.

» Both nations were divided between the North and the South: Israel between its northern and southern kingdoms and America's division of the North and the South during the Civil War.

» When the Hebrews took over Jerusalem as their capital, it didn't belong to a single tribe and was the center of the nation for all thirteen tribes. When America's founding fathers began to build Washington DC, it was considered a separate city with all colonies claiming it as their political center and capital.

» The city of Jerusalem was built up when Israel's second king, David, took control of the kingdom while his house in the mountains of Zion was built. While Washington DC was being built, it was America's second president, John Adams, who would be the first US president to live in the White House, home of America's presidents.

» Saul, the first king of Israel, and George Washington, America's first president, were both taller than the average man. Oddly, neither King Saul nor George Washington actually wanted to be the leader.

» The English spelling of *Jerusalem* has the letters *u, s, a* in the middle of the name.

These are unusual and interesting connectors linking American history with ancient Israel. Many years ago I began observing that America and Israel are spiritually linked. What occurred in ancient Israel can be repeated for modern America. In the late 1990s I saw a biblical pattern that I believed had a parallel for America. I began teaching that the years 2007 and 2008 would be the beginning of America experiencing major transition and change. I believed America was entering its climax as a global empire followed by an eventual, steady decline in status, toppling from its prestigious global position. It would break its economic influence and gradually shift economic momentum from the West to the East toward the Asian nations. This belief was based on economic and prophetic cycles, which are repeated sequences that reoccur in history. Certain historic events, as you will learn in this book, are on a rotational loop. Once a repetitive cycle is discerned, major events can be repeated in the circuit of human time, often with such precision that predictions of what is coming can be made in advance.

My prediction of *change and transition* coming to America hinged on many links between the patterns of ancient Israel being repeated in America, beginning with Abraham. I taught the unique parallels of America and Israel. God gave Abraham's descendants four generations, or four hundred years from Abraham's day to entering Egypt to Israel's departure called the Exodus (Gen. 15:13–14). With America mirroring ancient Israel, I noted that America's first colony was established on May 14, 1607, and four hundred years forward takes us to May 14, 2007. May 14 was the same day Israel was reestablished as a nation in 1948.

In retrospect 2007 introduced a major recession with high gas prices, millions of job losses, and the near collapse of the lending and auto industries. In 2007 we saw the beginning of an unsustainable national debt and a nation of people who are in *distress, debt,* and *discontented*—the exact three words found in 1 Samuel 22:2 when Saul became king. After predicting *change* and *transition,* I was amazed at what I saw in the 2007 United States presidential election. Candidate, then senator, Barack Obama's theme was "Change," with a promise to "fundamentally change America."

Recently, with America's stunning and often spiritually frightening *changes* and *transitions* (forced government health care and hundreds of new EPA regulations), we find our freedoms eroding, causing many to question, "How will America end up?" I believe the answer to this question can be found by examining the parallels between our nation, ancient Israel, and Imperial Rome.

America, Ancient Israel, and Imperial Rome

I have researched America's parallels with the spiritual, economic, and political cycles of Israel. I have also explored how America mirrors many economic and political patterns of Imperial Rome.

First, America's political and governmental patterns are now running parallel to the latter years of the Roman Empire—before its economic default and before invading foreign tribes seized control of its territory. However, with Imperial Rome the glorious and invincible empire gradually fell apart as Roman taxes oppressed economic growth, and eventually political Rome fell into the hands of ten pagan tribes. Yet, the Christian church in the West (Rome) and in the East (Byzantium) began dominating the empire as the Christian faith spread like wildfire throughout the civilized world.

Second, in Israel's case, like America, God's covenant people arose from a small tribal clan to a powerful nation of millions, after possessing the Promised Land and expelling the other tribes. In America our spiritual patterns begin with the founding documents of the early colonies. America reflects ancient Israel in its spiritual perception of God and its expansion of a monotheistic faith. *In Israel's history corrupt kings always gave rise for prophetic voices and the revival of faith.* If my cyclical thesis proves correct, the Christian faith will have its greatest opportunity in the near future as people can no longer trust their political leaders and lose confidence in the soft economic security built on sand that cannot endure coming storms. (See Matthew 7:26–27.)

These two templates, Rome and Israel, are so clear and unmistakable, that researching the outcome of their past significant events can actually reveal future events for America, unlike any other nation on earth. Some question the methods I use when examining a cyclical code and arriving at certain conclusions. The answer is simple: history repeats. Solomon understood how the future is concealed in the past when he wrote in Ecclesiastes 1:9–10:

That which has been is what will be, that which is done is what will be done, and there is nothing new under the sun. Is there anything of which it may be said, "See, this is new"? It has already been in ancient times before us.

A simple example of cyclical codes, exposing what has already occurred, being repeated in the future, is the history of Christ from His birth to His ascension. In the birth narrative there was Mary (His mother), Joseph (Mary's husband), and Herod (a Roman procurator), who put a death sentence on a newborn "King of the Jews." (See Matthew 1–2.) Approximately thirty-three years later the three same names appear but are three different people. There is a Mary, called Mary Magdalene; then another Joseph (of Arimathaea), along with a new Roman governor also named Herod, who participated in releasing Christ to the Jewish zealots for crucifixion. (See Matthew 27–28.)

At the beginning of Christ's ministry He fasted for forty days, and after His resurrection He appeared before many alive for forty days (Matt. 4:2; Acts 1:3; 1 Cor. 15:5–6). Christ ascended back to His Father from the Mount of Olives, and when He returns to earth, the first place He will touch down will be the last place He stood: the Mount of Olives (Acts 1:9–11; Zech. 14:4)! The end reflects the beginning.

There are many Old Testament stories with details that hide clues of future events. These events repeat in a different age, time, and often hundreds or thousands of years after the initial story occurred. One of many examples is the Esther code.

Esther—Deliverance for the Jews

The Book of Esther does not contain the name of God but is a book that hides secrets, including Esther's identity. While her Hebrew name was Hadassah (Esther 2:7), her Persian name *Esther*, in Hebrew, contains the three Hebrew letters: *samech, tav,* and *resh,* meaning "to conceal." Thus, Esther concealed her identity from the king because the Jews were in exile and there could be resistance to a Jewish queen, especially from the evil Haman (Esther 2:10).

The Book of Esther begins when the king of Persia, in his third year, hosted an international banquet. Queen Vashti refused to attend. Embarrassed by her rebellion, the king removed her from his inheritance. The king later conducted a "beauty contest" to find a new queen, with the main requirement being that she must be a virgin (Esther 2:1–2). In preparation to enter the contest, Esther was groomed, instructed, and anointed with oils. She won first place and was rewarded the position of queen in the kingdom. Their wedding celebration occurred in the seventh year of the king's reign (Esther 2:16). Notice the king selected Esther, a woman who was not Persian but was foreign to the Persian people. After Esther's ascent to the throne, Haman and his ten sons initiated a secret plot to kill the Jews (Esther 3:13). But the new queen, Esther, intervened by exposing Haman's plan, saving the Jews.

This historic narrative holds numerous prophetic layers, with Esther being a picture of the church and wicked Haman as the future Antichrist. First, Israel was married to God their King—just as Vashti was married to the Persian king. However, Israel became rebellious and stiff-necked, resisting God's commandments. They turned from His spiritual banquet invitation (as in the parable in Matthew 22:1–10). Notice Vashti received and rejected the banquet invitation in the king's third year (Esther 1:3). It was in the third year of Christ's ministry that He encountered the strongest opposition and rejection from His own people. (See Luke 13:7–9.) Because of Israel's sin and unbelief, God said He would divorce Israel (Jer. 3:8; Isa. 50:1).

After Israel's rejection, God the King selected a bride (for His Son), not from His own people but out of the Gentile nations. The Christian church of today is predominately a Gentile organism, thriving in nations throughout the world. (See Romans 11.) Christ's bride, the church, is espoused to Christ as a chaste virgin (2 Cor. 11:2), just as Esther was required to be a virgin bride. In the narrative, Esther's cousin, Mordecai, raised her up and continually instructed her in the kingdom. He was from the tribe of Benjamin, whose tribal name means "son of the right hand." Similarly, Christ is exalted in heaven, and today is seated on the "right hand of God" (Heb. 10:12) and is making intercession for His bride, the church.

At the end of days the Antichrist (a type of Haman) and the ten kings under him (a type of Haman's ten sons) will rise up with a plot to destroy the nation of Israel and the Jews; however, the conspiracy will not succeed. The bride of the King, the saints, will return to earth with Christ, the King of kings, and rescue the Jews from the Antichrist and his ten allies. Esther and the king were married on the seventh year, paralleling the marriage supper of the Lamb, which is celebrated in heaven on the final year—the seventh year—of the tribulation.

In the ancient Persian kingdom there was a group of wise men who understood how to discern the times and seasons (Esther 1:13). In David's day the sons of Issachar were men of understanding and could discern the times and what Israel ought to do (1 Chron. 12:32). Since (spiritual) knowledge and understanding will be increased at the time of the end, the Almighty will release greater understanding of His Word. The wonderful, prophetic layers and parallels will reveal *what has been is what will be* (Eccles. 3:15).

Connecting Israel's Past and Future

The spiritual events and journey of "father" Abraham serve as a pattern to discover the spiritual future of the nation of Israel. Abraham's early journey from Ur to the time of Lot gives us an amazing picture of Israel's passage into Egypt until the time of the Exodus from Egyptian bondage.

Abraham's Journey (Genesis 12)	Israel's Journey (Genesis 42–Exodus 12)
A famine sent Abraham to Egypt (v. 10).	A famine sent Jacob's sons to Egypt (Gen. 42:5).
Pharaoh went after Sarah (v. 15).	Pharaoh went after Israel (Exod. 1:8—16).
The Lord plagued Pharaoh (v. 17).	God plagued Pharaoh (Exod. 5—12).
Pharaoh sent Abraham away (v. 20).	Pharaoh sent Israel away (Exod. 12:31).

Abraham and Lot conceal the future patterns of Israel after the Exodus to the time of the Judges.

Abraham in the Land (Genesis 13)	Israel in the Land (Exodus–Judges)
Abraham departed from Egypt as a rich man (v. 2).	Israel left Egypt with gold and silver (Ps. 105:37).

Abraham in the Land (Genesis 13)	Israel in the Land (Exodus–Judges)
Abraham journeyed back to Canaan (v. 3).	Israel journeyed back to Canaan (Deuteronomy).
Strife begins among the workers (v. 7).	Strife arose among tribes (Num. 32).
Abraham divided the land with Lot (v. 9).	The land was divided among the tribes (Josh. 21).

Genesis 14 explains the wars inside the Promised Land and how Abraham defeated outside enemies, eventually meeting Melchizedek, God's first king and priest. The same process was repeated centuries later with Israel.

Abraham (Genesis 14)	Israel Among the Prophets
Lot was in bondage to four kings (v. 1).	Israel served four kings (Dan. 7–8).
Abraham returned with the goods (v. 16).	Israel returned with the goods (Ezra and Nehemiah).
Abraham went up to Jerusalem (v. 17).	Israel returned to Jerusalem (Ezra and Nehemiah).
Abraham met Melchizedek (v. 18).	Israel will meet Jesus the "Melchizedek" priest (Heb. 7:21).
Abraham's enemies were defeated (v. 17).	Israel will be delivered from their enemies (Zech. 14:1–2).

In Genesis 15:18 Israel was promised the land from the river of Egypt to the Euphrates, and in the millennial reign of Christ this promise will be fulfilled (Ezek. 44–47).

There are main personalities and prophets in the Bible whose lives correlate. This cannot be a coincidence but by divine design. Few would ever compare the links between the lives of Jacob and Moses, especially considering Jacob tricked his brother twice to get his birthright and blessing, had to wrestle with God, and came out of the fight with a limp and a name change (Gen. 27:36; 32:24–25). However, both Jacob and Moses were about forty years old when they went into exile. Notice the many other comparisons:

The Life of Jacob	The Life of Moses
Jacob sinned by lying (Gen. 27).	Moses sinned by murdering an Egyptian (Exod. 2:12).
Jacob fled for his life to Syria (Gen. 28).	Moses fled for his life to the Median Desert (Exod. 2:15).
Jacob journeyed to the East (Gen. 29:1).	Moses traveled east of Egypt (Median is east of Egypt).
Jacob met his wife at a well of water (Gen. 29:10).	Moses met his wife at a well of water (Exod. 2:16).
Jacob worked for his father-in-law (Gen. 29:14–29).	Moses worked for his father-in-law (Exod. 3:1).
Jacob tended sheep and cattle (Gen. 30:36).	Moses tended sheep (Exod. 3:1).
Jacob received an angelic visitation (Gen. 31:11).	Moses received a visitation from an angel (Exod. 3:2).
Jacob returned to the land (Gen. 31:21).	Moses returned to Egypt (Exod. 7).
Jacob took his family back to the land (Gen. 31:17).	Moses led Israel back to their land (Exod. 12–13).
Jacob was called a prince with God (Gen 32:28).	Moses became a prince over Israel (Exod. 2:14, KJV).

As an additional note, Jacob had two wives: Leah and Rachel. Not many realize that Moses had two wives: Zipporah, the daughter of Jethro, the priest of Median (Exod. 2:21) and an Ethiopian wife he married and left in Egypt.

The first forty years while Moses was living in Egypt, he defeated the king of Ethiopia in battle and married the king's daughter named Tharbis. Moses suddenly departed from Egypt at age forty; he left Tharbis behind, believing he would never return to Egypt. Moses thus married Zipporah, the daughter of Jethro in Median.

Forty years later Moses returned to Egypt, leading Israel out. Some suggest Moses may have brought his Egyptian wife Tharbis out of Egypt with him when he departed. This would be the Ethiopian wife that Miriam criticized (Num. 12:1). This "two wife" theory is interesting since Jacob also had two wives.

Moses's life mirrors one of Israel's greatest prophets, Elijah; rabbis consider both men two of Israel's greatest prophets.

» Both fasted for forty days (Exod. 34:28; 1 Kings 19:8).

» Both became depressed and requested to die (Exod. 32:32; 1 Kings 19:4).

» Both dealt with idolatry—Moses dealt with the *gold calf* and Elijah dealt with the *false prophets* on Carmel (Exod. 32; 1 Kings 18).

» Both saw the fire of God fall (Num. 16:35; 1 Kings 18:38).

» Both were threatened with death (Num. 14:10; 1 Kings 19:2).

» Both experienced God's presence in the cleft of a rock (Exod. 33:22; 1 Kings 19:8–9).

» Both left a successor in charge—Moses had *Joshua,* and Elijah had *Elisha* (Num. 27:10–22; 1 Kings 19–21).

» Both have no visible grave—Elijah went up, and Moses's grave was hidden (2 Kings 2; Deut. 34:6).

» Both sought God in a cleft and a cave on Mount Horeb (Exod. 33:21–23; 1 Kings 19:8–11).

» Both heard and saw the manifestations of God on Mount Horeb (Exod. 32; 1 Kings 19).

» Both appeared at the Mount of Transfiguration (Matt. 17:1–3).

» Elijah was translated alive in a chariot of fire in the same area where Moses was buried—in the plains of Pisgah—across from Jericho.

We have looked at how Moses and Elijah parallel. Now observe how Elijah's life is an example of a prophetic rotation or a looped event that repeats in the future. During Elijah's ministry he called *down fire* from heaven during a forty-two month *drought* (1 Kings 18). Elijah was received into heaven alive and will return to earth as one of the two witnesses during the tribulation (Mal. 4:5; Rev. 11:3). When Elijah returns, he will repeat the miracles and experiences he endured previously, serving as God's prophet when two wicked people ruled: Ahab and Jezebel. The second time the two evil ones will be the Antichrist and False Prophet

(Rev. 13:1–11). Below are the details of how Elijah's second appearance will reflect his first appearance.

In the Book of Kings: 1 Kings 17–2 Kings 2	In the Book of Revelation: Chapters 6–13
Forty-two-month judgment on Ahab (1 Kings 17:1)	Forty-two-month judgment on the earth (Rev. 11:2)
Forty-two months of no rain (1 Kings 17:1)	Forty-two months of no rain (Rev. 11:6)
A famine was in the land (1 Kings 18:2).	A famine will be in the land (Rev. 6:5).
Food was being rationed (1 Kings 18:4).	Food will be rationed (Rev. 6:6).
The brook of water dried up (1 Kings 17:7).	The River Euphrates dries up (Rev. 16:12).
Jews were hiding in caves (1 Kings 18:4).	Jews will be hiding in the wilderness (Rev. 12:14).
A faithful remnant exists (1 Kings 19:18).	A faithful remnant exists (Rev. 12:17).
Fire fell from heaven (1 Kings 18:38).	Fire will fall from heaven (Rev. 13:13).
A false religion swept the land (1 Kings 18:19).	A false religion will sweep the earth (Rev. 13:14).
Seven thousand would not bow down (1 Kings 20:15).	Seven thousand will die in Jerusalem (Rev. 11:13).
Elijah was caught up to heaven (2 Kings 2:11).	After dying, he will be caught up (Rev. 11:12).

Even the New Testament clearly demonstrates these patterns, both cyclic and repetitive, when examining the birth of Christ to the future millennial kingdom and the beginnings of Israel to the kingdom of Solomon. Observe how these events reflect off one another:

Israel From Their Birth to the Kingdom	Christ From His Birth to His Kingdom
Born in Canaan land	Born in Canaan land

Israel From Their Birth to the Kingdom	Christ From His Birth to His Kingdom
Suddenly moved to Egypt to save the nation	Suddenly moved to Egypt to save the holy family
Baptized in the Red Sea	Baptized in the Jordan River
Entered the wilderness for forty years of testing	Entered the wilderness for forty days of testing
Returned to Israel in power and miracles	Returned to Israel with power and miracles
Had twelve tribes	Had twelve disciples
Joshua (named Yeshua) died	Jesus (Yeshua) died.
The enemy was left in the land	The enemy was left in the land.
Began to possess the land	Saints began to preach the gospel.
Israel forsook the Lord	The church began to forsake the Lord.
God raised up deliverers.	God raises up reformers.
The nation chose men above God.	The nations look to men and not to God.
King Saul rose up persecuting the righteous.	The Antichrist rises up and persecutes Israel.
Saul stopped the priest's sacrifices.	The Antichrist stops the sacrifices.
King David comes and subdues enemies.	King Jesus comes and defeats Satan and the Antichrist.
Solomon built the temple in Jerusalem.	Jesus will build the temple in Jerusalem.
Solomon established a reign of peace.	Jesus establishes a thousand years of peace.

Scholars have stated for centuries that the Old Testament is the New Testament *concealed,* and the New Testament is the Old Testament *revealed.* It was God who declared:

> Let them bring forth and show us what will happen; let them show
> the former things, what they were, that we may consider them, and
> know the latter end of them; or declare to us things to come.
>
> —ISAIAH 41:22

The narrative on the ruling actions of biblical kings can also reveal future events. One such example is the pattern of King Jeroboam and the Antichrist. Nine comments the Bible makes about Jeroboam's rule are the same nine found in the biblical revelation of the final world dictator, the Antichrist.

Old Testament Reference	Pattern of Jeroboam and the Antichrist	Antichrist Reference
1 Kings 11:37	He rules whatever his soul desires.	Daniel 11:36
1 Kings 12:16	Ten tribes (kings) form an alliance, but three pulled away.	Daniel 7:8, 20, 24
1 Kings 12:20	He is appointed king by the ten other tribes/kings.	Revelation 17:12–13
1 Kings 12:28	He honors the God of forces or military power.	Daniel 11:38
1 Kings 12:28	He sets up idols and abominations.	Daniel 9:27
1 Kings 13:14	A prophet arises to challenge the wicked leader.	Revelation 11:1–14
1 Kings 14:9	He is the most wicked leader up until that time.	Daniel 11:36
1 Kings 14:11	He will be given to the fowls of the air.	Revelation 19:17–18
1 Chronicles 11:12–16	He will prevail against the holy ones.	Daniel 7:21

Cycles of Empires

These same prophetic loops and rhythmic repetitions are found not just among individuals, but also among the empires of prophecy. In early history, we read of the tower of Babel (Gen. 10:10; 11:4), the world's first global government. Hundreds of years later Daniel is a captive in the city of Babylon (Dan. 1). In Revelation, at the time of the end, the name Babylon reappears as a religious and economic force that is destroyed. Just as the tower of Babel fell, Mystery Babylon will also fall (Gen. 11 and Rev. 17–19).

In Daniel's time the Persian military machine captured Babylon, setting up the fourth major prophetic empire. Today the Iranians are the Persians and use the name *Persian* to identify their people. Persia is rising again and will lead an Islamic coalition against Israel at the battle of Gog and Magog (Ezek. 38:5). The patterns of the ancient Roman Empire have been repeated with the rise of the modern American empire. Thus, patterns of previous empires can move in repetitive cycles.

Cycles of Dates

Certain Jewish dates also have a replication cycle in history. Jerusalem and her temple were destroyed, first by the Babylonians in 586 BC. After the Babylonian captives rebuilt the sacred edifice, the temple again was leveled 656 years later in AD 70 by the Roman Tenth Legion—with both destructions occurring on the same day of the Jewish calendar, the ninth of Av.

The ninth of Av holds some of the worst Jewish catastrophes,[4] beginning with the negative report from the ten spies that kept Israel in the wilderness for forty years (Num. 13). In history Jews were slaughtered in a rebellion in AD 133 at the battle of Betar on the ninth of Av. In 1492 the Jewish deadline for leaving Spain was set for the ninth of Av (on the same day Columbus was set to sail) but was delayed one day, as there were numerous Jews on his ship. It would be the following day on the tenth of Av (on the Jewish calendar) that Columbus lifted anchor and by divine sovereignty discovered a new land that would later be named America—a nation serving as a safe land for future Jews.

Layers of Meaning in Scripture

Many believe the Scriptures only hold one layer of application. However, look at Hosea 11:1, KJV:

> When Israel was a child, then I loved him, and called my son out of Egypt.

In context Hosea was pointing back to when God led the children of Israel out of Egypt. However, pointing forward into the future, to protect the holy family, God directed Joseph to go to Egypt until Herod died (Matt. 2:13). Matthew quoted Hosea's prophecy as a fulfillment of Christ, God's Son, fleeing to Egypt (Matt. 2:15). This verse also has an application for all believers; as sons and daughters of God, we are commanded spiritually to leave "Egypt," a nation in the Bible whose imagery is a place of bondage, captivity, and sin. Thus, the verse has a historical application—the Exodus when Israel who was called God's son departed Egypt (Exod. 4:22–23); a prophetic application—Jesus would be taken and brought back from Egypt; and a spiritual or practical application—we as believers must be set free from places of bondage. Not all verses have a threefold relevance, but this view must not be rejected.

There is another way to identify the threefold layer of a passage or narrative. The first is the *primary* or literal meaning; a story from the past. The second is a *practical* meaning concealed within the narrative that can be utilized in personal application for your present spiritual life. The third layer is a *prophetic* meaning where the past veils the future.

Consider the story of Noah. The *primary* meaning is a literal story that occurred forty-two hundred years ago. The *practical* application is God will judge the ungodly and preserve the righteous in times of calamity (2 Pet. 2:9). The *prophetic* revelation would be as it was in the days of Noah, so will it be at the coming of the son of man (Matt. 24:37). In Noah's day the "*wickedness* of man was great in the earth" (Gen. 6:5, KJV). We are then told the "*imagination* of the thoughts of his heart was only evil continually…" (Gen. 6:5, KJV), and "the earth also was *corrupt before God, and the earth was filled with violence…*" (Gen. 6:11). One rabbi noted the Hebrew word *violence* is *chamas*, and one of Israel's modern enemies is an organization called Hamas.

It is also interesting to note that Noah was the *tenth* generation from Adam as certain biblical numbers can bring out key prophetic insight.

Prophetic Meaning of Numbers

Noah's ancestor Enoch provides us with two examples of the significance of biblical numbers. Enoch was the *seventh* man from Adam and, after living three hundred sixty-five years, he was translated alive, escaping death (Gen. 5:23-24; Heb. 11:5; Jude 14). Biblically the number seven always speaks of perfection; thus, Enoch walked with God and maintained a righteous life. The fact that he lived for three hundred sixty-five years is intriguing because a complete solar cycle is three hundred sixty-five days. This speaks to us that Enoch's life came full circle and concluded with a catching away to heaven.

Noah was the *tenth generation* from Adam. The tenth generation was a completion and represented the full existence of a nation or a family (Deut. 23:3). The biblical number ten represents spiritual completion:

> » Noah was "perfect in his generations" (Gen. 6:9).

> » After every ten years, a new decade begins.

> » God sent ten plagues to Egypt that eventually broke the power of the Egyptians (Exod. 9:14).

> » The tithe or the tenth is given to God (Lev. 27:30) as a witness of our complete trust and total confidence in God's provision for us.

> » God gave Israel a complete set of laws in Ten Commandments (Deut. 4:13).

> » God would have spared Sodom for ten righteous people (Gen. 18:32).

> » Abraham's servant loaded down ten camels with gifts for Isaac's future bride (Gen. 24:10).

> » Joseph's ten brothers bought grain in Egypt during the famine (Gen. 42:3).

> » The final global kingdom will have ten kings to complete the prophetic cycle of Daniel, and bring in the return of Messiah.

Because time is kept and predicated by numbers, then time also has dimensions connected with it as speed and distances are measured in numbers. The world we live in is three-dimensional; these three dimensions can measure width, height, and length. All objects, whether cabinets in the kitchen or carpet on the floor, contain these three measurements. The Bible is filled with threes, the number of unity.

One	Two	Three
Length	Width	Height
Egypt	Wilderness	Promised Land
Slaves	Sons	Soldiers
Body	Soul	Spirit
Faith	Hope	Love
Outer court	Inner court	Holy of holies
First heaven	Second heaven	Third heaven (Paradise)
Father	Son	Holy Spirit
Salvation	Sanctification	Holy Spirit baptism
Blood	Water	Spirit
Regeneration	Justification	Glorification

Biblical names, places, numbers, and patterns hidden in inspired narratives can all hold repetitive prophetic cycles as explained. Breaking these codes to discover how the future is concealed in the past can unlock the time or season of a future prophetic event approaching the horizon. While this method is not typically taught in North American Bible schools or among Western theological academia, it is understood in rabbinical circles. To reveal future events, look back at times and seasons marked in ancient history that parallel American history.

At times cyclical loops are subject to change and revision through intense prayer. King Hezekiah was given a death sentence, but he humbled himself before God, weeping, and God added fifteen years to his life (2 Kings 20:4–6). However, before delving deeper into this subject, let's take a look in the next chapter at understanding prophetic time, the methods God uses to count time, prophetic events, and God's cosmic calendar.

Chapter 2

THREE WAYS OF COUNTING TIME IN GOD'S COSMIC CALENDAR

MANY BELIEVERS WANT to understand the *signs of the times* while others are interested in the *time of the signs*; one answers the *what*, and the other the *when*. Multitudes believe in the literal return of Christ, the gathering together event (1 Thess. 4:16–17), and the advent when Christ returns to earth (Rev. 19:11–16). They often discuss the visible signs connecting prophetic movements and are naturally curious of the "time" when the signs of Christ's coming will all consummate, leading to the expected return of the Messiah.

The questions of *what* and *when* were also asked by Christ's disciples in Matthew 24:3: "Tell us, when will these things be? And what will be the sign of Your coming, and of the end of the age?" Jesus answered the *when* (time) by informing them of the *what* (signs). Prophetic signs are hands on the clock of redemption; once they begin to come to pass, they will eventually approach midnight as we hear the call: "the bridegroom is coming!" (See Matthew 25:1–6.)

Time is a dimension where specific events occur. Beginning with the creation of Adam to the present, it is always flowing forward into an unknown future, unless revealed to us in advance. We measure many of life's events— births, wars, political cycles, and key moments—using time intervals.

God has a systemic method of counting time that is quite different from the watches we wear, the automated time chips in our cell phones, or the satellite time running on our laptops. God's original time clock was, and continues to be, the *cosmic lights* of the sun, moon, and stars. This is clear from Genesis 1:14:

> Then God said, "Let there be lights in the firmament of the heavens to divide the day from the night; and let them be for signs and seasons, and for days and years."

The earth's rotation around the sun (notice it is cyclical) decides the years as it requires 365.25 days for the earth to begin and complete its orbit. From beginning to end this complete circle marks one year. The cyclic phases of the moon—from the new moon (total darkness) to a full moon, and back to a new moon (called a lunation)—were used to mark the 29.5 days that make up the average synodic month. Among the heavenly bodies (stars, comets, asteroids, blood moons, and specifically the constellations) the ancients observed the markers of heavenly signs, predicting major events, which included the rise and fall of kings and kingdoms.

In the Genesis Creation account these heavenly lights were for "signs and seasons" (Gen. 1:14). The Hebrew word for "sign" used here is *owth*, which translates into English as "a token, a monument; evidence or a prodigy." The word for "season" is the Hebrew word *mowed*, meaning "an appointed time, a fixed time, or season."

This is the very word used in the Torah (the five books of Moses) when describing the yearly festivals of Israel (Lev. 23:4). The Hebrew word *mowed* is translated as *feast* in Leviticus 23:2, 4, 37, and 44. There were seven festivals of Israel which were celebrated at appointed times (Lev. 23:2, 4, 37).

The other Hebrew word describing these festivals is *miqra*—translated in Leviticus 23:37 as "convocation." It can also be translated as "rehearsal." This is interesting in light of the fact that the seven main festivals of Israel were, and continue to be, a preview of future prophetic events. The original Passover was the rehearsal for the crucifixion of Christ as He died near *Passover*. The burial of Christ was during *Unleavened Bread*, and the resurrection of Christ occurred during *First Fruit*—the first three spring festivals of Israel. The Holy Spirit empowered a new entity on earth called "the church" on the same day as the *Festival of Pentecost* (Acts 2:1–4). Pentecost was the time Moses received the Law of God on Mount

Sinai. Major prophetic events, such as the Rapture, the Tribulation, and the coming Messianic Kingdom are patterned to align with the three fall convocations of Trumpets, Atonement, and Tabernacles (also known as the three fall festivals). In ancient Israel the moon cycles determined when the feasts began; therefore, God's calendar was visible in heaven from the beginning of creation.

The Calendar in the Heavens

Prior to receiving the Law of God on Mount Sinai, mankind experienced twenty-five hundred years without any divine, written revelation from God. The Almighty revealed Himself and His plans through dreams, visions, and angelic visitors. The ancient people and empires of early civilization all looked to the heavens to understand the movements of the heavenly lights. They often attempted—even *without* divine inspiration—to understand their purpose, meanings, and impact on humanity.

For the priest at the temple in Jerusalem, the new month began when two witnesses announced to the high priest they had seen the silver sliver of the moon. In Christ's time even the Pharisees understood weather patterns by observing the sky:

> He answered and said to them, "When it is evening you say, 'It will be fair weather, for the sky is red'; and in the morning, 'It will be foul weather today, for the sky is red and threatening.' Hypocrites! You know how to discern the face of the sky, but you cannot discern the signs of the times."
> —MATTHEW 16:2–3

Christ was asked for the sign of His coming, and in response He gave a series of prodigies that would indicate the seasons prior to His return. Christ noted:

> And there will be great earthquakes in various places, and famines and pestilences; and there will be fearful sights and great signs from heaven.
> —LUKE 21:11

> And there will be signs in the sun, in the moon, and in the stars; and on the earth distress of nations, with perplexity, the sea and

the waves roaring; men's hearts failing them from fear and the expectation of those things which are coming on the earth, for the powers of the heavens will be shaken.

—LUKE 21:25–26

From Luke's narrative, at the time of the end, the universal heavens will be shaken as strange, cosmic activity (both "great" and "fearful"), will be witnessed by those on earth. The Greek word for "great" is *megas*; it describes something big, very large, or exceedingly great. This indicates a cosmic sign or heavenly disruption that cannot be ignored and will be viewed throughout the entire earth.

Christ said there would also be fearful signs emerging from the heavens. The Greek word "fearful" here is *phobos*; it is used to describe something so fearful that it causes people to be frightened and filled with terror. In the Book of Revelation we see an example of a "phobos" cosmic event when John observed a large asteroid striking the earth, destroying a third of the sea life, trees, and grass (Rev. 8:10–12). When astronomers begin warning the world of a deadly asteroid approaching the planet, global panic will ensue. This will fulfill Christ's words that men's hearts will fail them for fear (Luke 21:26), as they look at what is coming on the earth, anticipating the asteroid's collision with earth and the massive destruction to follow.

God never wastes His signs, as there is purpose for every sign and wonder in the Bible. In Luke's account Christ said these cosmic harbingers are "signs"—indicating His soon return to set up His kingdom on earth (Luke 21:11, 25–27). The Greek word for "signs" (in both verses) is *semaino;* it comes from the word *sema* and means "a mark that indicates something." Thus, certain cosmic activity among the sun, moon, and stars at appointed moments in the future are actually cosmic markers pointing to prophetic events.

Scientists are continually observing the sun and its electromagnetic danger from solar flares, warning one day it could knock out satellites, which would impact all communication on earth. In 1969 astronauts walked on the moon, and in recent times we have watched the moon turning into blood (Acts 2:20). From a rabbinical view this refers to full lunar eclipses, especially those falling on Jewish feasts days.

The signs in the *stars* include meteorite showers, asteroids, and I believe there are even signs in some of the amazing pictures coming to us from deep space. They reveal astonishing designs that cannot be seen from earth. These pictures show "gaseous nebula" and "space dust" appearing like a man's hand, a crown of thorns, and one taken by NASA was coined as "the eye of God," appearing like a giant eye staring deep into space. God's cosmic calendar is speaking as the lights of heaven indicate various signs of Christ's return (Luke 21:11, 25).

The Original Calendar

Beginning with the biblical numbers listed in the genealogies of Genesis, from Adam to this present age, our calendar covers slightly more than six thousand years (on the standard calendar). Today's secular world uses a calendar called the Gregorian calendar, where a year consists of 365.25 days. This calendar is based on the time it requires the earth to make that "invisible circle" around the sun.

Early ancient history suggests that our present solar calendar—365.25 days in a year—was not the original calendar used in the beginning of time. At Creation God made the sun to rule by day and the moon by night, calling the morning and evening a complete day. This means that each orbital light sphere was given about twelve hours to "rule" its own light realm. Among the Jews, Christ said, "Are there not twelve hours in the day?" (John 11:9). The ancient Jewish workday began at sunrise (about six o'clock) and finished at sunset (about six o'clock in the evening)—a total of twelve hours. The moon would be a dim light near sunset, but ruled the night (except for the new moon) from six o'clock at sunset until sunrise the following morning, thus having twelve hours in a day.

There is indication the original months were twelve months of thirty days each. At the time of Noah's flood, Moses said Noah was in the ark for one hundred fifty days or for five months (Gen. 7:11, 24; 8:4). The internal evidence of the Genesis account reveals the months were thirty days each, the same time frame recorded in the Book of Revelation. The tribulation is a seven-year period of time (Dan. 9:27) divided into two parts of forty-two months each, or 1,260 days and 1,260 days (Rev. 11:2–3; 12:6; 13:5). For the time frame of 1,260 days to add up to forty-two months, the years are three-hundred-sixty-day years. If we use the normal solar calendar of 365.25 days consisting of one year, then the forty-two prophetic months (rounded off) hold 1,278 days—or eighteen days more than the prophetic 1,260 days connected with the tribulation. Thus, John's calculation of "tribulation time" is based on twelve months of three hundred sixty days a year.

The three-hundred-sixty-day year was the reckoning among the nations of antiquity before the eighth century BC. Thousands of years ago the ancient Greeks used twelve months of thirty days each. During the time of Muhammad, there were three hundred sixty idols in the Ka'ba in Arabia, representing one idol for each day of the year. The ancient Chinese used three hundred sixty days, as they understood a circle was three hundred sixty degrees. In India the early texts speak of a year being three hundred sixty days. Among the ancient Japanese there were three hundred sixty idols before the palace of Dairi. In Mexico the Mayans had seventy-two weeks of five days each, totaling three hundred sixty days. Among the ancient Incas there were thirty days to a new quilla (moon) and twelve quillas each year, equaling three hundred sixty days. In early Rome there were thirty-six days of ten months—making a year three hundred sixty days.

The question has been posed, what changed the original creation calendar from three hundred sixty days in a year to 365.25? While it cannot be proven, it is suggested that Noah's flood caused a decrease in speed of the earth's rotation or the upheaval did damage to earth's intricate orbit, including the alignment of the axis.

Others note astonishing miracles, such as Joshua's long day (Josh 10:13), and the supernatural occurrence where time was reversed on the sundial by ten degrees in the time of King Hezekiah (2 Kings 20:9–11). This may have caused a geological or cosmic change, impacting time as we know it. What differences have emerged by adding five days to the solar calendar, changing four months into thirty days each (September, April, June, and November), making seven months into thirty-one days each, and adding leap years? It will remain a discussion for the cosmologists.

In 46 BC the Roman Emperor Julius Caesar introduced the global calendar, recognizing the solar year as 365.25 days. A discovery came in 1582 that this calendar was off each year by roughly twelve minutes and fourteen seconds, exposing a ten-day error in time. Pope Gregory XIII dropped the ten days, and to correct the error he added a leap year—when one day is added to the month of February every four years. The Gregorian calendar, as it became known, was adopted by the American colonies in 1752.

Biblical Times and Seasons

In the lives of people or nations there are specific "set times" appointed by God Himself in which a major birth or event transpires, designed to change history or impact a nation. The phrase "set time" is used seven times in the Old Testament. Here are some biblical examples of set times:

> » Sarah became pregnant and gave birth at a set time the following year (Gen. 17:21).

> » The judgment that struck the animals in Egypt came at a set time (Exod. 9:5).

> » Job prayed that God would appoint him a set time to be remembered (Job 14:13).

> » David predicted that God would place special favor on Jerusalem (Zion) as a sign of the Messiah's return (Ps. 102:13–16).

> » At the pool of Bethesda in Jerusalem, an angel came down at a certain season (appointed time), stirring the waters for a healing miracle (John 5:4).

> » God's promises of blessings and warnings of judgments are marked moments of set times.

> » Even death comes to all men at an appointed "set time" (Job 14:14; Heb. 9:27).

As it relates to the time of a specific prophecy coming to pass (and leading to the return of Christ), the New Testament speaks of the significance of the *fullness of times:*

> That in the dispensation of the fullness of the times He might gather together in one all things in Christ, both which are in heaven and which are on earth—in Him.
> —Ephesians 1:10

There is a set moment identified as the fullness of the Gentiles.

> For I do not desire, brethren, that you should be ignorant of this mystery, lest you should be wise in your own opinion, that blindness in part has happened to Israel until the fullness of the Gentiles has come in.
>
> —ROMANS 11:25

This phrase "fullness of the Gentiles," according to numerous older Bible commentators, refers to a predetermined number of Gentiles from the nations of the world, converted prior to the return of the Lord, when the natural seed of Abraham will have the spiritual blindness removed from their eyes.

Another fullness of time is connected with the city of Jerusalem, linking the city's deliverance from Gentile powers. Jesus predicted:

> And they shall fall by the edge of the sword, and shall be led away captive into all nations: and Jerusalem shall be trodden down of the Gentiles, until the times of the Gentiles be fulfilled.
>
> —LUKE 21:24, KJV

Christ predicted Jerusalem would be in the hands of Gentile powers and trodden down (a term for continual wars and destruction). This resumes until the "times of the Gentiles" is fulfilled, when these nations would lose their grip, and Jews would control the city again.

In Luke 21:24 the Greek word for "fulfilled" is *pleroo*, and it means "to fill up, like cramming a net full; something occurring to coincide with a prediction." The prediction is fulfilled because it is considered a "fullness" of some type. A prophecy is fulfilled when the foretold event incurs particular circumstances, aligning at once with the prediction. Jerusalem's liberation from Gentile domination was a set time in June of 1967 after the Six-Day War, when the Holy City, once divided between Israel and Jordan, was united as one city, becoming the capital of Israel.

Some time frames are identified as "times and seasons." The disciples asked Christ if He would restore the kingdom to Israel:

And he said unto them, It is not for you to know the times or the seasons, which the Father hath put in his own power.

—ACTS 1:7, KJV

The Greek word for "times" is *chronos* and alludes to a fixed space of time, especially the time remaining from now until the coming of the Lord. The Greek word for "seasons" is *kairos* and signals a special season or event occurring within the fixed time. A third word is *moed*, or *moedim*, a Hebrew word meaning "appointed times." It is used for the seven festivals of Israel that were set yearly on a particular day and month. One amazing aspect of God's prophetic calendar is how major biblical and prophetic events fall in line with the same day or pattern of the seven festivals.

The Calendar of the Festivals

Beginning the night before Israel's exodus from Egypt, God began establishing seven yearly festivals. These are His appointed seasons, days, and months throughout the year. Here is a list of the festivals, the Jewish month, and their assigned seasons:

Name	Jewish Month	English Equivalent
Passover (Pesach)	First month, fourteenth day	March/April
Unleavened Bread (Hag HaMatzah)	First month, fifteenth through twenty-first days	March/April
First Fruits (Bikkurim)	First month, day after Sabbath of Unleavened Bread	March/April
Pentecost (Shavuot)	Fifty days from First Fruits	May/June
Trumpets (Yom Teruah)	Seventh month, first day	September/October
Atonement (Yom Kippur)	Seventh month, tenth day	September/October
Tabernacles (Sukkot)	Seventh month, fifteenth through twenty-first days	September/October

Because the Jewish calendar follows the lunar orbit, it has 354 days in its year; twelve months of six twenty-nine day months, and six thirty-day months. Lunar calendar variations allow the year to be 353 or 355 days. Since an average Jewish year is eleven days short of the global solar year of 365.25 days, periodically a thirty-day month is added to the Jewish calendar, called a *shanah meuberet* (pregnant year). It is added to the final month and called Adar. About every three years ("leap years") another month is added called Adar II. This ensures the feasts to fall on the same set day and appointed month. Otherwise, over many years, Passover would eventually come in the winter instead of the spring.

Throughout history major events often fall on parallel prophetic dates. There are twelve different months in the Jewish calendar. The month of Kislev commonly falls in the month of December and occasionally begins in late November. In the second century BC a statue of Zeus defiled the temple in Jerusalem on the twenty-fourth of Kislev. Oddly, the same temple was cleansed and rededicated three years later on the twenty-fourth of Kislev. After the Babylonian captivity, the rebuilding of the temple under Haggai was on the twenty-fourth of Kislev. Some suggest that Christ may have been conceived on the twenty-fourth of Kislev, during the time of the Festival of Lights (known as Hanukkah). Going forward in time and history, General Edmund Allenby liberated Jerusalem from four hundred years of Turkish rule on December 9, 1917, which was the twenty-fourth of Kislev.

As I mentioned in chapter 1, another date when negative, historic events repeat on the Jewish calendar is the ninth of Av. For centuries this day has been observed as a day of mourning for Jewish people. The following events occurred in Jewish history on the ninth of Av.

> » The twelve scouts sent out by Moses returned with a bad report.

> » The generation coming out in the Exodus was condemned to die.

> » Nebuchadnezzar set fire to the first temple.

> » The Romans destroyed the second temple.

> » The Romans plowed up the Temple Mount to convert it to a Roman colony.

> » The last independent outpost of the *Bar Kokhba* rebellion fell to the Romans.

> » King Edward of England expelled all the Jews in 1290.

> » The last group of Jews left Vienna in 1670 after expulsion from Austria.

> » The Turkish government banned immigration of Russian and Romanian Jews into Palestine in 1882.

> » World War I broke out in 1914. This was precipitated by the assassination of Archduke Francis Ferdinand.

> » A decree to expel Jews from parts of Hungary was issued in 1941.[1]

According to Jewish tradition, to undertake any enterprise on the ninth of Av is considered *bad luck*. In more contemporary times, on August 14, 2005, Jews were again removed from their settlements in Gaza (in Israel), and forced into other settlements to the north, weeping as their own soldiers forced them on buses to be resettled to other locations in Israel. This occurred on the ninth of Av.

Signals From the Moon

Before paper calendars how did the ancient people know when the month was beginning? The answer for Jews is in the moon. The moon actually has four cycles in each month. The first is the new moon, from the first to the seventh day of the month. The second is the waxing moon, from the eighth to the fourteenth day of the month. The third cycle is the full moon, falling on the fifteenth to the twenty-second day of the month; and the fourth, the waning moon, which occurs on the twenty-third to the thirtieth day of the month. This four-part process was known among some rabbinical sources as the moon being "reborn." The new moon is when the sky is totally dark, and the moon "hides its face" from the earth. When the moon's silver sliver appeared among the Hebrews it marked the beginning of the month, eventually leading to a quarter moon, followed by a full moon—from dark to full in slightly over fourteen days. The process is then reversed as the moon decreases, from full to quarter and back to dark. This is the renewal of the moon or the month. The link between the moon and the month is seen in the Hebrew word for both; the word *moon* is *chodesh* in Hebrew, and the Hebrew word *month* is also *chodesh* (Gen. 7:11; 8:4; 29:14; Exod. 12:2–6).

It is noted in rabbinical sources that the renewal cycle of the moon is a perfect imagery of Israel's national and spiritual progression and regression. From Abraham to Solomon is about fifteen generations. This indicates Abraham began the illumination of Israel in a time of total spiritual darkness, and fifteen generations later the kingdom of Israel was dwelling at its brightest fullness, with the climax of peace and prosperity under King Solomon. After Solomon's death, his son Rehoboam took rule, and the kingdom began to slowly diminish. Just like the moon in the sky, fifteen generations later, Israel was carried into the darkness of the Babylonian captivity; thus, the history of ancient Israel is linked to the twenty-nine-day or thirty-day cycle of the moon. This is why rabbis place prophetic significance on a total lunar eclipse (called a blood moon) falling on Jewish festivals. It is considered a bad omen for the Jewish people, including a sign of internal struggle or a foreboding war.

How Ancients Viewed the Cosmic Signs

Two of history's most noted Roman Emperors were Julius Caesar and Caesar Augustus. During Julius Caesar's reign, Roman settlers in Capua unearthed the ancient graves of Capua's colonists and a series of buried vessels. The founder of Capua had built a monument, which held a bronze tablet written in Greek with a prediction. It read:

> When once the houses of Capys is brought to light, then a branch
> of the Julian house will be slain by the hand of one of his kindred.

The strange prediction indicated the emperor would be slain by the hand of a relative. As if this prediction was not troubling enough, the wife of Julius dreamed their home fell apart. Believing the dream was a warning, his wife warned him to not go to the coliseum—which he ignored. It was there in the coliseum where Julius was stabbed twenty-three times, and met his death in 44 BC.[2]

Caesar Augustus was appointed Roman Emperor in 27 BC. He ruled until his death in AD 14. Augustus was emperor at the time of Christ's birth. His father, Octavius, had consulted an oracle about his son at a local temple. While offering a wine libation on the altar, the fire leaped to the roof of the temple. The priest told Octavius his son would achieve greatness, adding this sign had only happened one other time, when Alexander the Great was sacrificing.

In 2 BC Augustus was celebrating his silver jubilee and the seven hundred fiftieth anniversary of Rome. In 3 BC a worldwide census was conducted, and a tax levied to pay for the celebrations. King Herod in Judea required descendants of King David to return to Judea, register in Bethlehem, and pay the tax. Herod was so loyal to Rome they rewarded him with the title "King of the Jews." This was the same tax spoken of in the New Testament that brought Mary and Joseph to Bethlehem (Luke 2:1–5). Augustus was also called the "prince of peace" in his time, having resided over Pax Romana, or Roman peace throughout the empire. The Romans also titled Augustus, the "god of the nation." With such accolades, Augustus built a temple after being told he would rise to imperial power. Augustus traveled to the Delphic oracles in Greece to inquire how long his temple of peace would last. He was told, "Until a virgin gives birth to a child and yet remains a virgin."

Based on the impossibility of a virgin giving birth to a child, Augustus felt his temple would endure forever. He dedicated his own temple with this inscription: *Templum Pacis Aeternae.* Oddly, it was at the time of Christ's nativity that, without warning or cause, the temple collapsed on its foundation.

Ancient astronomers read the signs of the heavens when Augustus went to Palatine Hill. Located in Rome at the centermost hill of the seven hills, he asked the question to the oracle, "Will a greater one than me ever be born?" At that moment, a meteor lit the night sky. The woman put down her books and said to Augustus:

> It is a sign of the future which is revealed to you. One world is ending and another is beginning.[3]

This was alluding to the ending of a 2,150-year-old cycle of Aries the Ram—a heavenly constellation. Jewish tradition believes that the two skins with which God covered Adam and Eve were ram's skins, and the ram was the animal offered in place of Isaac (Gen. 22). At this time there was a sighting of the constellation of Pisces the fish, an emblem for Israel, at the same time Christ was born. This oracle was given to Augustus:

> A child has just been born, who is the king of the future millennia, the true God of the world. He is of humble birth and of obscure race. His divinity is unrealized; when he at last makes himself known, he will be persecuted. He will work miracles; he will be accused of trafficking with evil spirits, but I see him as victor in the end over death, rising from the place where his murderers entombed him. He will reunite all nations.[4]

Augustus reported the account to the Senate who then recorded the information, placing it in the Roman archives. It was read hundreds of years later by Emperor Constantine, who in his day legalized Christianity.

Since Israel is on the lunar calendar, any "sign" linked to the moon occurring on a Jewish feast date is an important omen for Israel. The Jewish sages indicate that a blood moon is not a good sign for Israel; it signified trouble in some form coming to the nation. Here is a brief list of historical eclipses:

Date of Eclipse	Event
January 10, in 4 BC	The death of Herod, the slayer of infants
September 27, in AD 14	Called Augustus's Eclipse because it occurred soon after the death of Caesar Augustus[5]
April 3, in AD 33	Possible time of the crucifixion—darkness over the land
March 4, in AD 71	The plowing of Jerusalem with salt by the Romans
May 22, 1453	The fall of Constantinople to the Muslims
March 1, 1504	Called the Columbus eclipse

Date of Eclipse	Event
July 31, 1776	After America's independence from Britain
January 15, 1805	The Lewis and Clark expedition
July 4, 1917	The time frame of World War I and the Balfour Declaration

Among the ancients, solar eclipses often brought superstition and fear. The ancient Chinese believed that solar eclipses were heavenly signs that foretold the birth of future emperors and leaders of the state. One of the famous eclipses occurred on January 27 in AD 632, and was visible in Medina, in Arabia. This was significant since the founder of Islam, Muhammad, had been expelled from Mecca and was living with his followers in Medina. It was in 632 that the founder of Islam died.

The Moon Turns Into Blood

One of the cosmic prodigies prior to the great tribulation is when the sun darkens, and the moon turns into blood (Joel 2:31). Taken literally the moon is a ball of cosmic dust and will remain a crater-covered sphere. This phrase is a metaphor that Jewish scholars interpret as a full lunar eclipse, when the moon appears as an orange-reddish ball in the sky. It is not just the natural phenomena that are significant, as lunar eclipses have occurred throughout history, but the timing of the event. Joel indicated both solar (the sun darkened), and lunar eclipses (moon turned as blood) occurring in the same time frame, before the day of the Lord. Apparently, from a prophetic view, these eclipses falling on significant time frames are cosmic marvels showing the coming of the day of the Lord.

In Moses's time and in Christ's day the set time of the seven festivals were determined each "month" by the positioning of the moon. Thus, when the moon is red on days of Jewish festivals, it is considered an omen that will impact Israel, the Jews, or Jerusalem in some manner.

In the twentieth century, on two occasions on the night of Passover, lunar eclipses were noted in Israel: on the Jewish year 5710 (1949–1950) and the year 5728 (1967–1968). These dates were prophetically significant for

Israel. In 5710 an eclipse occurred after Israel was reestablished as a nation and again in 5728, the date right after Jerusalem was liberated and reunited.

There has been much emphasis on the "blood moons" occurring in 2014 and 2015. However, Joel predicted both a solar and lunar eclipse occurring. It reads:

> The sun shall be turned into darkness, and the moon into blood, before the coming of the great and awesome day of the LORD.
>
> —JOEL 2:31

On average there are at least 2.4 eclipses somewhere in the world each year. On an average cycle of three and a half years, about five occur, and approximately every four and a half years, up to six can occur. The most that can occur in one year is seven. In 1917 there were seven eclipses—four of the sun, and three of the moon. This was a year of major prophetic events. Seven occurred in 1935, five being solar. This was during the Great Depression, the time of Hitler's rise, and just prior to World War II breaking out. Seven occurred again in 1982, which again saw a series of significant global events. In 3,600 years, from BC 1154 to the future AD 2485, two solar and four lunar eclipses will occur only fourteen times. For 3,600 years there have been three lunar and four solar eclipses thirty-four times up to 1982. Since the year AD 1000 there have been seven years in which five lunar eclipses occurred: 1181, 1246, 1311, 1676, 1694, 1749, and 1879.[6]

It is indeed rare when four lunar eclipses all occur on or near Passover, Israel's first festival, and Tabernacles, Israel's seventh and final yearly convocation. However, according to NASA, in back-to-back years (2014 and 2015), four blood moons coincide with these festivals. The blood moons are as follows:

- » First Day of Passover April 15, 2014
- » First Day of Tabernacles October 8, 2014
- » First Day of Passover April 4, 2015
- » First Day of Tabernacles September 28, 2015

Four solar eclipses also coincide with these festivals—April 29 and October 23 in 2014, and March 20 and September 13 in 2015.[7] The blood moons falling in line with these dates is certainly a prophetic prodigy for Israel; however, they alone are only one part of the Joel prophecy. The sun turning dark can be a reference to solar eclipses, which will also occur in the spring and fall cycles. Jewish rabbinical tradition gives a detailed list of eclipses that project to be omens:

» Solar eclipses are a bad omen for idolaters.

» Lunar eclipses are bad omens for Israel.

» A red moon at a lunar eclipse means a sword is coming for the whole world.

» A black moon at a lunar eclipse means the arrows of famine are coming for the whole world.

» At sunset the calamity will tarry in its coming.

» At sunrise the calamity is forthcoming.

Time will determine what these blood moons on festivals represent and if they are cosmic harbingers. Christ did say there would be signs "in the moon" (Luke 21:25). When the combination of signs in the stars, the moon, and the sun collide at the same time, then the signs in the heavens are evident.

Three Ways God Counts Prophetic Time

The lights of heaven are God's cosmic timepiece. Before there was a printed calendar, time was kept by the moon and sun. There were three biblical time cycles that were significant to the Hebrew people. The first is sabbatical cycles. The weekly Sabbath was set for the seventh day out of every week, called *Shabbat*, meaning "rest" or "cessation" (Exod. 20:10–11). This was originally Saturday. Today devout Jews and Messianic believers mark Friday at sunset to Saturday at sunset as the Sabbath.

A second cycle in Hebrew is called, *shmita* (meaning "release"); it is a cycle repeated every seven years, serving as an agricultural period allowing the land to rest and the ground to lay fallow the entire seventh year (Lev. 25:2–4). Because Israel did not keep the *shmita*, God sent them into captivity for seventy years to allow the land to rest (Lev. 26:32–35).

A third counting was to add up seven yearly cycles seven times (or, 7 x 7 = 49 years) and decree a *Jubilee* on the tenth day of the seventh month, every fiftieth year (Lev. 25:8–9). Many of Israel's prophetic movements and significant events are in patterns of sevens.

> » Jacob worked seven years and was given the wrong wife; he worked seven more years for his father-in-law, Laban, to marry his true love, Rachel (Gen. 29:18–20).

> » A seven-year famine brought Joseph's brothers to Egypt, eventually providing a home for them during the global crisis (Gen. 41).

> » Seven priests with seven trumpets marched around Jericho, and on the seventh day, after seven times, the walls collapsed (Josh. 6).

> » In the Esther story there were seven chamberlains (Esther 1:10), seven princes of Media and Persia (Esther 1:14), and seven maidens for Esther 2:9. It was Esther who saved the Jews in 127 provinces!

> » After giving an offering of seven bulls and seven rams, the Lord turned Job's captivity and gave him a double blessing (Job 42:8–10).

> » David declared that seven times a day he praised the Lord (Ps. 119:164)! Thus, seven is connected with Israel's breakthroughs and spiritual favor.

The second clear method of counting time is by *Jubilees*. In Hebrew the word for "jubilee" is *yovel*—a trumpet blast—as this represents the year of freedom. A release occurred on cycles of every fifty years, beginning on the Day of Atonement, by blowing silver trumpets (Lev. 25:9). This system of counting major events every forty-ninth or fiftieth year was so significant that an entire book was compiled called, *The Book of Jubilees*. It is believed a Pharisee between 135 and 105 BC wrote this Hebrew book. The introduction begins:

These are the words of the division of days according to the law and testimony, according to the events of the years, according to their sevens, according to their Jubilees, to all of the years of the world.[8]

The author begins his counting with the time of creation until his day, placing Israel's major events on Jubilee cycles (fifty years apart), attempting to demonstrate that Israel's major events fell on fifty-year intervals. The book is filled with traditions and changes in certain biblical narratives, filling in gaps of time not found in the Torah. Fifteen copies (or fragments) of *The Book of Jubilees* were discovered when the much-publicized Dead Sea Scrolls were discovered in the Qumran caves, now located in Israel (1948–1952). The writer begins his count from Creation and concludes it with the date of Israel entering the Promised Land, counting 2,450 years, dividing these years into fifty forty-nine year units, or Jubilees. I mention this book not to give credence to its contents, but to show how there was an elaborate scheme that emerged to promote the belief of the significance of Jubilee cycles in Hebrew history. The writer also frequently uses sevens, called *heptads*, meaning groups of sevens.

It has been noted that major events with Israel can fall on Jubilee cycles. The cycle began when Israel first took the Promised Land, which some suggest was in the year 1436 BC. Jubilee cycles have been discussed by scholars and some have attempted to discover when these significant events have occurred. Here are several examples that could be listed[9]:

» The seventeenth Jubilee fell at the time Nebuchadnezzar invaded Judea (606–604 BC).

» The thirtieth Jubilee fell at the time of Christ's crucifixion (AD 33–34).

» The forty-second and forty-third Jubilees fell when the Muslims took Jerusalem (AD 622–672).

» The sixty-eighth Jubilee fell at the time Zionism began to form (AD 1896–1897).

» The sixty-ninth Jubilee fell at the end of World War II (AD 1945–1946).

» The seventieth Jubilee fell at time of the Oslo peace treaties (AD 1994–1995).

Daniel reveals a prophetic cycle scholars call "Daniel's seventieth week." It is seventy years of seven cycles (four hundred ninety years; see Daniel 9). However, it can also be divided into ten forty-nine-year Jubilee cycles (totaling four hundred ninety years). There is much speculation involved in dating ancient events, unless they are specified in sacred or profane history. Modern dates, however, are clear. For example, in 1898 the Jewish Zionists movement, under Theodor Herzl, predicted within fifty years a Zionist state for the Jews would exist in the ancient Jewish homeland. Fifty years later (1948), the Jews were given a homeland they named Israel. In 1917 Lord Balfour (the British Foreign Secretary) signed a declaration promising the Jews a "national home" in Palestine. It would be fifty years later in June of 1967, following the Six-Day War, that East Jerusalem would be annexed from Jordan. East and West Jerusalem finally united as one city, the ancient and modern, forming the capital of Israel.

Horizontal, Vertical, and Circular Time

Time never changes; minutes, hours, days, weeks, months, and years only repeat over and over. All humans are eventually moving toward eternity where time ceases as we know it. But until then time is ever moving forward, as each of us can surely attest. We know our bodies fade, but time itself recycles. Forward time movement can also be compared to *horizontal, vertical, and circular* motion. Let's look first at *horizontal* time. Beginning with your birth, moving forward on an imaginary flat timeline, flowing from event to event until your earthly time concludes with death. This horizontal line marks human time with a set beginning and a set ending. Among the Greeks this would be *chronos*, or chronological time where life is ordered in a series of progressive events that can be dated and numbered.

The second is *vertical* time, or what I call climbing up Jacob's ladder. In Jacob's dream the base of the ladder was the "house of God," and the top was the "gate of heaven"—with angelic messengers going up and coming down at the same time (Gen. 28:12–17). Vertical time is in the spiritual dimension, where earthly believers can, at times, sit in "heavenly places" with

Christ (Eph. 2:6), receiving divine inspiration and revelation while abiding in God's presence. Vertical time emerges out of horizontal time. This is how prophets living on a horizontal timeline could be flowing from earthly movement, tapping into the heavenly realm, seeing visions of heaven and future events. The Greek word for this time would be *kairos*, which is an opportune or divine moment. We might describe *kairos* time as special "windows of opportunity" or "seasons" we have to accomplish certain tasks.

The third, and for our study, the most important flow of time is *circular*— when events repeat themselves, they have a cyclical pattern. The ancient people understood cyclical time far better than people do today. For them, time was on a loop that eventually repeated itself in pre-determined or divinely set seasons. Just as the four seasons of the year repeated annually, the solar cycles occurred yearly; the moon went through four monthly stages, and the Jews celebrated seven yearly festivals.

Politically we compare presidents with previous presidents: Bill Clinton with JFK, Obama with Lincoln, and so forth. There have also been families where both father and son served as president, although serving years apart: John Adams (the second president) and his son, John Quincy Adams (the sixth president), George H. W. Bush (the forty-first president) and his son George W. Bush (the forty-third president).

Spiritually the Bible uses comparisons, such as Christ with the first Adam (calling Christ the last Adam—1 Cor. 15:45), and compares the priesthood of Melchizedek (a king-priest) to the priestly ministry of Christ (Heb. 7:21). These are individuals whose futures are linked with the past.

As we begin to study cyclical patterns and how the past conceals the future, you will perhaps discover a new concept of how the future can be written in previous time frames. In the following chapters I will refer to past incidents and dates to demonstrate repetitive cycles and will compare these with future possibilities. It is time itself that reveals the true accuracy of prophetic time circles.

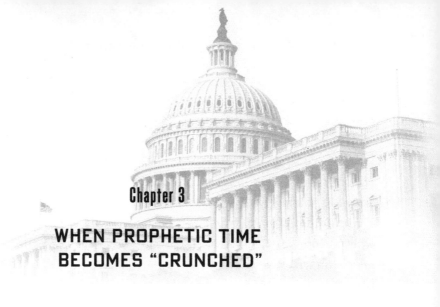

Chapter 3

WHEN PROPHETIC TIME
BECOMES "CRUNCHED"

AKE A PENCIL or pen and a piece of paper. Begin at the top in the center of the paper and draw a complete circle, meeting back where you started. The circle begins as a small mark, but as you form your 180-degree arc you are halfway to completing the circle. Once you begin moving around toward the starting point, the distance shortens, and eventually you close the circle, completing a cyclic drawing. The fulfillment of prophecy works in the flow of a circle; after it is spoken it can seem a long time before the actual fulfillment. However, once we reach the halfway point and arch back to the beginning, completing a full 360-degree circle of prophetic time, the signs and prodigies begin to merge causing the time component to be "crunched."

The completion of a cyclical pattern is best identified as the culmination, or fullness of time. Paul spoke of this in Ephesians 1:10, KJV:

> That in the dispensation of the fulness of times he might gather together in one all things in Christ, both which are in heaven, and which are on earth; even in him.

The New International Version reads:

> To be put into effect when the times reach their fulfillment—to bring unity to all things in heaven and on earth under Christ.

A biblical prophecy can be interrupted with gaps between one part of the fulfillment and the other. The best example is the prophecy of Daniel's seventy weeks. Based on Daniel 9:24–26, the Babylonian exiles returned to Jerusalem, and from the time of the decree to build the city until the death of the Messiah there are no interruptions in the flow of time for 483 years. Christ died at the close of the sixty-ninth prophetic week (69 x 7 = 483 years). The final seven years, which will complete the four-hundred-ninety-year cycle, lies in the future—in the seven-year tribulation. Thus, there has been a huge gap in time between Daniel's sixty-ninth and seventieth week. This "gap" has been over 1,982 years as believers continue to teach and warn others of the coming Antichrist and Tribulation. The numerous latter-day and end-time prophecies of the Bible will all be fulfilled as we move toward closing the gap in the circle and complete the final cycle of the fullness of times.

The prophet Ezekiel saw a vision called the valley of dry bones (Ezek. 37). Scholars, noting the vivid description and wording of his vision, believe it predicted the Jewish Holocaust, or rather how the Jews would survive and return to their land becoming a united nation and greater army. Gentile nations felt compassion for the Jews after the Holocaust, and the United Nations partitioned Palestine for a Jewish state, called Israel. This fulfilled Isaiah 66:8, where the prophet predicted that a nation would be born in a day.

At the same time in 1948, a great healing and restoration revival erupted in the United States, continuing for seven years until 1955. This was considered by followers one of the latter rain outpourings, mentioned in Joel 2:28–29. From 1939 to 1948 a series of worldwide events, including wars, thrust entire nations into unexpected transitions, shifting global powers and aligning events for the greatest prophetic fulfillment since the resurrection of Christ—the resurrection of Israel as a nation.

Think back to the concept of "fullness" that I discussed in chapter 2. Five distinct predictions about Christ's return are connected with the concept of being "full." First is the *fullness of the gospel*—the preaching of Christ must spread around the world (Matt. 24:14). This can now be done through the Internet, satellite, and other amazing technology linking the world. According to Romans 11:25, there must come a "fullness of the Gentiles" when the full number of Gentiles reaches their predetermined numbers in the kingdom of God. There is also the dispensation of the "fullness of time," or the management of the grace of God during the church age that will climax (become full) leading to the coming of Christ. Daniel spoke of the "fullness of iniquity," meaning when the global cup of iniquity becomes full. This is when the Antichrist will be revealed on the earth (Dan. 8:23). Jerusalem is also an important key as Christ revealed the city would be in Gentile hands until the time of Gentile dominion would be broken; when the "time of the Gentiles are fulfilled" (Luke 21:24). The fullness of time is like water being poured into a glass. As the fulfillment of the event comes closer, the glass becomes fuller, until the overflow signals the fulfillment has arrived.

The first prophecy of the future was given to Adam, direct from God in Genesis 3:15, predicting the seed of the woman would bruise the head of the serpent. The first warning prophecy, according to Josephus, was given to Adam. Adam passed it to his son Seth, revealing the earth would be destroyed twice: once by water and the next time by fire.[1] From Adam's prophecy until Noah's warning of the flood, 1,556 years had passed. Once a warning is given, a set time is established until the destruction comes. As that time approaches, time becomes crunched.

The Flood in Noah's Day

Adam to Noah's warning of a flood	1,556 years	Genesis 5–6
Man's time to repent	120 years	Genesis 6:3
Time it took to build the ark	100 years	Genesis 5:32–7:11
After the ark was finished	7 days	Genesis 7:4
The ark door was shut	1 day	Genesis 7:16

For one hundred years, the people did not know the day the flood was coming (Luke 17:27). However, when the appointed moment arrived, in one day, the door was shut; the floodgates of heaven and the fountains of the deep were opened.

The same "crunch sequence" is evident in connection with God's plan for an exodus from Egypt. In Genesis 15:13 God says He would bring the descendants of Abraham out of a strange land back to the Promised Land after four generations (four hundred years). The fulfillment of those four hundred years can be divided into the following flow of time:

From Abraham (Gen. 15:13) to the Exodus (Exod. 12)

Abraham to Moses fleeing from Egypt	360 years	Counting the genealogies
Moses watching flocks in the wilderness	40 years	Exodus 7:7
God initiating the ten plagues in Egypt	About 26–50 days	Exodus 7–12
The Exodus from Egypt	Within 24 hours	Exodus 12

The process of going down to Egypt began when Jacob sent his sons during a famine for grains. Joseph, the youngest, was sold by his brothers at age seventeen and kept in bondage until age thirty. Joseph later regained freedom while in Egypt, and prepared for a famine for seven years. Two years into the famine his brothers arrived. After being in Egypt for twenty-two years, Joseph revealed himself to his brothers, and they returned to their father, bringing the entire clan back to Egypt. They lived in the land for hundreds of years, populating from seventy souls to six hundred thousand men (Exod. 1:5; 12:37); however, when time struck at full circle, we read:

> And it came to pass…even the selfsame day it came to pass, that all the hosts of the LORD went out from the land of Egypt.
> —EXODUS 12:41, KJV

God's promise to Abraham was executed to the very day.

Both Isaiah and Jeremiah predicted the Babylonian captivity, many years before the actual invasion. Jeremiah revealed the Jews would be taken captive for seventy years (Jer. 25:11–12; 29:10). About one hundred eighty years before the event, Isaiah warned Hezekiah that in a future generation, the Babylonians would come and take the golden treasures to Babylon (Isa. 39:7). Nearly twenty-three years before the Babylonian armies arrived, Jeremiah pronounced doom on Jerusalem and Judea (Jer. 20:4). When the moment arrived, there were three invasions on Judea, the final attack coming to Jerusalem (601 BC, 597 BC, and 587 BC). Scholars say there were

fourteen years from the first invasion until the overthrow of Jerusalem. As
the divinely appointed moment arrived (the fullness of time) the key scenes
begin merging together, triggering the actual episode predicted decades
earlier.

Events and Circumstances Must Be in Proper Order

As a young minister, I wondered why God did not send Christ to the earth
earlier. Why did He wait four thousand years before bringing the Messianic
prophecies to pass? Part of the answer is God waited until the message of
the gospel could be spread throughout the known world, which was possible after the rise of the Roman Empire. Rome laid out roads connecting
the major cities, built and bought ships that sailed from major ports, and
there was one language that could be spoken throughout the Empire: Greek.
Consequently, the New Testament was written in Greek to ensure all could
read it. The circumstances necessary to spread the gospel merged at one set
season, at the time of Christ's birth:

> But when the fullness of the time had come, God sent forth His
> Son, born of a woman, born under the law, to redeem those who
> were under the law, that we might receive the adoption as sons.
> —GALATIANS 4:4–5

From the first "Messianic" prediction, the seed of the woman (Gen. 3:15)
to the moment of the Crucifixion, prophetic time is spread out over four
thousand years. In that time Hebrew prophets foresaw bits and pieces of
the puzzle that finally fit together with the appearing of Christ. As time of
Christ's appearing drew near—time moved faster with fewer gaps.

Scripture	Prophecies	Time Frame Before the Fulfillment
Genesis 3:15	The seed of the woman prediction	Four thousand years before Christ's birth
Genesis 49:10	The scepter, Shiloh, and Judah predictions	Seventeen hundred years before Christ's birth
Psalm 22:1–31	The crucifixion prophecies by David	One thousand years before Christ's birth

Scripture	Prophecies	Time Frame Before the Fulfillment
Micah 5:2	The Savior comes from Bethlehem	Seven hundred forty years before Christ's birth
Isaiah 53:1–11	The suffering servant prophecies	Seven hundred years before Christ's birth
Malachi 4:2	The Sun of Righteousness would arise	Four hundred fifty years before Christ's birth

I mentioned gaps of time between a prediction and a fulfillment. Malachi was the last of the Old Testament prophets; there are an estimated four hundred years of "silence" with no major prophetic voice in Israel until the appearing of John the Baptist. Once Christ reached age thirty, there was an acceleration of "prophetic movement" preparing to initiate God's set plan of redemption. Here is the order:

From Christ's birth to the beginning of His ministry	Thirty years (Luke 3:23)
The length of Christ's ministry	Three and a half years (He celebrated three Passovers)
The end of Christ's ministry to the Crucifixion	Seven days of the passion
From Christ's death to the Resurrection	Three days and nights (Mark 8:31)
When Christ took the keys of death and hell	One minute (the moment of the Resurrection)

After Christ's resurrection, He was seen alive for forty days (Acts 1:3). At the conclusion, He told His disciples to tarry in Jerusalem until they received power from on high. We read:

> Now it came to pass, when the time had come for Him to be received up, that He steadfastly set His face to go to Jerusalem.
> —LUKE 9:51

There was an appointed time for Christ's ascension, and a set time for the Holy Spirit to come. The disciples waited for seven days until the festival of Pentecost had arrived. The day of Pentecost had to "fully come" before the

Holy Spirit blew into Jerusalem, like a mighty rushing wind. This "promise of the Father" came on one day, in one hour and descended like tongues of fire upon the disciples in one second (Acts 2:1–4).

Israel's Restoration Process

Jerusalem was destroyed, and the Jewish people scattered in the year AD 70. It was 1,878 years from the destruction of the temple to the restoration of Israel as a nation in 1948. Once this ancient nation was raised from the dead, the end-time prophecies related to Christ's return began jumping from the pages of Scripture. Psalm 102:16 teaches that Jerusalem must be built up before the Messiah could return. From 1948 until the reunification of Jerusalem in 1967, nineteen years passed. Beginning with the prophetic marker of 1967, moving forward eighteen years brings us to 1985, when the Ethiopian Jews were airlifted in Operation Moses back to Israel. Four years later (1985 to 1989), Russian Jews began flying out of Russia and Eastern Europe—the northern countries (Jer. 16:15), returning Jews to Israel.

There are two powerful prophetic triggers that will be pulled at the same time, thrusting the nations into the final episode of God's end-time drama. First, the gospel message must be preached in all nations as a witness and then the end shall come (Matt. 24:14). Coinciding with the gospel covering the earth will be a universal outpouring of the Holy Spirit that will also reach into every nation, impacting the sons and daughters from around the globe (Joel 2:28–29). These twin predictions collide together at the same season as evidence of the last days and the return of Christ.

One is the *fullness of the gospel,* and the other is the *fullness of the Spirit.* The gospel was first preached in Jerusalem and Judea; then the message spread to the uttermost parts of the earth (Acts 1:8). As the fullness of time comes in a complete circle, the gospel must return to its original headquarters: Israel and Jerusalem.

It is interesting to note that not far from the Mount of Olives and the ancient city of David are two buildings where the gospel is reaching nations: Daystar and TBN studios. These two stations, whose networks are headquartered in America, provide twenty-four-hour teaching, singing, and preaching of the gospel worldwide. Christ ascended from—and shall return to—the Mount of Olives; and Jerusalem will be the focal point of blessing and conflict at the time of the end (Zech. 14:2).

America's Fullness of Time

In the 1600s the Turkish Ottoman Empire was a powerful influence in the world influencing three continents and twenty-seven provinces, including Palestine. In the 1700s the British Empire was a dominating global force. The 1800s saw the rise of the French and their arms stretching throughout Europe, even as far as the United States. The 1900s experienced a new "bear" on the block as the paws of Russia (the Soviet Union) and Communism trampled nations in Eastern Europe, including parts of Asia and China. The late twentieth century without a doubt belonged to America. Now in the twenty-first century the economic power, influence, and structure of democracy are slowly transferring from America to the East—including the Asian nations of China and Indonesia along with India and Japan.

In 1669 Nathaniel Morton, the secretary of Plymouth Colony,[2] called those coming to America "the seed of Abraham his servant, and the children of Jacob his chosen…"[3] With the exception of Israel, no other nation other than America, has acquired such large masses of land in a short time and gained world influence and power in such a brief span of history. No other country in modern history has built such a spiritual foundation, based on biblical principles, supporting the gospel around the world, as has America.

It is our Christian principles that motivate us to feed the hungry and bring relief in famine-stricken, third-world nations. It is our Christian compassion that invests in digging freshwater wells, building orphanages, and ministering to the poor. Because of special favor from God upon those who care for the fatherless and widows, believers are actively involved in assisting those who are suffering. Even in times of war, our soldiers attempt to protect the innocent, and when possible go above and beyond to preserve edifices of religious significance in the nations they occupy. America is blessed and unique because of its faith in the Bible and the New Testament Christian principles. Eventually America's fullness will arrive and be accompanied by the same patterns as previous empires that also reached their fullness.

Empires only have a set season and are then replaced by other empires or a new coalition of nations. Only when you understand this fact can you have peace about where America is going—knowing God is in control, and the nation inside the nation—the church—is where the influence and strength must be manifest. (See 1 Peter 2:9.)

During prophetic "crunch time"—the space required for the prophecy to be fulfilled shortens and combined prophecies merge all at once. At the "time of the end" (a phrase used by Daniel in Daniel 8:17; 11:35, 40; 12:4; 12:9), the hundreds of remaining biblical prophecies concerning Israel, the Antichrist, the Tribulation, and the return of Christ will begin to merge into a set time frame. Human time will merge with God's prophetic time. Paul said it this way:

> For He will finish the work and cut it short in righteousness, because the LORD will make a short work upon the earth.
> —ROMANS 9:28

The Greek word translated here as "cut" is *suntemno*, and it means to "contract something by cutting." An illustration would be taking a baggy garment with excessive cloth, cutting a section out, and then sewing the two parts together. You have reduced the amount of cloth and the wide space has become smaller. This same Greek word is also translated as "short," indicating God will contract time, bringing man's rule to an end. At this point in time He will establish His kingdom on earth.

It took 1,878 years from the destruction of Jerusalem to the reestablishing of Israel as a nation in 1948, and the reunification of Jerusalem nineteen years later in 1967. Because we are in the time of the end, what would normally take centuries to fulfill will before our eyes occur within months, weeks, or hours—as we have entered prophetic crunch time.

To continue understanding the times in which we are living, let's take a closer look at the prophecies hidden in the Hebrew alphabet and numbers.

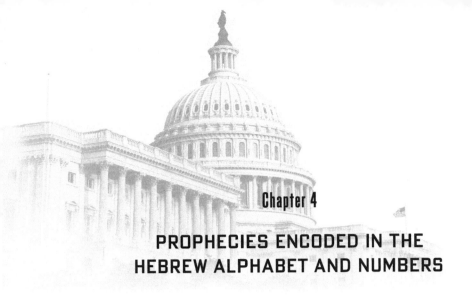

Chapter 4

PROPHECIES ENCODED IN THE
HEBREW ALPHABET AND NUMBERS

IT WAS A warm morning with clear skies over Jerusalem in the early summer of 1985. I clearly recall standing outside the Israeli Larome Hotel, when my tour guide handed me the *Jerusalem Post* with a small, but newsworthy, story. It told how researchers in Jerusalem had discovered "coded messages" in the Bible's first five books—the Torah. Hebrew professors and researchers placed the Hebrew version of the Torah in a computer and programmed it at equal distances and skip-sequences. They ran the program, beginning with the first letter in a sentence or verse, skipping every third, fifth, seventh, tenth, and fiftieth letter; all were biblically significant numbers. They were stunned to see not only word patterns emerge, but also how, contained within the verses, the "code words" or combined phrases could be applied. The article said this included naming thirty-one kinds of trees discovered inside the narrative of the Garden of Eden.

Years later, Michael Drosnin wrote a best-selling book called *The Bible Code*, which explained the method used to decipher these encoded messages. He printed charts with the information showing the Hebrew letters that formed phrases or sentences in the form of various matrixes. In many cases the chance of finding these particular words that connect with the verse was quite astonishing. While the codes were scrutinized by critics, it only added more wood to the burning belief that the Bible is truly a divinely inspired manuscript to believers.

During my studies of rabbinical methods of interpretation, I have learned two other methods of unlocking "encoded information." Not yet exposed to the average Westerner, these techniques are quite fascinating and give direct clues to the events transpiring in the year of the prediction.

Before revealing this method and the messages, please note that these particular "codes" only work with the Hebrew language. Many know Hebrew is a holy language and was created and chosen by God. He chose it to communicate His written Word, the Torah, to speak to His people and His prophets. Christ spoke to Paul from heaven in the Hebrew tongue (Acts 26:14), when the common language of Paul's day was Greek; the Romans spoke Latin, and many commoners in Israel spoke Syriac-Aramaic. As evident in the New Testament, Christ used this language, and the Gospel writer Mark had to interpret it for his readers (Mark 5:41; Mark 15:34). While Greek, Latin, and Aramaic were languages in Christ's day, the mysteries of God are concealed in the Hebrew language and Hebrew text.

Called the *alef-bet*, there exists a sacred mystery shrouding the Hebrew alphabet. The alphabet consists of twenty-two letters that are all consonants. There are no vowels among these twenty-two letters. Around AD 600 a group called the Masoretes placed dots and dashes, called *nikkudim*, under and above the individual Hebrew letters to indicate how the text was to be chanted in the synagogue. These marks assist in adding the correct vowel sounds with the word to be pronounced.

In the opening verse of the Bible, we read in English, "In the beginning God created the heavens and the earth" (Gen. 1:1). In Hebrew it reads, *"Bereshit bara Elohim et hashamayim ve'et ha'arets."* The fourth word in that sentence, *et*, is formed from the two Hebrew letters, *aleph* and *tav*, which are left untranslated. By using these letters throughout the Hebrew Scriptures, you can connect one thought to another. In the middle of the phrase are the first and last letters of the Hebrew alphabet, the *alef* and *tav* (pronounced "et"). In Hebrew grammar this nontranslatable word is used to mark a point, identifying the word that follows it as the direct, definite object.

The original form of the Hebrew alphabet was actually in word pictures. The older text, called the Proto-Canaanite script, consisted of twenty-two forms that represented common images. In speaking of the *alef tav*, the *alef* is the first letter in the alphabet and the last Hebrew letter is *tav*. The word picture for *alef* is the head of an ox, and the word symbol of the *tav* is a cross, or a + sign. This first and last letter of the Hebrew alphabet cryptically reveals an early imagery of the redemption plan, which began with animal sacrifices at the tabernacle and concluded with the final sacrifice of Christ on the cross. In the New Testament Jesus said, "I am Alpha and the Omega" (Rev. 1:8), which are the first and last letter of the Greek alphabet. In Hebrew, He would have said, "I am the *alef* and the *tav*."

When reading Genesis 1:1 in Hebrew, Jewish mystics say the *alef tav* is speaking of the Hebrew alphabet; thus, the verse is saying: "In the beginning God created the *alef tav*..."—the twenty two letters of the alphabet. Thus, He is using Hebrew words and letters to speak out His entire creation. Some Messianic believers note that Christ is the Alef Tav (Rev. 1:8 in the Hebrew text) and the Genesis phrase could imply, "In the beginning God created the Alef Tav" (or "His eternal Word") that would manifest in the form of flesh—Christ Jesus. (See John 1:1–3.)

Another significant picture is the twenty-first letter of the Hebrew alphabet, called the letter *shin*. From its earliest inception, its form is similar to our letter *w*, although it is an *s* sound and not a *w* sound. In Moses's time the high priest was commanded to bless the people with a blessing called the priestly blessing, recorded in Numbers 6:25–27. Jewish tradition teaches that the priest recited the blessing placing both hands, palms outward, with his thumbs touching and the four fingers of his hands split. His hands created the form of the letter *shin* and represented the name *Shaddai*, the name revealing God as the most powerful one (Gen. 17:1).[1]

Moses taught that God would bring His people to a place marked by His name (Deut. 12:11, 21; 14:23–24). That place remains Jerusalem, where three mountains, Ophel, Zion, and Moriah merge to form the area of the ancient city of David.[2] When examining the topography of these three areas, the hills merge to form a similar shape of the letter *shin*. Since *shin* represents *Shaddai*, the true name for God (translated as *Almighty* in Gen. 17:1), then the features of these three mountains in Jerusalem visibly reveal where God "placed His name."

The Alphabet-Number Exchange System

Greek and Hebrew are two languages in which each letter of the alphabet is given a numerical value. In Hebrew the first letter, *alef,* is matched with the number one, and the numbering continues until you reach the final letter, *tav,* the twenty-second letter, whose numerical value is four hundred.

There are thirty-two principles of biblical exegesis used by Jewish sages to interpret the Torah. The twenty-ninth principle is called *gematria.* Jewish commentaries teach that this method of giving the alphabet numerical values was given to Israel on Mount Sinai.[3] The word for "gematria" is derived from the Greek word *geometria* meaning "earth measure," from where we derive the word *geometry.* The ancient alphabets of both the Hebrew and Greek use this system as they interchange the letters of the alphabet with numbers and the numbers also are exchanged back to the letters. In Hebrew every letter has a value, every word has a sum value, and at times, entire sentences can have a total, specific numerical value.

Here's an example of how the value is calculated. Using the name *Jesus,* *Yeshua* is transliterated as *Iesous* in Greek. The chart shows the English letter transliterated from Greek; the Greek letter and its Greek numerical value, as both Hebrew and Greek use the alphabet-number exchange system.

The English Letter	The Original Greek Letter	The Value in the Greek
I	Iota	10
E	Eta	8
S	Sigma	200
O	Omicron	70
U	Upsilon	400
S	Sigma	200
		Total: 888

The biblical number eight was researched years ago by E. W. Bullinger (1837–1913), who noted the patterns of eights in the life of Jacob, Abraham, and others.[4] He also noted eight classes of furniture in the temple, and other patterns of eights:

> » Jewish male infants were circumcised on the eighth day (Gen. 17:12); and the firstborn son was to be given to God on the eighth day (Exod. 22:29–30).

> » Noah was the eighth soul among the eight lives spared in the ark during the flood (2 Pet. 2:5).

> » After eight days, Moses and Elijah appeared and Christ was transfigured (Luke 9:30).

> » Thomas saw Christ, and his faith was restored eight days after the resurrection (John 20:26).

Thus, eight is the number for a new beginning; Christ began a new covenant (Heb. 12:24), making us new creations (2 Cor. 5:17), promising us a home in the New Jerusalem (Rev. 21–22).

On the Jewish Festival, Feast of Trumpets in 2008, the Jewish New Year began at sunset, September 29. Israel is on a seven-hour difference from Eastern Standard Time. On that day the Dow Jones lost 777.7 points in one day while the Standard & Poor's Index (S&P 500) lost 8.8 percent the same day. It was the *seventh* worst day of losses ever on the S&P.[5] Around that same time gold was selling at $888 an ounce. These numbers, 777, 8.8 percent, 888, are significant in biblical numerology and also in prophetic terms. Seven is God's number of completion and the number eight represents a new beginning. Again in Greek, the name *Jesus* totals 888, and gold was selling for $888 an ounce. I immediately thought of God's message to the wealthy Laodicea church:

> Because you say, "I am rich, have become wealthy, and have need of nothing"—and do not know that you are wretched, miserable, poor, blind, and naked—I counsel you to buy from Me gold refined in the fire, that you may be rich; and white garments, that you may be clothed.
>
> —Revelation 3:17–18

God was warning America that a *refining fire* was coming! This stock market shock occurred the first day of the ten "Days of Awe" on the Jewish calendar. This is a time where devout Jews believe God is setting in motion His judicial decisions related to the repentance, or lack thereof, among His people.

In Jewish thought it is within these ten days that God is examining the *reaction* of His people. They will either turn (repent) and forsake their sins or stubbornly remain in their disobedience to face consequences. During this season, decisions are made by God for His people for the upcoming twelve months.

In 2008 Americans showed no repentance or humility following this warning and here is what resulted:

Mortgage crisis	Loss of millions of homes as home values dropped
Banking crisis	Government bailout of banks and lending institutions
Wall Street crisis	Market began collapsing with people losing millions of dollars in investments
Transportations	Major auto companies needed government bailouts
Job market	Highest unemployment in years
Recession	Greatest recession began since the Great Depression

Biblical Names With Prophetic Significance

When a combination of numbers that holds biblical and prophetic significance is evident at once, this can be a prophetic layer that is encrypting a message, such as a warning or an attention getter. Such an "attention getter" is found when the numbers are assigned to the Hebrew and Greek letters in the names *Lord, Jesus,* and *Christ.*

In the New Testament our Savior has three names: Lord, Jesus, and Christ (Acts 11:17). This exact combination is used in eighty-one verses. In Greek the word *Lord* refers to a master or owner. The name *Jesus,* from the Hebrew form *Yeshua,* means "God (Yahweh) saves." The name *Christ* in Greek is *Christos* (meaning "the anointed one," a Greek word similar to the Hebrew word *Mashiach*). It is a name used for the Jewish Messiah, or the anointed one at the end of days. Each of the three names has a Greek and Hebrew numerical equivalent.

	LORD	JESUS	CHRIST	
In Hebrew	37	397	358	Total: 792
In Greek	800	888	1,480	Total: 3,168

Thus, the sum total of these three names is 3,168 in Greek and 792 in Hebrew. Christ was God made flesh; thus, divinity took on humanity, to introduce a new redemptive covenant. Biblically, four is an earthly or carnal number, and Christ's name in Hebrew totals 792; multiplied four times, it equals the Greek total of 3,168.

Notice, some interesting numbers begin to emerge when totaling the Hebrew *gematria* of the names of the original twelve tribes of Israel. Below they are presented in English for the reader, but using the Hebrew alphabet prior to Ephraim and Manasseh, notice the interesting outcome:

Tribal Name	Numerical Value in Hebrew
Asher	= 501
Benjamin	= 152
Dan	= 55
Gad	= 8
Issachar	= 830
Joseph	= 156
Judah	= 30

Tribal Name	Numerical Value in Hebrew
Levi	= 46
Naphtali	= 570
Rueben	= 259
Simeon	= 466
Zebulon	= 95
	Total: 3,168

These twelve men formed the twelve tribes of Israel, the nation from which the Messiah would emerge. Christ is called the seed of the woman (Gen. 3:15), and the ruler from the tribe of Judah (Gen. 49:10). Amazingly the numerical value of the twelve tribes, from the original Hebrew alphabet, totals 3,168, encoding the name Lord Jesus Christ.

Christ and David both were born in Bethlehem in the tribal territory of Judah. The numerical value of Judah is thirty. David was thirty when he became King of Israel (2 Sam. 5:4), and Christ was thirty when He was baptized and began His public ministry (Luke 3:23).

Christ was born in Bethlehem and from the Temple Mount in Jerusalem to Bethlehem is about six miles. Six miles equals 31,680 feet. Bethlehem was the place where lambs that were selected for the daily offerings at the temple were born and raised, and the farmland in Bethlehem was believed to provide the wheat for the grain used to make the bread for the priests at the temple. The Hebrew name *Bethlehem* means "house of bread." Christ was born in Bethlehem in a stable, a place where lambs abode, and He was the "bread which came down from heaven" (John 6:41). From the place of His birth to the place where He would die and rise again, the distance between these two cities encodes Christ's three New Testament titles: Lord, Jesus, and Christ!

Creation Reveals a Divinely Ordered Numeric Code

Christ's fingerprint is found throughout creation. The atmosphere containing oxygen that we breathe is sixty miles from the ground to the sky. One mile is 5,280 feet, so multiplying sixty miles with 5,280 feet totals 316,800 feet. In Hebrew, if zeros are at the end of a number they can be dropped as they hold no numerical value; thus, we have the root number 3,168, which is the sum total in Greek for *Lord, Jesus, Christ.* This fact reminds me of this verse, "He gives to all life, breath, and all things" (Acts 17:25).

David wrote, "I will praise you, for I am fearfully and wonderfully made" (Ps. 139:14). Man was created in God's image. His likeness encoded throughout our own bodies is a message to whom we belong. Certain biblical numbers with spiritual meanings also are connected to the human body. For example:

» There are 60,000 miles of blood vessels, which convert to 316,800,000 feet; the root number 3,168 being *Lord Jesus Christ* in Greek.

» The brain of an average man weighs approximately 3.168 pounds, which to me speaks of a believer having the mind of Christ.

» The Jewish rabbis teach there are 365 sinews in the human body—holding all things together, parallel to the 365 days a year that God sustains a man's life.

» The foot has twenty-six bones. The sacred name of God, YHVH, consists of these Hebrew letters: *Yud, Hei, Vav* and *Hei,* totaling twenty-six. This speaks to us that we must, like Enoch of old, *walk* with God by faith.

» The human rib cage has twenty-four ribs—twelve on each side. In heaven there are twenty-four elders—twelve on each side of God's throne, representing the twelve sons of Jacob and the twelve apostles of the lamb. The ribs in the body represent the divine order God has established regarding the major organs in the human body as the ribs protect the heart, lungs, and other vital organs.

» The arms and legs all have thirty bones each, or a total of one hundred twenty bones. God said to Noah that a man's days would be one hundred twenty years (Gen. 6:3). The body of Christ was formed with one hundred twenty believers (Acts 1:15).

» The pelvic bones have three fused bones holding the torso together, three being the number of unity.

» We are created with a divinely ordered numerical flow as the foot has twenty-six bones, the hand twenty-seven, and the skull twenty-eight.

» The average heart weighs slightly over ten ounces. The Ten Commandments are to be obeyed with the heart and not just the mind.

God's Name Is Written on Our Hearts

"The life of the flesh is in the blood" (Lev. 17:11), and the *heart* is the center of the body, pumping an average of seventy milliliters of blood each heartbeat, providing oxygen and keeping us alive. The heart is divided into halves. Both halves have two chambers inside, the left and right atrium and the left and right ventricle. If we could cut a heart in half and see the inner shape of the chambers, the heart walls form the profile of the twenty-first letter of the Hebrew alphabet—*Shin*, the uniquely sacred Hebrew letter that represents the name of God. This letter has maintained a principal shape, even though the form of the twenty-two Hebrew letters has evolved over the centuries. The *Shin* is placed on the outside of every mezuzah, the small object holding Scripture placed on the right side of the doorpost in Jewish homes. This letter represents the first letter in God's name, Shaddai. The name *Shaddai* is a name that serves as an acronym for "Guardian of the doorways of Israel."

The four chambers in the human heart form the Hebrew letter representing God's name. God marked His name in your heart when you were formed in your mother's womb. In the Torah, God commanded His people to "Love the LORD your God with all your heart and with all your soul and with all your strength. These commandments that I give you today are to be on your hearts" (Deut. 6:5–7, NIV).

Searching for Biblical Codes

The idea that the Bible contains encoded layers is not just some contemporary concept. Before the birth of Christ, the Essenes, a group of men living in a self-sustaining community at Qumran near the Dead Sea (50 BC to AD 70), were said to have an understanding of exchanging letters to reveal future events.

> The "Essenes"... [had] the gift of Prophecy. They had knowledge to give numerical values to letters.... They exchanged certain letters with opposite letters.... They could not only predict the details of the fulfillment of a Sacred Writing, but could determine the exact time of the prophecy's fulfillment with astute accuracy. Rarely, if ever, did their predictions prove wrong.[6]

Using this value exchange method and their interpretation of certain passages in the Book of Enoch, the Essenes predicted a restoration of Israel after seventy generations from Babylonian captivity, which did occur. Dating Nebuchadnezzar's first invasion around 606 BC and moving forward to 1948, the years of Israel's complete restoration is 2,554 years using a standard calendar. Seventy generations of 2,554 years would average thirty-six years for a generation.* The seventy generations to restore Israel was understood among religious Jews, including the father of Menachem Begin (Israel's prime minster 1977–1983), who told his young son that he would be a leader one day in the Jewish state that God would restore—as his son was the seventieth generation.[7]

In the seventeenth century Sir Isaac Newton was a Christian who spent many of his years researching the Bible. Many of Newton's theories still stand the scientific test today. Newton regarded the universe as a "cryptogram set by the Almighty." Some have suggested that Newton was familiar with the Jewish studies of his day, where rabbis were attempting to discover

---

* Earlier in this book I referred to a generation as one hundred years. This was in reference to generations before the flood. The average length of man's days was reduced after the flood, changing the length of a generation.

codes within the biblical text. They believe he may have set forth his own research—although some Newton historians deny this.[8]

An actual Torah scroll is handwritten on kosher parchment under strict rules and standards. The scroll has no numbered verses or verse divisions, but each page has forty-two lines of hand written letters inscribed on sheets of animal skin sewn together. In antiquity the Hebrew texts were divided into paragraphs identified by two Hebrew letters; the letter *Pe* to begin a paragraph and the letter *Samech* to close a paragraph. Stephen Langton, Archbishop of Canterbury, added chapters divisions to the Bible in AD 1227. The Wycliffe English Bible of 1382 was the first to use the chapter and verse headings. The first Hebrew Bible to be divided with chapters and verses was in 1448 by Rabbi Nathan. The verse numbers change as the thought structure in the sentence changes, and the chapter heading divided the thoughts and stories.

Among the rabbinical methods of interpretation, the verses in the Torah (first five books), which are numbered in our Bible, at times can match the same Jewish year, and reveal the historic date in which the prediction in the verse was fulfilled. Keep in mind that the Jewish reckoning of time is different from our Gregorian calendar. For example, the Gregorian year 2015 is the Jewish year 5776, and each new Jewish New Year begins in fall months (September or October) on our calendar.

To understand how this method works, we need to start with an understanding of the number of verses in the Torah. Below is a list of the total number of verses in the Torah in a standard English Bible:

Genesis	1,533
Exodus	1,213
Leviticus	859
Numbers	1,288
Deuteronomy	959

5,852 total verses

Next, if we look at a Jewish year and match it with the corresponding verse number in the Torah, we will discover the Jewish year and verse number combination reveals a prophetic event that occurred during that year. It's also interesting to show the matching Jewish and Gregorian years as many Gentile events occurred on a particular year on the Gregorian calendar. Here is how it works:

Jewish Year	Matching Gregorian Year	Matching Verse
5708	1948	Deuteronomy 30:5 (the 5,708th verse)

Using this method, we examine the 5,708th verse in the Torah, Deuteronomy 30:5 (KJV), which predicts:

The LORD thy God will bring thee into the land which thy fathers possessed, and thou shalt possess it; and he will do thee good, and multiply thee above thy fathers.

This verse is God's promise that Israel would return to the Promised Land after being dispersed. This return to the land occurred after the Holocaust, at the end of World War II. The British mandate ended at midnight May 14, 1948, and the Jews were given a homeland, called Israel, after almost 1,878 years of being scattered throughout the Gentile nations. Notice how the verse number 5,708 matched the Jewish year 5708, and how accurately the verse described what occurred on the Gregorian calendar, May 14, 1948.

Using this method of matching the Jewish year to the verse in the Torah and interchanging that year for the same Gregorian year, we notice there are several single or combined verses that predict events involving Israel and Jews; each conceals a clue, which we can unlock by matching dates with verses. The next verse is connected with the Jewish year 5712, which is the Gregorian year 1952. The 5,712th verse in the Torah is found in Deuteronomy 30:9, KJV:

And the LORD thy God will make thee plenteous in every work of thine hand, in the fruit of thy cattle, and in the fruit of thy land, for good; for the LORD will again rejoice over thee for good, as he rejoiced over thy fathers.

After Israel returns to their land as promised in the Hebrew year 5708, four verses later (representing four years later) God promised to increase the land of Israel with cattle and agricultural prosperity. History reveals that it was in the early 1950s when David Ben Gurion initiated a program to make the desert (Negev) blossom like a rose (Isa. 35:1–7). Today in the southern half of Israel, in the heart of the Aravah desert, there are thousands of acres of farming communities that have turned the desolate places into a garden of fruits and vegetables. In the region north of the Dead Sea, thousands of acres of date trees, vineyards, and other forms of fruits have carpeted the once barren desert with agricultural prosperity.

Moving nineteen years forward from 1948, the Jewish year of 5727 brings us to the year of 1967. The Jewish year changes in the middle of our Gregorian year, as the Jewish New Year begins in the fall on the Feast of Trumpets (also called Rosh Hashanah), meaning the "head of the year." Below are two verses, which would be 5726–5727 on the Jewish calendar, and 1966–1967 on the secular Gregorian reckoning. The 5,726th and 5,727th verses in the Torah are found in Deuteronomy 31:3–4 (KJV), which reads:

> The LORD thy God, he will go over before thee, and he will destroy these nations from before thee, and thou shalt possess them: and Joshua, he shall go over before thee, as the Lord hath said. And the LORD shall do unto them as he did to Sihon and to Og, kings of the Amorites, and unto the land of them, whom he destroyed.

In the time of Moses, Sihon was a strong king ruling in Jordan, and Og was the King in Bashan, the mountainous land in North Israel; today it borders Syria and Lebanon. Back in 1966 the West Bank in Israel, known as Transjordan, the Bashan area, or the Golan Heights, was under complete Syrian control. One year later, during the 1967 Six-Day War, Israel mounted an offensive attack in which these ancient areas—the West Bank (Judea and Samaria) and Bashan (the Golan Heights) were annexed into Israel. Just as ancient Israel defeated the kings Og and Sihon, taking their land for Israel's inheritance, in 1967 both regions were captured by Israeli forces, fulfilling Deuteronomy 31:3–4 by taking possession of their Promised Land. Modern Israel in 5727 defeated the armies in surrounding nations, taking possession of the same land promised to Abraham and Moses.

Moving another nineteen years forward from 1967, the Jewish year 5746 matches our year of 1986. The 5,746th verse in the Torah is penned in Deuteronomy 31:23:

> Then He inaugurated Joshua the son of Nun, and said, "Be strong
> and of good courage; for you shall bring the children of Israel into
> the land of which I swore to them, and I will be with you."

This prediction speaks of the Hebrew people returning to the land of
Israel from their forty years of wandering in the wilderness. Although
modern Israel as a nation was reborn in 1948, a multitude of Jews were
still living in Eastern Europe and in the Soviet Union, unable to get visas
to leave the oppressive Communist nations and return to their homeland.
These Holocaust survivors were like the ancient Hebrews who wandered in
the dry wilderness, dreaming of the day when they could cross the border
of their own "Jordan Rivers" to settle in the land of their ancestors. After
forty years in the wilderness Joshua brought the people into their spiritual
inheritance, and toward the end of Israel's first forty years as a nation Jews
began being airlifted back to their original Promised Land.

In 1984 Israeli military conducted a covert airlift called Operation Moses,
evacuating Ethiopian Jews from famine-ravaged Sudan and granting permanent visas to 8,000 individuals. In the Soviet Union, under the leadership of Mikhail Gorbachev, the borders of the Soviet states were opened,
enabling the Jews to leave. Between 1989 and 2006 about 1.6 million Jews
migrated to Israel. Before this time, if a Jew attempted to acquire an exit
visa from the Soviet Union, they were often rejected, branded a traitor, fired
from their jobs, and marked for harassment and persecution.[9]

From 1989 moving another nineteen years forward and matching the
Torah verses with the Jewish year, there is sudden transition in thought that
occurs in the Torah beginning with our Gregorian year 2008. Deuteronomy
32:15 (KJV) states:

> But Jeshurun waxed fat, and kicked: thou art waxen fat, thou art
> grown thick, thou art covered with fatness; then he forsook God
> which made him, and lightly esteemed the Rock of his salvation.

The word *Jeshurun* is a word for the upright or those who were walking
righteous before God. This indicates that God's people would rebel and
fight against God because they are "fat"—a word used as a metaphor for
prosperity and success. Deuteronomy 32:17 says they sacrificed to devils
and took up new gods. Sacrificing to devils is not just idolatry but it can

also allude to Molech worship—where the ancients offered their infants to the idol Molech, by passing them through the fire (Lev. 18:21; 20:2–4). This evil act would be considered the modern practice of abortion today.

There has been a shifting in the church since 2008. Since extreme liberals have been in control in every level of government, many have shifted their opinions favoring iniquity and changing their convictions as to what is right and wrong. In some circles ministers are publicly accepting abortion as a birth control option, while some "financially rape" their members by demanding offerings that are not used for outreach or ministry but their personal lusts and lifestyles. Christ was concerned that when He returned people would have *no faith* (see Luke 18:8). Also, in Deuteronomy 32:20 (matching 2013), the Lord says, "They are a forward generation, children in whom there is no faith" (KJV).

Some may be thinking that these are historic verses that deal with Israel and one cannot force them to apply to America. This is like saying, "I know America has numerous patterns of ancient Israel, but that is insignificant." Perhaps to the Western scholars this method is futile, but not to rabbinical hermeneutics where the past repeats in the future and past empires are reborn in future empires. Israel and America have a spiritual umbilical cord that releases the same blessings on both nations for obedience. Likewise, this same lifeline can unleash "curses" or disfavor for their unbelief or because they turn away from God.

If we match Deuteronomy 32:22 (2015) and move forward through the next several verses, which fall on the Gregorian years 2015–2023, the people are warned to consider their "latter end" (v. 29), a reference to the warning of the "latter days" in Deuteronomy 31:29. Biblically the phrase "latter days" refers to the return of the Messiah.

In these passages God warns that strange nations will rise against God's chosen (Deut. 32:21). God will send a fire that will consume the increase. This can be natural disasters and fires burning the land (v. 22). The Torah predicts arrows will be sent, which is a metaphor used for wars and fighting (a prediction of internal fighting or involvement in a war around 2016–2017). Something will affect the food supplies (v. 24) and burning heat can allude to a drought or famine (v. 24). God warns of terror within the nations (v. 25), which brings us to our Gregorian year of 2018–2019 (adding the Jewish year changes in the fall of our year). We read where the people do not acknowledge that these combined disasters are judgment from God, and in verse 29 God said that they should consider their "latter end." This verse matches the time frame of our year 2022.

Based on previous matching verses, many of these scenarios and warnings apply to national Israel. However, because America is the mirror of Israel in founding documents, religious beliefs, and patterns, what applies to Israel can have a parallel application for America. As observed, the thoughts change from blessings to warnings and predictions of severe trouble, including fire on the earth, hunger, sword, and terror without and within its borders.

The Significance of One Hundred Twenty Years

The Torah and Deuteronomy wrap up with the death of Moses and these words:

> And Moses was an hundred and twenty years old when he died:
> his eye was not dim, nor his natural force abated.
> —DEUTERONOMY 34:7

There are specific numbers used throughout the Bible that have meanings. The number three always represents unity; six is the number of man, and seven is perfection and completion. Forty is identified with biblical accounts where there is a temptation, test, or trial. The number one hundred twenty is found in several biblical narratives. The first reference is where God gave man one hundred twenty years before the flood struck the earth (Gen 6:3). Moses's life ceased after one hundred twenty years (Deut. 34:7). There were one hundred twenty priests blasting trumpets at the dedication of the temple (2 Chron. 5:12). The church was birthed on Pentecost, and the initial prayer meeting in the Upper Room consisted of one hundred twenty believers (Acts 1:15). After Moses's death at age one hundred twenty, Joshua, whose Hebrew name was Yeshuah, led the people from the wilderness into the Promised Land.

Hebrew students have noted this biblical number and the multiple layers or combinations that can total one hundred twenty. Moses was in Egypt forty years; he spent another forty years in the wilderness watching sheep, and then became Israel's pastor after the exodus for yet another forty years—totaling one hundred twenty years.

Using one hundred twenty and multiplying it with other biblically significant numbers reveals a possible pattern. God's law established a Jubilee cycle that was every fiftieth year (Lev. 25). One hundred twenty Jubilee cycles (120 multiplied 50 times) is six thousand. This is interesting considering that from the creation of Adam to the present time is about, or slightly over six thousand years. It was after one hundred twenty years that Moses passed away and Joshua, whose Hebrew name is Yeshua, led the "church in the wilderness" (Acts 7:38) to their Promised Land. At a set future moment in time, King Jesus (Rev. 19:16), whose Hebrew name is also Yeshua, will lead the saints into their Promised Land, and together we will rule with Him in His kingdom for a thousand years (Rev. 20:4).

These parallels are all found in the Book of Deuteronomy, which also lists the numerous blessings for obeying the commandments of God and the curses pronounced for those who willfully choose to turn from the ways and instructions of the Lord. In my previous books I have explained how the same blessing provided for Israel, from obedience, will follow any nation who commits its laws to align with God's social, moral, and judicial laws. However, the same disfavor will apply to those who act in arrogance as ancient Israel did, only to watch their national and personal blessing fade like fog in the heat.

The Years Exchanged Back to Letters

Another method of rabbinical interpretation I encountered through the teaching of a noted rabbi was taking the Gregorian year, transferring it back to the Jewish year, and matching the number with the proper Hebrew letter in its alphabet. This method was taught and used by a Lubavitcher Rabbi, Menachem Schneerson, from Brooklyn, New York. He was a noted scholar in the Torah, mathematics, and science, and before his death had hundreds of thousands of followers and students. Schneerson used a system of taking the Jewish year and transferring the numbers back to the letters of the Hebrew alphabet to see if they formed words or acrostics with messages. His research was quite amazing.

We begin with the Gregorian years 1909 through 1910. (Remember, the

Jewish calendar begins in the fall months.) The year that began in the fall of 1909 was the Jewish year 5670. Taking these numbers and translating them back to the Hebrew alphabet, the numbers produce the letters that have the meaning of "Hat'reah," which means to sound an alarm—from the word *teruah,* which is a sound from a shofar. This word indicated that some form of trouble was brewing in the near future and warning signs were on the horizon. Global trouble did strike four years later with the beginning of World War I.

Note: It was during this same time (February 1910), looming in the darkness of a poor house for men in Vienna, that a young Adolf Hitler began to develop his demonic taste for anti-Semitism. "I owe it to *that period* that I grew hard," Hitler stated in *Mein Kampf.* He immersed himself in anti-Semitic literature. Then he went out and studied Jews as they passed by, stating, "The more I saw, the more sharply they became distinguished in my eyes from the rest of humanity." Hitler affirmed in his book, "For me this was the time of the greatest spiritual upheaval I have ever had to go through. I had ceased to be a weak-kneed cosmopolitan and become an anti-Semite."[10]

World War I began in 1914, on the Jewish year 5674. When exchanging these numbers for Hebrew letters of the alphabet, the letters spell the Hebrew word for *tremble.* August 1, 1914 was the start of World War I. This date on the Jewish calendar was also the ninth of Av, meaning that Word War I began on the most negative date of the year on the Jewish calendar.

Moving forward to the years 1938 and 1939, we arrive at the initial Hebrew year 5698. Exchanging these numbers for the corresponding Hebrew alphabet, the letters spell the word *murder.* The prophetic implication of these years, corresponding with circumstances leading to the beginning of the Holocaust, was the greatest seven years of the murdering of innocent people in world history.

Using this system, the former noted rabbi from Brooklyn, New York, Menachem Schneerson, noted that 1947–1948 (the Jewish year 5708) spells an acrostic for "seasons of the birth pains." It was the birth pains of the Holocaust that gave birth to a new Jewish state, Israel, in 1948. The term *birth pains* is used both in Judaism and Christianity. The initial signs of Christ's return are called the "beginning of sorrows" (Matt. 24:8, KJV). The Greek word *sorrows* literally means "birth pains." Among Jewish rabbis, parallel signs are called "birth pains of the Messiah." Isaiah wrote about this when he saw the birth pains leading up to the restoration of Israel as a nation in Isaiah 66:7–8:

> Before she was in labor, she gave birth; before her pain came, she delivered a male child. Who has heard such a thing? Who has seen such things? Shall the earth be made to give birth in one day? Or shall a nation be born at once? For as soon as Zion was in labor, she gave birth to her children.

Another year that stands out is the Gregorian year 1973, the Jewish year 5734, whose numbers are exchanged for letters containing the word *sheled* which means skeleton. A skeleton implies death. It forms an acrostic for "seasons of the skeleton." It was in 1973 that the Supreme Court voted to legalize abortion, which to this point has taken the lives of more than fifty-five million infants in America alone.[11] The same year, in October, the Syrian and Egyptian armies launched a surprise assault on Israel on their national fast day, Yom Kippur.

I recall the same New York rabbi announcing in 1989 through 1990 (the Jewish year 5750) that, based on the Jewish calendar year, exchanging it for the letter, it formed an acrostic "Season of Miracles." In retrospect this was the beginning of a marvelous miracle as the Jews from the Soviet Union for the first time were granted permission to return in mass numbers to Israel, also fulfilling numerous Old Testament prophecies (Ezek. 20:34; 36:24; 37:12).

In the years 1997 through 1998 the Jewish year 5758 had arrived. This was a significant year, as the last two numbers of this Jewish year are 58. The Hebrew letter *chet* has a numerical equivalent of eight and the Hebrew letter *nun* has the value of fifty, totaling fifty-eight. *Nun* and *chet* spell the Hebrew name *Noach*, or in English, *Noah*. During 1997 and 1998, the emphasis was "the seasons of Noah."

An interesting cosmic prodigy occurred in 1997–1998. During this year a bright comet called Hale-Bopp was visible for months. A Jewish tradition stated that Noah saw a great comet pass by when he was building the ark. It was reported that Hale-Bopp would have been the same comet that was visible on earth at the time prior to Noah's flood! The year, the name of Noah, and the comet are all prodigies that reminded me of the words of

Christ: "As it was in the days of Noah, so it will be at the coming of the Son of Man" (Matt. 24:37, NIV).

I realize this method of interpretation is controversial, especially to Western scholars, and it is only taught in certain rabbinical schools of thought that emphasize the secret or mystical level of biblical interpretation. However, to me this only proves that each word and phrase in the Bible, every "jot or one tittle," are inspired—placed in divine order by God (Matt. 5:18; 2 Tim. 3:16). It should also remind us of the words of Daniel:

> But you, O Daniel, shut up the words, and seal the book, even to the time of the end: many shall run to and fro, and knowledge shall increase.
>
> —DANIEL 12:4, KJV

The Nineteen-Year Cycles

Many of these Torah predictions, whose verse numbers and calendar dates run parallel with Israel, often emerge within nineteen-year cycles. The greatest prophetic fulfillment in modern history was when Israel became a nation in 1948, as no end time or Second Coming prophecy could be fulfilled until the Jews had a homeland. If we move forward and backward every nineteen years from the pivotal prophetic year 1948, history records events that affected the Jews, and at times America. There are so many dates that the list would be pages. I have selected a few for examples.

Israel's Nineteen-Year Cycles— Moving Backward From 1948

1948	Israel was reestablished as a nation after eighteen centuries.
1929	The year of the beginning of the stock market collapse and the Great Depression.
1910	Return of Halley's Comet—which often appears throughout history four years before wars.
1891	The International Socialists Congress met in Brussels to answer the "Jewish question."
1872	Russian Zionists begin setting up Jewish settlements in Palestine.

If we continue counting back, using the nineteen-year cycles starting from 1948, we will eventually come to the years 1530, 1606, and 1492. In 1530 the Turks already had possession of Jerusalem and were making plans to rebuild the walls of the old city, which would fulfill Isaiah 60:10, "The sons of strangers shall rebuild thy walls" (KJV). Here the Hebrew word *strangers* is not Gentiles but *foreigners*. For America, some of our first ancestors set sail from England in 1606, arriving at the American mainland on April 26, 1607. They founded the Jamestown colony on May 14, 1607, as our first colony. In the year 1492 two major events were occurring the same month: Jews were being expelled from Spain, and Columbus was discovering a new continent—America. These significant occurrences were separated by nineteen-year cycles.

Now, let us explore what comes to light if we mark 1948 and move forward every nineteenth year. We will see that significant prophetic years emerge.

Israel's Nineteen Year Cycles— Moving Forward From 1948

1948	Israel was reestablished as a nation after eighteen centuries
1967	After the Six-Day War Jerusalem was reunited as the capital of Israel
1986	Jews began returning from Gentile nations, especially from the northern countries
2005	Jews were forcibly removed from settlements in Gaza; Hurricane Katrina struck New Orleans
2024	The date is yet to be seen

Prophetically, Israel will have strong birth pains and sorrows in the time of the end with surrounding Islamic nations, many who are descendants of Ishmael, Abraham's son through Hagar (Gen. 16:15). In Hebrew the name *Ishmael* consists of the words *yishma*, meaning "hear," and *El*—El being a two-lettered name of God. The original name Ishmael was given to his mother, Hagar, as she cried out to God in the desert to spare her and her young son, and God heard her. The Jewish Midrash comments that at the end of days the Arabs will cause much trouble for Israel and the Jewish people will cry out to God and He will hear them—(*yishma-el*).[12]

The Alignment of Future Crunch Cycles

All biblical prophecy in the sixty-six books of the Bible are addressed to one of four groups, or at times a combination of the four. The Scripture references are too numerous to list so I will keep the list simple and short:

» Prophecies addressed to the nation of *Israel*

» Prophecies addressed to the *Gentile nations*

» Prophecies addressed to the *church* and *believers*

» Prophecies addressed to *individuals*, including *leaders*

Prophecies not only speak words revealing future events, but can also provide instruction, give direct warnings, and reveal "signs" or "triggers" that will occur. When these signs are fulfilled, they pull the curtain back and release onto the world stage the events predicted. When the Bible lists particular signs, they too are layered in the context of the prediction for distinct nations, people or moments in history. There are six different types of signs:

» There are signs concerning the nation of *Israel, the Jews, and Jerusalem*—its past, present, and future.

» There are signs concerning the alignment or the dealings of *nations* with Israel, the Jews, and Jerusalem.

» There are signs concerning the *first appearing of the Messiah*—fulfilled in Christ.

» There are signs concerning the *second coming of the Messiah*—being fulfilled now and in the future.

» There are signs and warnings given to the *church and believers* to observe prior to Christ's return.

» There are signs given to *individuals* as a witness of God's will, direction, or miraculous power.

When the time and appointed season approaches for a prophetic event to be fulfilled, the prophecies linked with that event will merge quickly and accurately. The fulfillment is undeniable to the student of Scripture. Here are two major events coming full circle in our time that should alert prophetic students.

1. The fall of Egypt and Libya

When the alleged "Arab Spring" spread throughout the Middle East and President Mubarak was arrested, I stated that if we were truly in the last-day cycle, then Libya would fall next and both nations would have internal struggles for government control, military power, and financial authority. I based this prediction on Daniel, where the future Antichrist seizes power in both Egypt and Libya—something impossible under the leadership of former Presidents Mubarak in Egypt and Gadaffi in Libya. Daniel predicted:

> He shall stretch out his hand against the countries, and the land of Egypt shall not escape. He shall have power over the treasures of gold and silver, and over all the precious things of Egypt; also the Libyans and Ethiopians shall follow at his heels.
>
> —DANIEL 11:42–43

Daniel and John saw the rise of ten kings ruling ten kingdoms in the years prior to the Messiah's return (Dan. 7:24; Rev. 17:12). When the Antichrist comes to full power, he will uproot—or take over—three of the ten nations. According to Daniel and several of the early church fathers, the three nations will be Egypt, Libya, and Ethiopia, all located in the northern horn of Africa. Presently, Egypt is under the Egyptian military command, and Libya is a country where three main tribes are competing to be the controlling group. Ethiopia was once a strong Christian nation, but recently has seen a rise in Islam and Islamic radicals attempting to make inroads. The shakeup of Egypt and Libya, within months of each other, was a definite preparation season for coming events.

2. The rise of the Persians

The biblical name *Persia* is the ancient name for modern Iran. The Iranians have at times been viewed by the West as a rather backwoods, oil-producing nation. However, the Iranians are made up of predominantly

Shi'ite Muslims, and their spiritual leaders have strong Islamic traditions on the signs of the end of days and the rise of the Mahdi. They believe the Mahdi is the final Islamic leader who will emerge from Iran or Iraq, uniting Muslim nations under one banner and finalizing a global conquest, including the forced conversion of multitudes to Islam. In the Shi'ite tradition, the "cross" (Christians) and the "swine" (the Jews) must convert or be exterminated by death.

For several years, the Persians have been acquiring and enriching uranium for nuclear power, but they are also involved in a clandestine attempt to create nuclear warheads. According to my sources in Israel, it is believed they have already obtained several nukes, and have been working on building a missile delivery system to reach Israel, Europe, and eventually the United States. Ships from North Korea have been intercepted with material and needed parts to assist the Persians in their nuclear ambitions.

The significance in the military strength and rise of the Iranian nation is the fact they are specifically mentioned by their ancient name, Persia, as being one of the main instigators in the future war of Gog and Magog in Ezekiel 38. We read:

> I will turn you around, put hooks into your jaws, and lead you out, with all your army, horses, and horsemen, all splendidly clothed, a great company with bucklers and shields, all of them handling swords. Persia, Ethiopia, and Libya are with them, all of them with shield and helmet.
>
> —EZEKIEL 38:4–6

All three monotheistic world religions (Christianity, Islam, and Judaism) believe in this future conflict, and all three identify this battle with the name, "the war of Gog and Magog," although all three have a different interpretation of the final outcome.

The "Codes" in the Gog and Magog War

Informed prophetic students have often asked me if I believe this battle of Gog will occur *before, during,* or *after* the catching away of the church. This is a difficult question to answer, but the Bible gives three important clues about the circumstances linking the *timing* of the war. The prophet foresaw the war occurring in the "latter days" (Ezek. 38:16), a term used in connection with times and seasons prior to the return of the Messiah. The New Testament would call this same phrase the "last days" (Acts 2:17; 2 Tim. 3:1; 2 Pet. 3:3; James 5:3); both terms are synonymous with events before Christ's coming. The second "timing" clue is when Israel is dwelling safely in their land (Ezek. 38:14). This was impossible prior to Israel's reestablishment as a nation in 1948, but today with advanced technology and a strong military, Israel has secured its borders, and Israelis can live normal lives. A third and interesting clue concerning life in Israel, when the war is unleashed, Israel will dwell in cities with "unwalled villages" and in cities "without walls, and having neither bars nor gates" (Ezek. 38:11).

In the Old Testament period all cities were built on hills surrounded by walls with gates, as this was the only way of ensuring protection from invading armies or enemies wanting to rob and pillage. Excavations in Israel, such as in Megiddo, have uncovered massive stone walls that once surrounded the city with evidence where huge gates were hung—opened in the day and closed at night, with watchmen keeping a careful eye from stone towers. Modern Israel is dwelling safely in cities without walls. Also, this war occurs after Israel is regathered out of the nations (Ezek. 38:12), and is in possession of cattle and other "goods" (Ezek. 38:12); the Hebrew word for *goods* used here means wealth, riches, and acquisitions.

Another clue that this battle did not happen in the past and is yet in the future is the verse dealing with cattle and the area of Bashan. First, the Bashan area is also called the Golan Heights. This area begins north of the Sea of Galilee and extends toward the high mountains, bordering Lebanon and Syria. Along the travel route, off the main road, are hundreds of cattle, nicknamed "cows of Bashan." This is significant—before the 1967 Six-Day War the entire Golan Heights (Bashan) was Syria, and many hills in the area were actually Syrian artillery bases and military bunkers. For this Islamic coalition of nations mentioned by Ezekiel to cover the "mountains of Israel," the battle must occur *after 1967*—otherwise these Islamic nations would be battling Syria and not Israel, as pre-1967 this was a Syrian and not an Israeli position! In the 1967 war and then in the 1973 Yom Kippur war, Israel took possession of Bashan, placing underground bunkers, military command centers, and communications hubs on numerous mountains—protecting Israel from future invasions from the north.

Bashan is one area where Persians and invaders from the North Country would bring their troops to fight against Israel, as this area borders two troubled nations: Lebanon and Syria. Ezekiel also indicated a second area that would be greatly impacted with large numbers of slain soldiers, known as the "Valley of the Passengers on the east of the sea" (Ezek. 39:11). This area is located on the east side of the Jordan River, and can be seen from Jericho as a person looks east, toward the mountains of Jordan. In the time of Ezekiel it was a valley between the Abarim mountain ranges (Num. 27:12; Deut. 32:49). This was the mountain range where Moses went up to view the Promised Land. The valley where Gog's armies will fall is below Mount Nebo (Num. 33:47)—the same valley where God buried Moses.

On my first Holy Land tour in 1985, I stood on Mount Nebo in Jordan looking over into Israel, the way Moses did thirty-five hundred years ago. There was a patch of green surrounding Jericho as the town has a freshwater spring that can be tapped into for growing produce. On my more recent trip, we were driving along the Jordan River, and I viewed miles and miles of farmland on the Jordanian side. I was informed this was the area where the majority of food for the entire nation of Jordan was grown.

Immediately I recalled the passage in Ezekiel, when God said He would bring down the Persians and their coalitions of nations by putting "hooks in their jaws" (Ezek. 38:4). This metaphorical phrase can imply God using their need for food to pull the attackers into the land. There are three possibilities of why a food shortage in Persia (Iran) could be the hook in the jaws. Years ago, a wheat rust (a deadly fungus) struck in Iran destroying portions of the wheat crop—a necessary staple in that part of the world. Iran has experienced several earthquakes recently, toppling cheaply made homes and buildings and causing casualties. One quake was not far from a main nuclear power facility. If these nuclear facilities were impacted in an earthquake or an air strike and radiation leaked out, it could pollute the farming lands for years, causing a serious lack of food and possibly a mini-famine for the people.

Israel has had great success in growing enough food to feed their entire population and selling tons of produce to other countries. On the east side of the Jordan River is the long Jordan Valley that runs along the massive Jordanian mountains where incredible amounts of food sources are available. Portable greenhouses can be seen for miles and have brought a sevenfold increase in productivity. Since Jericho has become a major city with twenty-five thousand people and is now under control of the Palestinian authorities, the invading armies could tap into tens of thousands of Palestinians, moving through the Jericho valley, to assist in this conflict as the majority of the invaders come from other nations, which today are Muslim.

The Seven Years "Code"

One of the most significant verses that may be a *code* is in Ezekiel. It may reveal how this battle connects with a peace agreement. The future Antichrist will initiate the peace agreement when the war concludes and will require seven years to burn the piles of weapons.

> Then those who dwell in the cities of Israel will go out and set on fire and burn the weapons, both the shields and bucklers, the bows and arrows, the javelins and spears; and they will make fires with them for seven years. They will not take wood from the field nor cut down any from the forests, because they will make fires with the weapons.
> —Ezekiel 39:9–10

The significance of burning weapons for seven years is threefold. In Daniel 9:27 the future Antichrist will make an agreement (covenant) with Israel for seven years. This agreement will involve a deceptive peace treaty (Dan. 8:25; 1 Thess. 5:3), connected with stopping future wars and dividing Israel's land (Dan. 11:39). This is the central conflict between Israel and the Palestinians today: Who truly owns the land and the rights to call it their homeland—the Jews or the Palestinians? The signing of this agreement begins the time clock for the seven years of tribulation mentioned (at times with various names) by Old Testament prophets (Nah. 1:2; Isa. 63:4), by Christ (Matt. 24:21, 29), and by the apostle John (Rev. 7:14).

When the battle concludes in Israel after God Himself intervenes and destroys all but one-sixth of the invading armies, the Islamic nations will be prepared to compromise, signing an agreement with Israel. The destruction of the weapons is noted since, in Ezekiel's day, modern, chemical, biological, atomic, or nuclear weapons were nonexistent. What Ezekiel saw he wrote in terms that his ancient readers could comprehend and understand. However, not taking wood to burn weapons is an important phrase as in the prophet's day, when the spoils of war were collected, the cities were burned and many of the weapons, spear handles, bows, and arrows could be piled up and burnt to ashes or kept as spoils of war. However, when a nation disarms today, with the metal tanks, metal shell casings, and modern equipment it would take much longer to destroy the weapons. Also, if Israel would be required to disarm, then this would take years of ridding of certain "materials," just as it takes substantial time to remove WMDs or nuclear materials.

The emphasis here is the *"seven years"* (Ezek. 39:9). If the return of Christ for the overcoming church were to occur at the beginning of the seven-year tribulation, and Daniel described a seven-year agreement with the Antichrist and Israel (Dan. 9:27), the question is then posed: Are these two sevens, in these separate prophecies, referring to the same event—seen by two different prophets at different times? Is the treaty of the Antichrist signed following this war, and is part of this agreement a demand to destroy and disarm the weapons from this battle that could be used in future wars? Daniel 9:27 indicates the Antichrist will keep the agreement for forty-two months and break it in the middle of the seven years. Based on the Apocalypse, this will be when the Antichrist will make his move toward Jerusalem (Rev. 13).

The Phrase, "It is Done"

I had read the narrative of Gog and Magog hundreds of times and overlooked one passage that was pointed out to me by a ministry partner, Tim Castellaw, while taping programs in Israel. He said, "Have you ever noticed this verse in Ezekiel?" He read the following:

> Behold, it is come, and it is done, saith the LORD GOD; this is the day whereof I have spoken.
>   —EZEKIEL 39:8, KJV

In the context God has predicted the utter destruction of Gog's invaders on the mountains of Israel. They fall upon the mountains (Ezek. 39:4)—which refers to the mountainous Bashan region and in the open field (v. 5). It is also the valley previously mentioned on the east of the Jordan River across from Jericho. God will send a fire against Magog and those dwelling in the isles; indicating land outside of Israel will be impacted during this same conflict (v. 6). God declares that He will make His name known, and the heathen will know He is God (v. 7). This is when God announces "It is done," and confirms it is the day of which He had spoken (v. 8).

It is interesting that a time frame of *seven years* is mentioned in this prophetic war, and the return of Christ for the church (1 Thess. 4:16–17; Eph. 1:9–10) could occur prior to the *seven-year* tribulation. Are these "seven years" connected? Could "it is done" in the destruction of Israel's enemies connect to another seven-year event? Perhaps the day of Christ's return coincides with the timing of this battle—part of the reason God announces, "This is the day whereof I have spoken."

As Christ breathed His final breath from the cross, He cried out, "It is finished!" (John 19:30). Commentators point out that Christ was summing up the following: *He had fulfilled the will of His Father in heaven, He fulfilled the predictions of the prophets, met the demands of righteous judgment, and ratified a new covenant through His death.* These three words, "It is finished," closed a chapter on the law and the prophets and began a new chapter called the new covenant and the kingdom.

The phrase, "It is done," is found twice in the Book of Revelation. The first is where the Euphrates River dries up preparing a path for the kings of the East to cross as they move their armies toward the Valley of Megiddo, the site of the final battle in a two-hundred-square-mile valley in central Israel (Rev. 16:16). When global armies marched toward Israel, an angel from the heavenly temple cried out saying, "It is done," (v. 17). Note, the final cry of Christ, "It is finished," from the cross produced a sudden earthquake in Jerusalem (Matt. 27:51). In Revelation the greatest earthquake in world history strikes shortly after the angelic messenger announces "It is done" (Rev. 16:17–18). During the war of Gog and Magog, one of the main manifestations is when God sends a violent shaking on the mountains so strong that the living creatures tremble, and mountains are thrown down (Ezek. 38:20).

The second reference to "It is done" is when Christ closes His remarks in the Apocalypse after the creation of a new heaven and a new earth (Rev. 21:6). I do not wish to overemphasize the significance of Ezekiel's reference to "It is done" when the armies of Gog are defeated; however, I would suggest that this would be an excellent time for the sudden and unannounced return of Christ to gather together His body, the church. The world's attention would be on this war and the massive hailstorms, earthquakes, and other disruptions fit well in distracting the nations from numerous missing individuals.

Back to Crunch Time

Biblical prophets often would look for a combination of odd circumstances merging at once to reveal specific events. Seldom is the exact time frame given for the monumental prediction to come to pass. Jeremiah knew Israel would be in Babylon for seventy years (Jer. 25:11), and Christ predicted the destruction of Jerusalem within one generation (Matt. 23:36; Mark 13:30). The body of Christ can discern the times, and as events collide, time becomes squeezed and shortened; we know that we have entered the time of the end at this time.

> And unless those days were shortened, no flesh would be saved; but for the elect's sake those days will be shortened.
> —MATTHEW 24:22

On August 6, 1945, when America dropped a secret weapon, an atomic bomb on Japan, the United States became the lone superpower of the world and was respected among all nations. Shortly thereafter, the Soviets began a secret program to develop atomic weapons. Now, fast-forward to this present time. Nations such as India, Pakistan, and North Korea all have nuclear weapons. Islamic nations such as Iraq, Iran, and Syria all possess deadly nerve agents and biological weapons. It is only a matter of time until the genie will slip out of the bottle, and the world will enter the gates of hell—a land of no return. Without Christ's intervention and His return to earth, unless the days be shortened—or cut—no flesh would be saved—another example of "crunch time."

In the West religious academia uses a more traditional, systematic method of interpreting scripture. From a rabbinical level, however, there are layers of understanding, and dimensions, with patterns, cycles, numbers, and individual letters—as you have just read—that reveal present and future prophetic truths.

Chapter 5

VISIONS AND DREAMS
CONCERNING AMERICA'S FUTURE EVENTS

THE INSPIRED SCRIPTURES indicate, at the time of the end, that there will be an increase in visions and dreams, with the messengers being sons and daughters, servants and handmaidens (Acts 2:17–18). On many occasions, after deep prayer, my father, Fred Stone, would receive a warning dream and sometimes vivid visions, revealing events that were coming to America. On one occasion he saw how terrorists were plotting an attack on Washington DC.

Just after 9/11 Dad and I were staying in a hotel while ministering in the panhandle of Florida. The next morning he was burdened and distressed after experiencing a troubling dream during the night. In the dream he saw a federal building in Washington DC. He noticed a certain type of truck (that I prefer to keep nameless) on a road near the building, when suddenly a massive explosion occurred. Plastic, military-type explosives had been placed in the wall panels of the truck by terrorists. Dad also saw where the truck had been prepared, inside a barn on a farm in the state of Maryland (Washington DC connects to Maryland). In the dream Dad saw the truck gutted, and new panels were installed with explosives inside the entire truck. The explosion he saw in the dream was devastating, creating a second wave of panic in the nation.

Fortunately I was able to call a high-level executive in the federal government to whom the information was relayed. Follow-up action was taken on the information in the dream, as there was, at the time, some evidence that Washington was again being targeted for an attack. However, the intelligence needed to confirm the details was vague. Dad's dream provided the needed details to fill in the missing links. The insight Dad gave was recognized and classified as a "tip" and given the same level that intelligence agencies use for "inside information."

To some, the idea of God speaking through a vision or a dream seems odd and has been theologically relegated to a former time frame known as the "Bible days." For those in the full-gospel movement, however, a spiritual dream can be a part of the Holy Spirit's warning or personal instruction for a believer or a nation. Throughout the years praying men and women have received valuable insight, information, and warnings through this spiritual manifestation.

In my own life I have experienced two visions that came to pass in detail. The first vision was in June of 1996. It was of what appeared to be the Twin Towers (the upper part), shrouded in black with five gray, spinning tornadoes almost as tall as the buildings, emitting sparks of fire forming in front of one of the large towers. This imagery later proved to be the black smoke from the plane that poured out of the hole in the building, flowing upward to the top of the buildings. The gray spinning smoke funnels became obvious when the buildings collapsed. The five spinning, gray-colored clouds were also representative of the other five buildings, trade centers three through seven, that were affected when the gray clouds of spinning dust poured into the buildings, making them uninhabitable. I openly spoke of this vision for about four years before the attack.

The second vision occurred years later. Standing off the coast of Louisiana, I saw a series of five different storms. In the form of black tornadoes, the storms were spinning and impacting four particular things: restaurants, shopping centers, small-town "mom and pop" stores, and trucks delivering goods. The fifth, dark funnel was distinct, as it was unfolding on top of the water at an oil rig. I saw a black whirlwind of oil spinning on the water, striking an oil rig and shutting it down. I knew something detrimental would happen involving oil, and it would impact Louisiana.

Six months after this night vision, I called a pastor from Baton Rouge and shared with him this troubling vision, predicting something would occur off the Louisiana coast that would impact the state's economy. It would be over a year later that the British Petroleum oil rig exploded, breaking the pipe underneath the water. When the underwater camera revealed the place where the oil was leaking, it looked exactly like the vision—a small spinning oil tornado! The oil spill affected trucks that once delivered seafood and impacted tourist shopping and the fishing industry as restaurants in certain areas were shut down, creating a negative economic impact. Thankfully, in the vision I was instructed to pray, and I shared this vision in Baton Rouge two months after the disaster struck. That night over twenty-five hundred people prayed for a solution to the crisis, and within a few weeks the underwater spill was capped. However, there was a devastating economic impact to the coast, to towns, and to the state for a season.

Seeing Cities Burn

I have known for several years, by revelation of the Holy Spirit, that, at some point in the future, something will trigger rioting in America. Masses living in certain inner cities will ignite riots leading to massive fires breaking out. I observed this clearly in a night vision in Pigeon Forge, Tennessee, during one of our major Partner's Conferences several years ago.

In the vision it was night outside as I was standing at a large river, scanning American cities in front, to the left, and to the right of me. I remember sensing tension, and I saw fires beginning to break out; I could see fire in the heart of what appeared to be about ten different cities. The entire city was not burning, but certain sections were definitely on fire. After I had awoken, I pondered on five different events that could trigger such violence. This is what I wrote down:

> » If government welfare or food stamps were cut off or hindered from reaching the masses, it might cause this.

> » If a federal government shutdown continued for months due to a national crisis, it might cause this.

> » If the power grid failed for days, or an electromagnetic pulse bomb was detonated in the nation, it might cause this.

> » If there was a disruption in fuel or truck deliveries in major cities which impacted food supplies, it might cause this.

» If, God forbid, there was an assassination of the president, it might cause this.

As troubling as this night vision was, I was told a noted man of God who has since passed to heaven, David Wilkerson, had received a series of warnings. In these warnings he had seen fires burning in the cities, especially in New York. After researching, I discovered Wilkerson began warning America as far back as 1985 in his book *Set the Trumpet to Thy Mouth*.

America is going to be destroyed by fire! Sudden destruction is coming and few will escape. Unexpectedly, and in one hour, a hydrogen holocaust will engulf America—and this nation will be no more.[1]

Later he wrote, "An attack from Russia and the great Holocaust follows an economic collapse of America...the enemy will make its move when we are weak and helpless...America will not repent..."[2]

On September 7, 1992, Wilkerson wrote about seeing one thousand fires in New York, and explained his interpretation of this terrible event:

I have had a recurring vision of over one thousand fires burning at one time in New York City. I am convinced race riots will soon explode! New York is right now a powder keg—ready to blow...Federal and state welfare cutbacks will be the spark that ignites the fuse...100,000 angry men will be on the streets enraged because they have been cut off from benefits...fires will rage everywhere...[3]

Wilkerson gave a final warning in March 2009:

An earth-shattering calamity is about to happen. It is going to be so frightening, we are all going to tremble—even the godliest among us....Major cities all across America will experience riots and blazing fires—such as we saw in Watts, Los Angeles years ago. There will be riots and fires in cities worldwide....There will be looting...[4]

A close friend of Wilkerson told me that this last warning was not just a vision or a dream, but Wilkerson confided in him that this message and warning came from an angelic visitor.

Some may suggest that Wilkerson may have "missed this prediction," since it has not yet occurred. However, most prophetic warnings don't happen immediately. When a national crisis is on the horizon, God gives people time to repent and turn to Him. Christ predicted the destruction of Jerusalem and the temple, which did occur, about forty years after His prediction in Matthew 23 and 24 (AD 30 to AD 70).

Jeremiah warned his generation the Babylonians were coming and the city would be in ruins. His warnings continued for twenty-three years until finally the Babylonians sent an army the Jews could not overpower.

Imagine when Elijah warned Jezebel that the dogs would eat her. The prophet disappeared from the world scene, and Jezebel thought God forgot the prophecy. Elisha replaced Elijah. However, over time another man of God, Jehu, ensured the prediction was fulfilled when he commanded this evil queen to be thrown over the wall, where wild dogs fulfilled Elijah's prophecy (1 Kings 21:23; 2 Kings 9:33–37).

Predictions, including biblical prophecies, can have gaps of time before their fulfillments, especially if their fulfillments are not predicted to occur within specific time frames.

In the distinct vision of the Twin Towers shrouded in black, it was five years later before the vision came to pass. The oil rig vision was given to me several years before it occurred. One possible reason for delays is to send a warning out to as many as possible, so people have an opportunity to *pray* and *prepare*. Warnings provide time for believers to intercede, which at times can save lives and in some instances delay the event for a future time.

The act of prophetic preparation was evident in the Book of Acts, where believers began selling their property and distributing the money to the needy and poor within the church. Why would Ananias (Acts 5:1–10) and Barnabas (Acts 4:36–37) sell personal property in or around Jerusalem, when no doubt they had families when the profits from the sales were being distributed among the widows and needy?

The answer may be in statements made by Christ in Matthew 23 and 24. In these two references Christ revealed the Jewish temple would be destroyed with no stone remaining upon another, and Jerusalem would be desolate. He warned believers to flee out of the city and not return to their houses (Matt. 24:16–18). With this advanced warning, believers began selling their property knowing that in a future time, within one generation (Matt. 23:36), the property would be useless once the siege and destruction of the city occurred.

Ample time—about forty years—was provided to sell their possessions and leave the city before Jerusalem's destruction. Christians heeded the warnings of Christ, left Jerusalem, and settled on the other side of the Jordan River in a community called Pella. Most warning dreams or visions are revealed to give believers time to plan, prepare, and make wise decisions before it's too late.

Dad's Final Dream

Throughout his life, from age seventeen until his death at age seventy-eight, my father, Fred Stone, was gifted in visions and dreams—seeing events before they would happen. While being interviewed on the Sid Roth program, Sid asked me if the Lord revealed anything about the future to my father prior to his death. I immediately recalled one of the final dreams he had which, I believe, was a warning about a food disruption in the future.

From the time I can remember, Dad loved gardening and often would plant a small garden in the backyard, growing tomatoes, peppers, onions, and other vegetables. On this particular night he had a dream of seeing three sets of utensils, a plastic fork and knife, buried one-third deep into the ground, leaving two-thirds of the objects exposed on the surface. He immediately felt he understood its meaning.

The three sets of the knife and fork represented the three basic meals we eat: breakfast, lunch, and dinner. Seeing one third of all knives and forks buried indicated at some point, a famine, natural disaster, or another unforeseen challenge would impact a third of the food supply, leaving two thirds of the food remaining. He received no time frame or further insight into the matter. What would cause a food shortage in America, the world's breadbasket?

One possibility is the disappearance of hundreds of millions of honeybees, which are nature's pollinators for numerous fruits and vegetables. There has been a "colony-collapse disorder" (CCD),[5] leading to the deaths of 30 to 90 percent of the worker bees in hives in America and other parts of the world. The missing bees are a concern to those in the agricultural and food industry, since without these bees one third of the foods we eat cannot be pollinated. The proposed reasons for the collapse range from pesticides, parasites, stress, or possibly cell phone towers, according to some. Famines were a troubling event in biblical cities of both testaments. In Acts a prophet named Agabus predicted a global famine, giving believers time to organize financial relief for the churches in Judea (Acts 11:28–29). Often as time passes we see the fulfillment of prophetic events; thus, over time the interpretation is understood.

Another possibility is supervolcanoes. They have the ability to devastate the world's agriculture, causing severe disruption of food supplies and mass starvation. These effects would be sufficient to brutally threaten the fabric of civilization. They can rain hellfire across thousands of miles and cause worldwide climate changes. There are several found throughout the world; however, one of the biggest is in Yellowstone National Park.[6]

Situated in Wyoming, scientists have recently discovered Yellowstone's supervolcanic magma reservoir is at least two and a half times larger than previously believed. Before these reports came out, scientists said if Yellowstone's supervolcano were to erupt, an area the size of North America would be devastated, and pronounced deterioration of the global climate would be expected for a few years following the eruption. Half of the United States would be covered in up to three feet of ash.[7] This was said *before* these new reports were realized.

The new reports from the Seismological Society of America tell how they had thought the magma chamber was covered in pockets. Studies now reveal a single connected chamber about fifty-five miles long, twenty miles wide, and six miles deep.[8] This would cause utter devastation, and the study is still inconclusive to the actual vastness of the underground activity. LiveScience reports, "Additional molten rock, not imagined in this study, also exists deeper beneath Yellowstone, scientists think."[9]

Furthermore, a global drop in temperature would occur from the release of volcanic material and gases in the atmosphere—blocking the sun. Yellowstone sits on a very seismic active area, experiencing fifteen hundred to two thousand earthquakes a year. "The most likely hazard in Yellowstone is from large earthquakes," said James Farrell, analysis team scientist of the University of Utah in Salt Lake City.[10]

The Most Recent Warning

During my ministry, there have been significant moments in which I received a night vision of a future event. Occasionally I did not fully understand the symbolism or the full meaning. The most recent night vision was very striking and remains clear in my mind, months after the initial experience.

In this vision I was carrying a set of ministry books into a two-story duplex located in an American city. Through the window of the living room I could see the large skyscrapers of the downtown area. Outside, directly below the duplex, was a woman who appeared to be a tourist, taking photographs of the city. My wife and both of my children entered the room. I asked my wife if she had heard from her sisters, who were on their way to where we were. At that moment I looked out over the city and saw tiny black tornadoes forming in the atmosphere on the edges of some of the higher buildings. Suddenly a round, disk-like, dark cloud formed—just above the city—with the outer sky remaining a clear blue. I began tapping on the window trying to warn the woman outside to seek shelter.

I quickly ran into another room in the upper level of this two-story duplex. I looked out from a huge window to the right and noticed a road with a large bridge over water that appeared to lead out of the city. It connected to another land area several miles away. At that moment I saw two ghostly images of the World Trade Center rising out of the water. They appeared part light and part transparent, slowly breaking the water's surface and extending upward. However, before becoming as tall as the former structures in New York, they vanished like a vapor into the atmosphere. Immediately I thought of a terrorist's attack and wondered if terrorists had targeted this city.

At that moment three things happened. I saw the bridge suddenly shake and then collapse into the water. On the bridge I saw a green interstate sign with the name of an East Coast city on it. The sign, with the bridge, suddenly collapsed and slid into the water. All of a sudden a massive wave began forming in the water and was headed straight toward the shore—similar to the high waves of a tsunami. The wave was strong and high enough to come to shore and crash into the glass—where I was on the second-floor level. Stunned, I continued to watch the shocking events. I was uncertain if terrorists planned to destroy a bridge, or if some natural disaster would come.

Some have asked me for the name of the city that was on the sign. I have refrained from giving it for this reason: I am uncertain if the name on the sign was the city I was in or was in the direction of the bridge, which led in and out of that city. Also, in the past, when I have named a state or a location, people within that area began calling and e-mailing me wanting more information, asking for my opinion. Uncertain anticipation creates unfounded fears, leading to irrational decisions based on possibilities that are imagined and not fact. Therefore, until I receive an inner release, I am only at liberty to say this particular city is located on the East Coast with large bridges in its region.

Some forewarnings are given to initiate prayer assignments, seeking God's mercy to prevent or expose the attack. This should be the first reaction to any warning dream or vision: to intercede, to expose, or to prevent the danger from developing. At other times the warning is revealed to demonstrate God's ability to show the future to mere humans, providing evidence that God exists and is in charge of the affairs of men. Some events are preventable, and some are set unchangeable, but we are never wrong to intercede when we are shown future events.

The New York Car Bomb Attempt

Jerry Collins, a pastor friend from Pulaski, Virginia, provides us with an example of intercessory prayer. In May of 2010 Jerry and his wife were in Times Square, walking along the busy streets of New York City. They passed by numerous parked cars, when suddenly they heard what sounded like gunfire or fireworks, startling both of them and causing them to duck. They continued walking another two blocks to their hotel. Then they noticed a large presence of New York City police officers lined up with barricades and trucks with additional barricades.

Jerry said, "We assumed they were controlling traffic for a movie production. We made it back to the hotel and changed our clothes to attend a Broadway show that evening. When we headed back to Times Square, there was a four-block perimeter of barricades in place."

Jerry continued, "When I asked an officer what was happening, he said it was a possible bomb threat. I commented to him about hearing the loud sounds earlier, and he asked me if I had noticed anything unusual as he was pointing toward a black SUV. As it turned out, my wife and I were only forty feet from a car bomb that failed to explode."

Had the bomb gone off, Pastor Collins and his wife would have been in the line of fire, and could have been seriously injured or killed.

After returning home, he learned that two of his leading prayer intercessors had come under a very heavy burden to pray for him and his wife. They sensed great danger prior to and on the day of the planned attack. These intercessors were standing in the gap (Ezek. 22:30), seeking divine protection for their pastor. When Jerry relayed this to me, I said, "I always wondered what prevented that car from exploding; now I believe it was prayer—especially from your intercessors seeking God's protection."

A Message to Eisenhower—From Mary

In 1982 I was preaching a revival for Pastor Joe Edwards at the North Cleveland Church of God. On their staff was a respected elderly minister, Dr. C. E. French. Following one service, Dr. French invited me to sit down to hear an amazing story that occurred when he had preached for Pastor Jack Matthews, who pastored a Church of God in Wrens, Georgia from 1960 to 1965. He told me about a woman he and his wife met on a Sunday morning named Mary Rouse. She was a 98-year-old faithful church member. Mary had married a Methodist minister. Her occupation was a schoolteacher, but her spiritual calling was a prayer intercessor, spending hours each day in prayer.

French and Pastor Matthews were invited to dinner at the home of Mary and her husband. Mary approached them from the kitchen, looked at French and blurted out, "God told me something about you today." When French asked, "What did He say?" Heading back into the kitchen, she shot back, "If you were close enough to Him, He would have told you." Then Mary's husband immediately began telling French that his wife was a unique woman and related to him an amazing story about her.

That night Dr. French recounted the story to me. Years ago Mary had been in prayer, and in a dream she saw President Eisenhower in a late-night, secret meeting. It was at the White House with the head of Turkey and another foreign national, discussing disturbances in the Middle East. The Lord told her the president was going to sign a secret agreement with these two nations, and it would be the wrong decision.

Mary, this simple praying woman, contacted an operator at the White House. She began explaining to the operator her warning. She went on to tell how the president was in a secret meeting, and then revealed in great detail the conversations occurring in the secret meeting. Shortly thereafter, federal agents were at Mary's home asking her how she obtained her information. Her insight was so detailed that at first she was accused of being a "Turkish spy." After a lengthy "interrogation," the agents realized Mary's information really had come through prayer. The revelation was passed along to Eisenhower, changing his plans to sign the secret agreement. Even the local paper published the information of the government's visit to Mary. That day Mary's husband showed Dr. French cards that President Eisenhower's wife had sent to Mary, thanking her for her prayers.

The Dream of the Birds With Padlocks

Prior to 1960 Mary had a dream about the future. She predicted the next president would be a Catholic. However, she saw in a dream the dome of the White House in Washington surrounded with black birds on top with padlocks in their mouths. In the Scripture birds (called "fowl" in the King James Version) can be a metaphor for evil spirits that steal the seed of the Word of God planted in a person's heart (Matt. 13:1–9).

The Lord spoke to Mary about a time coming when there would be an attempt to place a padlock on every Protestant church in America. Remember, this was before 1960, and at the time such an occurrence seemed almost impossible. In fact, many Christians probably would have laughed at the idea that individuals in high places would attempt such a feat. Yet, since that time America has become a post-Christian nation as pure Christianity is declining and interest in biblical truth is sinking in a cesspool of unbelief.

Today a very liberal, anti-Christian spirit manipulates the minds of many individuals in our nation's universities. Students sitting in these classrooms become teachers in colleges, journalists, news reporters, lawyers, or members of political movements that influence national legislation. There is no question that many of the major papers and news organizations are flooded with professionals whose moral and spiritual beliefs conflict with the moral-social practices and instruction of the Bible. Some would actually rejoice if those "lame brained, intolerant Christians" were forever silenced from having influence over laws, dictating social issues such as abortion or "same-sex lifestyle issues." Thus, a generation is brainwashed into thinking America must fundamentally be changed by breaking up the original foundations of faith and recreating a new foundation with its new world order. How could Mary's dream come to pass?

First, certain laws can be passed that place unwanted regulations on religious organizations. We've seen this with a recent battle of the new health care laws. The government is requiring Christian organizations to pay for contraception and abortion pills for their workers. How can they demand something so contrary to the very core of their religious teachings? This law is the first time in the history of the United States that the government has sought to override the religious beliefs and convictions of a major Christian religious group. In short the law is saying, "We do not care what your religious beliefs are—we can, and will, pass laws contrary to them, and you will obey, or we will close your hospitals and businesses." After an outcry, some changes were made, but the compromises were still unacceptable to many Christian leaders. Just remember, today it is the Catholics, tomorrow the Protestants, and eventually the Jews.

Mary's other encounters were so accurate that I have pondered: What events or laws could shut down Protestant churches? One way is the inability for a local church to make their mortgage payments to their local banks. Recently about three thousand churches in one year were unable to meet their monthly payments, mostly Protestant churches in and around the Atlanta, Georgia, area. There have been several megachurches that have had to close their doors or sell their properties, as their debts to the banks were unsustainable. In Maryland the pastor of a large church was told by their lender that the bank's national headquarters had instructed them to no longer make large loans to churches. Another church in Maryland had never missed a payment, but suddenly had their loan "called in." They searched for months for a new mortgage lender and nearly lost their mul-timillion dollar property in the process. Since many large lenders are now puppets with new laws pulling their strings, banks can now call in loans under pressure from the federal government or banking lenders.[11]

During the recent recession, I was in contact with many pastors with church memberships from three hundred to as high as thirty-five hun-dred. Some told me they were experiencing an impact on the giving levels at their church due to members losing jobs or having their hours cut. This was happening on a level where the monthly income had, at times, fallen short from 20 percent to as high as 60 percent in some areas. Months of financial shortfall and missed mortgage payments can eventually motivate banks to step in, suddenly calling in loans and causing churches to default, losing their facilities. Because churches are supported by tithes and offer-ings, and with the economy wavering in some cities, financing church proj-ects can now be considered high loan risks. Without advanced building or construction loans, a congregation is unlikely to initiate or complete a project.

The third event impacting every church is the possible removal of a church's or ministry's tax-exempt status—also from their buildings and properties—across the board. The government could easily do this with future taxation by imposing new tax codes that could be forced on churches. Right now a church is officially recognized as a nonprofit orga-nization. Thus, the charitable giving of tithes and offerings to a church is tax deductible. Washington lawmakers are discussing the possibility of removing charitable deductions from churches to collect additional, tax-able income from their citizens. Talks are now being entertained to remove the tax exemption from churches, church-owned land, and parsonages (minister's homes). In fact, here at Voice of Evangelism, which is a not-for-profit 501(C)(3) organization, the ministry has paid over $60,000 a year just in property taxes. Our income goes back into ministry projects. We have challenged the issue several times in Nashville, Tennessee, but each time the same liberal judge has struck it down. We were told because we sold product and our donations were lower, we must pay the property tax on both facilities (even though on some years, more was spent for min-istry projects than came in). With the tax revenue being sponged from the ministry, we could build churches on the foreign field, or support our five missionaries in major overseas evangelism events.

Many local congregations, especially in the inner city, or major churches with high monthly payments will be crushed financially if the new laws are passed by the liberal left who desire churches to pay taxes. In Mary's dream the birds were sitting on the White House dome at 1600 Pennsylvania Avenue with padlocks in their beaks. The implication is whatever future laws are passed, they must be approved by the elected official living in the "people's house" before becoming law. These three combined scenarios are quite possible, and if believers are silent we will lose our authority and influence to prevent controlling powers from clicking padlocks on our mouths.

The padlocks in the mouths of the birds illustrate attempts to silence the mouths of ministers, whose voices are used to proclaim the gospel. Prophetically we are informed in the Apocalypse of a False Prophet who will arise as a lamb with two horns, meaning he will represent a false form of Christianity. The two horns indicate he will be recognized by two major religions: perhaps Islam and apostate Christianity. (See Revelation 13:11–16).

From the beginning, our ministry has chosen to operate without bank loans. When there is debt, the borrower is a servant to the lender (Prov. 22:7). Excessive money borrowing brings pressure to ministries and churches to maintain a specific level of income required to meet obligations. By paying as you go or setting aside a financial war chest in advance, ministries can pay for land, equipment, and buildings without the pressure of a fifteen- to thirty-year monthly payment with interest.

There may be regulations and pressure in the future that none of us can escape as the nation moves from a republic to a dictatorship. However, God is with His people and His church, and if the gates of hell cannot prevail against it, neither will corrupt governments. The true church feeds itself off the opposition of its adversaries, using it as fuel for soul winning. Jesus has the keys of death and hell and has the keys to any padlocks men would place on the mouths of His servants.

The Seven Prophetic Visions

As I said, some predictions can be altered through prayer. For example, 185,000 Assyrians surrounded Jerusalem to destroy the city. The night before the assault Isaiah and Hezekiah conducted a serious prayer meeting and by morning all Assyrian troops were dead (2 Kings 19). Other biblical prophetic warnings are set in time, such as the ones linked with the "time of the end" and the last days, which will come to pass as predicted.

My father was converted to Christ in a revival that continued nightly for over three years. From Dad's earliest ministry, the Holy Spirit imparted a gift of dreams and visions to Dad, as he would spend hours on end in prayer. Dad's ministry began at the same time of a national revival, known as the *healing revival*. Many men were called of God during this time, and some were blessed with unique gifts that set them apart from "normal" ministers.

One quite controversial minister from Dad's era was William Branham. My father never knew Branham, but I have met numerous people who knew him, worked with him, and sat under his ministry, including his organ player. Those judging him negatively today often read opinionated Internet blogs from people who never knew him, but formed biased opinions based on certain doctrinal issues or actions by some of his followers.

Branham was a leading minister in the wave of healing revivals erupting in America in the 1940s and 1950s that was the seed sprouting into the charismatic movement of the 1960s. A small, meek, middle-aged servant of Christ, Branham's life was filled with out-of-the ordinary, supernatural encounters with God; had there not been eyewitnesses and close associates to personally authenticate them, some miracles would seem too far-fetched.

One of Branham's most noted visitations occurred one morning, in June of 1933, as he was preparing to teach a Sunday school lesson in a rented hall in Jeffersonville, Indiana. Just before he stood to minister, the Lord revealed to him in seven consecutive open visions what would come to pass before the return of Christ. Most have already been fulfilled, and some are yet come. They are listed in the order they were written.

1. Branham saw and publicly predicted that Benito Mussolini, the Italian dictator, would establish a fascist state in Italy and invade Ethiopia. Thirty months later, the vision came to pass. Branham said the dictator would die a horrible death, and his people would spit upon his corpse. This was fulfilled on April 28, 1945, when the people seized the dictator at an airport

attempting to escape to Switzerland. He was hung upside down and spat upon by his own people![12]

2. In the second vision he saw the Siegfried Line two years before it was built. He saw an Austrian named Hitler rising in Germany and saw numerous American lives lost in a war with Germany, which Roosevelt would declare after his election for a fourth term. All of this happened.[13]

3. The third vision revealed three major "isms": Fascism, Nazism, and Communism. The first two would come to naught, but Communism would flourish. A voice told him to keep his eyes on Russia, because Fascism and Nazism would end in Communism.[14]

4. The fourth vision predicted advancement in technology right after the war. He saw automobiles shaped like eggs, and a car with a plastic looking bubble on top being run by remote control. The driver turned and began playing games with the folks in the backseat. This type of car has been invented, and in the future we will have self-driving automobiles. I have a vehicle with DVD screens in the back of the headrest where the kids can play games or watch videos. This technology did not exist until over sixty-five years after Branham's vision.[15] The fifth vision in 1933 involved women. He witnessed the moral decay of women in America as they would enter worldly affairs, bob (cut) their hair, and adopt the clothing of men. He then saw where women were all but stripped-naked, merely covering themselves with tiny aprons about the size of a fig leaf (this was long before bikinis), and how they would wear clothes that were too revealing.[16]

5. The sixth vision involved a woman rising to power in the United States. Branham was quoted as saying:

> Remember, in that day before the end comes: before the end time comes, that a woman…now you all keep this wrote down. There'll be a powerful woman raise up, either to be president, or dictator, or some great powerful woman

in the United States. And she'll [America] will sink under the influence of women.[17]

Thirty-one years later, on July 26, 1964, Branham remarked in a sermon:

> The morals of our women are going to fall in such degraded things till they're going to be a disgrace to all nations.... I seen a woman stand in the United States like a great queen or something. And she was beautiful to look at, but wicked in her heart. She made America's step—go to her step.[18]

Because of the accuracy of the previous five prophecies, and countless words of knowledge given to Branham, those who recalled these visions are inclined to pay careful attention to them; one must interpret them in literal terms and not in an allegorical sense. I have discussed this sixth vision with a minister who personally knew and traveled with William Branham. Branham believed the vision could allude to a "Jezebel Spirit" that will seize the church and the nation in the future. After writing down this vision, Branham made a note in parenthesis that this woman could be the rise of the Catholic Church in the future. He believed this system was the woman riding the beast in Revelation 17. Others point out the wording of the vision mentions a "dictator or a president, or some powerful woman." These words imply more than just a "spirit" or a religious empire, but an actual woman who will sit in great authority in America prior to the return of Christ. According to the vision, America will morally and spiritually sink during the time of this woman's season of authority.

Also note, these events are to unfold before the end comes. Be aware that even if a woman is elected as president, she may not necessarily be the *specific woman* noted in this vision, since the future will hold numerous elections and opportunities for women to rise into positions of authority. Since the other visions were so accurately fulfilled, it appears that this one will also see its completion in the future.

The biblical correlation of a powerful woman influencing a nation was the rise of Ahab and Jezebel. Although her husband was king in Samaria, Jezebel controlled the major decisions. She targeted her hatred toward the ultraconservative prophet Elijah, who challenged her self-appointed four hundred fifty prophets of Baal on Mount Carmel. In the narrative Ahab is removed from office (by death), yet Jezebel retained control, living in the ivory house (1 Kings 22:39). Amid enjoying her security in the ivory palace, she is overthrown and another takes her place (1 Kings 22:39; 2 Kings 9:30–37). During the reign of Ahab and Jezebel, Elijah the prophet became their thorn in the flesh, as he exposed their iniquity and warned the Israelites not to be divided between two opinions. After Elijah's departure to heaven (2 Kings 2), Jezebel had to encounter Elisha, who had received a double portion of Elijah's anointing (see 2 Kings 2).

God will always have a *voice*, a *people*, and a *remnant* in these final days, especially in America. Only time will tell how this sixth vision will play out. When the sixth vision occurs, then the seventh, which is the most frightening, will be on the horizon.

6. In the last and seventh vision Branham saw a great explosion destroy the entire land, leaving the United States smoldering and in ruins. He commented that as far as his eyes could see, he saw craters and smoking piles of debris.[19] He said he saw no people in the area of the destruction. Then the vision faded away. Many godly men and women have seen this type of final destruction over the years. A major, internal civil war is possible, but the devastation is more likely from major terrorist attacks from Islamic nations, a future invasion from China or Russia, or major volcanic eruptions.

America is not mentioned specifically in biblical prophecy but would fall in line with the end-time biblical prophecies given to the Gentile nations. Such prophecies could include:

» Kings shall fall and serve Him (the Messiah), and all nations shall serve Him (Ps. 72:11).

» The Lord's house shall be established in Jerusalem and all nations will flow into it (Isa. 2:2).

» The indignation of the Lord is upon all nations, and His fury upon all their armies (Isa. 34:2).

» "I will gather all nations, and bring them down to the Valley of Jehoshaphat" (Joel 3:2).

» "I will shake all nations" (Hag. 2:7).

» "The nations were angry, and thy wrath is come" (Rev. 11:18, KJV).

When the tribulation judgments are sent from God to earth, some will only impact certain areas as we read where a third of grass, trees, and water are destroyed in one region (Rev. 8:7). However, one earthquake affects all nations: "And there was a great earthquake, such as was not since men were upon the earth, so mighty an earthquake, and so great. And the great city was divided into three parts, and the cities of the nations fell" (Rev. 16:18–19, KJV). This global quake will impact the entire world and not just a selective area. This would include America.

The Bible tells us that the Holy Spirit can instruct and warn through dreams, visions, and inspired insight. It tells us that we are not to despise prophecy (1 Thess. 5:20), and that we should weigh these warnings carefully. The prophet Joel predicted in the last days God would release visions and dreams (Joel 2:28). These dreams are for instruction, direction, and warning.

Not all dreams or visions are warnings or instructions from God; therefore, wisdom and understanding are required to discern correctly any vision or dream and its meanings. A true spiritual dream often has biblical symbolism connected with it, which must be interpreted in line with the scripture. Time is the interpreter of a vision or a dream, but we should be aware God does use visions and dreams to speak to us today. (I wrote more about this in my book *How to Interpret Dreams and Visions.*)

While a dream, vision, or a prophetic word is never on the same level of divine inspiration as the Scripture, God has and continues to reveal His progressive will to His children, in each generation, instructing them in righteousness. With that in mind, let's take a closer look at the patterns of past presidents and world leaders.

Chapter 6

AMAZING PROPHETIC PATTERNS OF AMERICAN PRESIDENTS AND WORLD LEADERS

I N A SMALL booklet printed in September 1960, Gordon Lindsay posed a prophetic question: "What about the new president? Will he also die in office? You will want to have this book to check out events to come." In the book Lindsay documented a rather bizarre "cycle" connected to US presidents elected in a year ending in zero that he called "the presidential zero curse." Lindsay noted in his booklet, "If this cycle of the presidents continues then the president elected in 1960 will die sometime between 1961 and 1969."[1] Lindsay's observation proved correct. The president-elect in 1960, John F. Kennedy, was assassinated in Dallas, Texas, by two bullets from an assassin hiding in the upper corner of a book depository building.

After the death of Roosevelt, this strange cycle was first placed in public print. Few paid attention until after the death of John F. Kennedy. It later resurfaced after the assassination attempt on Ronald Reagan, who was elected by a landslide in 1980—another zero year.

I once asked a dear friend and former Secret Service agent Lewis Mason, who was with Reagan during his administration, if the Secret Service agency was aware of the "zero year cycle." Mason, being a Spirit-filled Christian, replied that a few of the Christian men had heard of it, but to his knowledge it was never discussed in any detail.

This odd cycle appears to have begun after the death of men who fought in the Revolutionary War. Three early presidents who signed the

Declaration of Independence all died on the Fourth of July. John Adams and Thomas Jefferson both died the same day, July 4, 1826, fifty years after signing the Declaration. James Monroe passed away five years later on July 4, 1831. William Henry Harrison was elected president in the year 1840. After his inauguration, which took place in inclement weather, he caught a severe cold that developed into pneumonia. He died a month after his inauguration. Harrison was America's first president to die in office.[2]

The Dream of Abraham Lincoln

Twenty years passed, and Abraham Lincoln was elected president in 1860. While living in Springfield, Missouri, Lincoln became friends with Rev. James Smith, the pastor of the Presbyterian Church of Springfield. It was Rev. Smith who recalled memories of Lincoln before he became president. The pastor had placed the book *The Christian's Defense* in the hands of the young lawyer, who examined and read it several times. Rev. Smith said:

> From then on Mr. Lincoln attended church regularly, even the prayer meetings and the revival meetings.[3]

After his nomination as president, Lincoln gave a farewell speech in Springfield in which he said:

> Unless the great God who assisted him [speaking of General George Washington] shall be with me and aid me, I must fail; but if the same omniscient mind and the same Almighty arm that directed and protected him, shall guide me and support me, I shall not fail, I shall succeed.[4]

Lincoln believed that future events could be seen through dreams and omens. The day after the election in 1860, he went home and threw himself on a haircloth sofa. Across the room sat a bureau with a swinging mirror. As he looked into the mirror, he saw a reflection of himself with one body, but two heads. One head was very pale. He jumped up, and the illusion vanished. When he reclined again, he saw the same image in the mirror, this time much more clearly. He told Mrs. Lincoln what he saw. She interpreted the omen: he would be elected for two terms. In his second term, the pale "death face" meant he would not live through his second term.[5]

At the end of the Civil War Lincoln had another dream. He saw a coffin in the White House with thousands of people sobbing and weeping. When asked who had died, the answer was, "the president."[6] After this experience he felt his death was imminent. On Good Friday, April 14, 1865, an actor named John Wilkes Booth shot Lincoln behind the left ear while he and Mrs. Lincoln watched a play at Ford's Theatre. Lincoln, though unconscious, lived another nine hours before he took his final breath.

Having studied the detailed history of Lincoln's life, one comes away with the conclusion that he was not appreciated until after his death. In fact, before his untimely departure, even his own Republican Party spoke of electing another president. It was under Lincoln's leadership that the spirit of slavery broke in the nation, through his Emancipation Proclamation. Yet it would be more than one hundred years later, after Kennedy's death, that the spirit of racism would visibly begin to break in America.

James Garfield—Wrong Place at the Wrong Time

Twenty years later, in another zero year (1880), James Garfield was elected president. At the Republican Convention of that same year, not one vote was cast for him on the first ballot. On the next four he received one vote. His name disappeared entirely on the fourteenth through the eighteenth ballots. On the thirty-third ballot, he received one vote. Oddly, he ended up winning the nomination by a landslide! Three months later, after being elected president, Garfield was shot at the railway depot in Washington, by a despondent office-seeker named Charles Guiteau. The terrible zero cycle had struck again.[7]

William McKinley and the Pan American Exposition

The twenty-year pattern went unbroken with William McKinley elected in 1900, becoming the twenty-fifth president of the United States. The Pan American Exposition was being held in Buffalo, New York. The vast crowds sought to shake hands with the president. The president's personal secretary, George Cortelyou, tried to cancel the handshaking event, but President McKinley overruled him. In the crowd that day was Leon Czolgosz. He entered the line wearing a dark suit with a bandage on his right arm. No one noticed a .32 caliber, nickel-plated revolver hidden inside the bandage.

While standing face-to-face with McKinley, Leon fired at point-blank range. The president slumped to the floor as panic hit the crowd.

The president did not die at that moment. Doctors immediately operated, but the wound turned into gangrene. A few days later the nation was once again grieving the untimely departure of another beloved leader. Another American president had fallen to the mysterious zero cycle.

The Cycle and the 1920 Election

The cycle continued with the election of Warren Gamaliel Harding in 1920. Harding, the twenty-ninth president, is said to have surrounded himself with unscrupulous men, who were willing to sell the nation's resources to the highest bidder. The men in Harding's administration were considered some of the most corrupt in America's history. For example, Albert B. Fall, Secretary of the Interior, was convicted of accepting a bribe for $100,000 from Edward Doheny, connected with the Elk Hills Naval Oil Reserve in California.

In 1923 Harding set off on a speaking tour. As the tour progressed, people noticed he seemed older than the stop before. On the way back he suddenly became violently ill and rapidly died. Rumors spread the president had been poisoned. Some believe those who were afraid of what might happen to them in the 1924 campaign poisoned him. Others rumored that Mrs. Harding had something to do with the death because she refused an autopsy and had the body buried immediately. It must be pointed out that there was no evidence to the rumors. Harding became the fifth president in a row elected on a zero year to be struck down while occupying the White House.

Roosevelt and His 666 Votes

After receiving 666 votes on the first nomination, Franklin Roosevelt became the nation's president-elect in 1932 and was reelected in 1936. Because of his immense popularity, he announced a run for his third presidential term in 1940. While Roosevelt did not die in his third term, he was elected for a fourth term and died during that term. The president was stricken while sitting for an artist in Warm Springs, Georgia.

It is interesting that Roosevelt ran against Wendell Willkie in the general election. What if Willkie had won in 1940? Would Willkie have survived the presidency? History shows that Willkie suffered a heart attack and died on October 8, 1944. Therefore, whoever won in 1940—from either the Democrat or the Republican ticket—they would not have lived out their full term!

The Death of John F. Kennedy

After six presidents elected on a zero year had died in office, followers of the cycles wondered what would occur on the next zero-year election. When that election concluded in November 1960, it was one of the closest in many years. Richard Nixon and John Kennedy went head to head. Nixon had served under Eisenhower as vice president and Kennedy was a senator from Massachusetts. Although there were voting irregularities and definite voting fraud in Illinois,[8] Kennedy triumphed and became the first Catholic president in American history.

During his brief time in office, Kennedy overcame one of the most frightening conflicts in American history—the Cuban Missile Crisis. The racial conflicts in the South were causing social division in the nation, and the unions were challenged for their corruption. Although his handsome appearance and charming personality were making him one of the most popular presidents in American history, Kennedy's aggressive leadership was creating a host of enemies.

Several weeks before his untimely death, he spoke to Baptist evangelist Rev. Billy Graham. During a television interview on *Larry King LIVE*, Graham remembers Kennedy asking him if he believed in the literal return of Jesus Christ. When Graham replied he did, Kennedy said, "Why don't we hear about this in the Catholic church?" Graham said he believed Kennedy was hungry for spiritual knowledge, and was searching deeper—for spiritual truth.[9]

The Curse Against the Kennedys

For many years tragedy has struck down several members of the Kennedy family. To list just a few examples: Joseph Kennedy Jr. was killed in a military plane crash. John Kennedy was assassinated in Dallas, and Robert Kennedy was assassinated in California during the 1967 primary. Ted

Kennedy was humiliated by an incident in Chappaquiddick, and John Kennedy Jr. was killed in a fatal plane crash. The trend has led many in the media to ask: "Is there a curse on the Kennedy family?" My intent is not to dissect the historic tragedies to discover any conclusion, but to expose how non-Christians in the secular public often ponder such questions.

What is unknown among many is the alleged "curse" placed on John Kennedy after his blockade of the island of Haiti. At the time Haiti, an impoverished nation, was under the control of "Papa Doc," a dictator and self-acclaimed witch doctor. According to a former missionary to Haiti, Papa Doc claimed he and a group of witch doctors came together and cast a voodoo spell on Kennedy. In this act the group made a voodoo "doll" to represent Kennedy. They drove sharp voodoo needles into an area of the doll where the curse was to have the greatest impact—allegedly in the head of Kennedy. A "spirit" was sent to take the life of Kennedy. Several weeks later Kennedy was shot in the back of the head by an assassin.

It is also interesting that Papa Doc feared going outside and remained indoors at all times. The only time he went outside was on the twenty-second day of each month, as he believed there was some type of spirit protection working in his favor.[10] Oddly, it was on November 22 that Kennedy's life was taken.

Reportedly two weeks before his trip to Dallas, Kennedy had an inner feeling that his life was in danger. His own secretary warned him not to go to Dallas. She did not feel good about the trip. Kennedy overruled the restlessness and inner nudges and traveled anyway. It was a beautiful, clear day in Texas. With thousands of people lining the streets, a lone shooter hid in a book depository window, waiting for the presidential motorcade to turn the corner, where Kennedy would be in clear site of the scope of his rifle. The cracking of shots soon echoed from the window, sending Kennedy slumping with part of his head missing, bleeding on the backseat. The year of 1963 saw another president fade into eternity! The zero cycle had circled the White House again.

I have toured the building in Dallas, now housing a museum on the top floor. The eerie feeling that in six seconds history was changed from that small room still permeates the air. Often people stand in silence and stare for a lengthy time as the questions of how and why still flood the visitors' minds.

In preparing her husband's funeral, First Lady Jackie Kennedy asked aides to research the Library of Congress for information concerning the death of Lincoln and how they prepared the final internment for the slain president. They placed Kennedy's coffin in the East Wing to lie in repose, his casket being only one of two presidents to lay in the White House: President Lincoln and Kennedy. Kennedy's closed coffin was then taken to the nation's Capitol building and placed on the catafalque built to hold Lincoln's casket in 1865. His body lay in state in the Rotunda, where a statue of Lincoln hovered silently over the slain leader. Kennedy was buried at Arlington National Cemetery in Virginia.[11]

This terrible repeat of history takes an even more strange twist, considering that Lincoln was shot in the Ford Theatre, and Kennedy was shot in a Ford Lincoln Limousine. The question posed by Gordon Lindsay, "What will happen to the president elected in 1960," was answered in Dallas, Texas, November 22, 1963. Oddly, Lindsay, who posed the question, housed his ministry headquarters, Christ for the Nations, in Dallas, Texas. One scripture in Ecclesiastes 1:9 explains why there are so many parallels between the life and death of Lincoln and Kennedy.

> The thing that hath been, it is that which shall be; and that which is done is that which shall be done: and there is no new thing under the sun.
>
> —KJV

1980—The Attempt Upon Ronald Reagan

With the 1980 election of California governor Ronald Reagan, I was fully aware of this "zero cycle." With Reagan's age, many believed the risk of possible death by heart failure was greater than all former presidents. I was conducting a revival in Asheboro, North Carolina, when the news flashed across the television screen, "President Reagan has been shot." I recall my heart seemed to fall to my stomach, and my eyes were glued to the news reports in utter disbelief. Soon the world saw a tape showing the assassin's attempt. Despite a bullet lodging one inch from Reagan's heart, it turned out his life was spared, and he continued to work out his first term, being reelected for a second.

Was it luck that this attempt failed? When discussing Reagan breaking this cycle with a noted Christian musician and singer, he shared with me that Reagan's inner circle included a secretary who was a Spirit-filled Christian. That secretary prayed in the Oval Office and was "interceding for the president each morning." He also pointed to a large number of praying Christians who were a part of Reagan's staff.

Without doubt, Reagan broke the cycle in his administration, I believe, because of his personal commitment to Christ, and praying Christians who covered the president with a "prayer covering."

In retrospect the prevailing questions have been:

» Why has this cycle seemed to come on a zero, every twenty years?

» Why does it impact the president of America?

» Who or what may be the reason for this "curse"?

Cursed When Shedding Innocent Blood

The Book of Proverbs says, "So the curse causeless shall not come" (Prov. 26:2). The question arises, "Why did this repetitive pattern emerge, impacting presidents elected every twenty years?" If this cycle has a spiritual foundation, the answer may be concealed in the Scripture. For instance, the Lord established, at the age of twenty, every young man was required to become a soldier in the Hebrew army. This instruction was a direct command given to Moses from the Lord, recorded in Numbers 1:18–45.

> From twenty years old and upward, all that are able to go forth to war in Israel: thou and Aaron shall number them by their armies.
> —NUMBERS 1:3

With all the greatness of this country, we must be aware that America's early history carries a trail of war blood. Throughout history America has fought wars to defend freedom, to stop the cancerous spread of atheistic communism, or to deliver the earth from the scourge of a heartless dictator; however, the early history of America goes beyond just defending the Union from invaders. Much innocent blood was shed on America's soil from the time of its beginning.

Anyone who has studied American history is aware that multitudes of Native Americans were slain by the hands of settlers in America who migrated from Spain, France, and England. They arrived at different times, searching for gold. It was Columbus who called the natives from the Islands "Indians" since he thought he had landed in India. Columbus, impressed with the Indians' gold ornaments, searched the islands for gold. Rumors of gold quickly spread throughout Europe, and the Spanish explorers led by Hernán Cortés (1519) sailed to Mexico searching for the treasures. Cortés killed thousands of Aztec Indians sending their gold back to Spain. The English and French soon followed, sending ships to South America, Mexico, and America searching for rumored lost cities with hidden gold. Needless to say, any Indian attempting to defend his village from any violent intruder met the swift punishment of death.

May I add, there were missionaries to the Indians including John Eliot (1631), Roger Williams (1636), David Brainerd (1700), and John Wesley (1735). These men traveled, committed to teach the Indians the gospel, and to bring the message of Christ's love to the numerous tribes. It was difficult because white men were invading the land and running the Indians from their native territory. While some Indians became friends of the white men, many tribes were disbursed from their homes and land. This was especially true with the Cherokee tribe, forced from the "Cherokee nation." They were sent walking to Oklahoma on what would be called the "Trail of Tears," relocating them to the Midwestern states. The struggle between the new Americans and the Native Americans continued during the administration of many early presidents.

The Curse of Tippecanoe

The first president to die in office elected on a zero year was William Henry Harrison. It is noted:

> When Harrison had arrived on the scene, "most of the Indians had been reduced to poverty, their hunting lands had already been carved up by the new farmers in their midst, and they were regularly victimized by traders....Harrison...had added more than fifty-million acres to the public lands. The Indians weren't paid of course, but the official government price to the white settlers was two dollars an acre."[12]

During Harrison's time, the Shawnee Indians had a chief known as Tecumseh. He and his brother Tenskwatawa, also known as "The Prophet," were the leaders among the Shawnee and had set up a village in the middle of the land the US government wanted to take from the Indians. It was Harrison who moved in on them with a thousand soldiers.

According to legend the Prophet pronounced a curse on the future leaders of the white men. After the battle of Tippecanoe in the late 1830s, Shawnee Chief Tecumseh sent a message to Harrison (by a released prisoner) that, "Harrison will not win this year to be great chief…but if he wins he will die in office. Every twenty years, the leader will die to remember the death of my people…" It was reported the Indian Prophet said, "Every twenty winters the days of the great chief they elect will be cut short…" When Harrison, who went by the nickname Tippecanoe, became president, he was elected on a zero year (1840) and died in office.

The "Indian Connection"

There is a strange coincidence relating to the deaths of former presidents and the Native American Indians. From the early 1600s through the time of Lincoln, Indians were being slain and driven off the land. Oddly, it seems most of the slain presidents were from states where fierce battles were fought with the Indians. These included the states of Ohio, Illinois, Kentucky, Indiana, New York, and Massachusetts. Below is a list of presidents elected in a zero year. Notice each one was from a state known for their struggles and wars with the Native Americans:

> » William Henry Harrison was born in Virginia but lived in Ohio when elected; he also led a major Indian battle in Indiana.

> » Lincoln was born in Kentucky but lived in Illinois.

> » James Garfield was from Ohio.

> » William McKinley was from Ohio.

> » Warren G. Harding was from Ohio.

> » Franklin Roosevelt was from New York.

» John F. Kennedy was from Massachusetts.

» Ronald Reagan was born in Tampico, Illinois.

Of these eight, seven presidents who died in office were born in areas where some of the most severe bloodshed occurred as white settlers attacked Indians. In fact, four of the presidents were from Ohio. The territory of Ohio, along the Ohio River, was one of the regions where violent battles ensued with thousands of Indians being killed.

In 1830 a law was passed stating the Indians had to move from their land and were forced to go westward. Ten years later in 1840 tens of thousands of Indians had walked the "Trail of Tears" and many had died along the way. The frontiersmen had fought natives, annexed their land, and conquered them through wars. The Trail of Tears is a sad example of how our government moved Native Americans from their original lands, making room for the white settlers.

These removals were approved under President Andrew Jackson. In 1840 William Harrison was elected as president. He was known as an Indian fighter, leading battles against well-known tribes and seeking to kill the Indian chiefs. He served as a congressman in Ohio, and was later elected president of the United States, even using the nickname associated with his famous battle against the Indians in his presidential campaign "Tippecanoe and Tyler Too." As I have written, he was also the first American president to die in office, only thirty-two days after being elected.

Slavery—More Bloodshed

It was not just a conflict with the Indians that impacted the country. The scourge of slavery had plagued our young nation, and the president elected in 1860, Abraham Lincoln, was determined to set slaves free. Most slave owners mistreated, verbally abused, and beat the slaves; some to the point of death. The soil of the young nation was stained with innocent blood. By 1860 the country divided, with brother turning against brother in the Civil War, as the northern Yankees battled the southern Confederates. Battlefields were covered in corpses, cities burned to the ground, plantations ravished, and blood soaked the land. The Civil War brought an end to slavery, but took a huge toll on Lincoln.

The Commander in Chief

The president of the United States is the Commander in Chief of America's military. God scolds Israel in Hosea 13:11 and announces, "I gave thee a king in mine anger, and took him away in my wrath" (KJV). Twenty is the biblical age of a male soldier, and every twenty-year interval on a zero year brought about the deaths (or in Reagan's case, near death) of our Commanders in Chief. Could this cycle have been a sign of disfavor from the Almighty, regarding the shedding of innocent blood?

The Bible teaches, "Cursed be he that taketh reward to slay an innocent person. And all the people shall say, Amen" (Deut. 27:25, KJV), and "You shall not follow a crowd to do evil…" (Exod. 23:2). Israel was warned, "Keep yourself far from a false matter; do not kill the innocent and righteous. For I will not justify the wicked" (Exod. 23:7). God's judgment for the iniquity of the fathers continues up to four generations.

Cursed to Four Generations

The Scripture reveals examples of "the curse of shedding innocent blood." In the time of Christ He rebuked His generation for their unbelief and predicted God would allow their sacred temple and the city of Jerusalem to be destroyed. The reason was the Hebrew leaders had shed the blood of righteous men of God. Christ said, "That upon you may come all the righteous blood shed on the earth, from the blood of righteous Abel to the blood of Zachariah…whom you murdered between the temple and the altar" (Matt. 23:35). Jesus said destruction would fall upon His generation (Matt. 24:34). About forty years later, in the year AD 70, the Roman tenth legion destroyed the temple and city, toppling the huge stones and slaying men, women, and children.

A powerful warning is given in Scripture that God will visit "the iniquity of the fathers upon the children to the third and fourth generations of those who hate Me" (Exod. 20:5; 34:7; Num. 14:18). A generation of unbelief as expressed here is considered forty years (Ps. 95:10), and the first president to die in office was William Harrison, elected in 1840, then four generations of forty years (up to the fourth generation) would bring us exactly to the year 2000. This brings us to a serious question in retrospect, after seven presidents were impacted by the zero curse. Reagan broke the cycle, and after President Bush's election in 2000, this particular curse should have been totally broken. I say "should have been" because ungodly leadership breaks the covenant that our forefathers established. When that happens we become open to other forms of curses and disfavor that can impact national leaders.

The Scriptures tell us how to break national curses: through national repentance, both to God and to those of whom we may have mistreated, harmed, or done evil to in the past. This would include repenting to the Native Americans and their tribal leaders, and seeking restitution for the many terrible actions such as the Trail of Tears, when the Cherokee and other first nations were forced out of their land. An example of a national curse that was eventually stopped by repentance is found in 2 Samuel 21.

National Curses—The Gibeonites

In 2 Samuel 21 a severe famine was devastating Israel during King David's reign. As David sought the Lord for this reason, the Lord answered him saying, "It is for Saul, and for his bloody house, because he slew the Gibeonites" (2 Sam. 21:1, KJV). The previous king, Saul, slew a group of innocent people from the area of Gibeon, initiating a divine curse, manifested as a famine under Israel's next king, David.

God revealed, "The life of the flesh is in the blood" (Lev. 17:11). The Hebrew word for "life" is *nephesh*, alluding to the soul. We could say, "The life-giving force of the body is found in the blood." When an innocent person's blood is shed, the Scriptures teach that blood has a "voice" that cries out to the Lord. When Cain murdered his brother Abel, the Lord inquired of Cain saying, "Where is Abel your brother?" Cain replied, "Am I my brother's keeper?" Then the Almighty replied, "The voice of your brother's blood cries to me from the ground" (Gen. 4:9–10). In Hebrew the word for *blood* in Genesis 4:10 is plural and not singular. It reads, the "voice of thy brother's bloods." Rabbis teach that Cain not only killed one man, Abel, but also all the future children of Abel that would never be born.

This is why shedding innocent blood is so tragic, whether the victim is an infant or a mature adult. The legacy of an entire family is erased from the earth. Descendants from that lineage that will never be born could have impacted lives changing the course of history. Since the blood type of a child comes from the father's "seed," God heard the secret voice that is hidden in the DNA of Abel's blood crying out from the ground.

Apparently in David's time the blood of the Gibeonites was crying out from the earth as well. The Gibeonites were not Israelites but were a remnant of the Amorites, whom Israel had sworn an oath not to harm. Yet Saul in his zeal had broken the oath and slew many of them.

Under the old covenant, if a man shed innocent blood, then the murderer, if proven guilty without a doubt was to be sentenced to death. In David's time, since Saul was now dead, the sons of Saul received a death sentence in order to remove the curse of the famine. This punishment seems extreme; however, on the altar, blood was offered to make atonement for sins under the old covenant (Lev. 17:11). Human blood was sacred as it concealed the DNA code that can produce an entire nation, such as with Abraham, whose descendants today are the Jews.

Breaking the Curse Under the New Covenant

We are now living under the New Covenant that was ratified through the death and resurrection of Jesus Christ. The Scripture says, "Christ has redeemed us from the curse of the law being made a curse for us" (Gal. 3:13). This redemption is as though we were held in prison, guilty as charged, and facing execution. Suddenly the jailer unlocks the door and says, "You are free if you want to be, because a man named Jesus has been executed in your place!"

The two main keys of redemption are repentance and forgiveness. To repent means to be regretful for your actions, but it also means to turn around from the direction you are heading. To be forgiven means to "release yourself and others from any harm, hurt, or injury done." If I ask you to forgive me, I am saying I regret the words or deeds done against you and I am asking you to release me in your heart.

If there is a connection with this past "zero cycle" and America's mistreatment of the Native American Indians, then the highest leader of the land, the president (with members of Congress), should repent, ask for the Native Americans' forgiveness, and make proper restitution when possible.

Some counter my observation, by pointing out certain Indian lands were purchased with money. However, this is not the issue. Has any American president ever publicly repented and asked for forgiveness on behalf of the "sins of the fathers"? Remember, the unchanging Word of the Lord says that the iniquity of the fathers will be visited upon the third and fourth generation (Exod. 20:5). The Hebrew prophet Daniel understood this spiritual principle when the Hebrews were led away into Babylonian exile, over twenty-six hundred years ago. As he predicted, seventy years of captivity were coming near the conclusion, when Daniel began interceding, asking God to forgive Israel for the sins of the fathers (Dan. 9:4–19). Daniel's intercession paved the trail for the Hebrew captives to walk the road leading to the Promised Land.

It has been common throughout history in times of national crisis, wars, or disaster for leaders to call the nation to prayer. Only a few, such as Abraham Lincoln, called the nation to repent for its sins. Today's society is so ignorant of spiritual truths, if the president called for national repentance, many would say, "Repent of what?" or, "What have I done wrong?" Then of course, the ACLU would announce a lawsuit for forcing "religion" on Americans. The truth remains: God honors His Word and those who obey it. They may not be the most popular in the nation, but they will become the greatest in the kingdom.

There is one more interesting observation about the "sins of the fathers" in Exodus 20:5 and how it might pertain to this zero curse. Exodus 20:5 says the sins of fathers will be visited upon the third and fourth generation. In the Book of Job four generations totaled one hundred forty years (Job 42:16). If the iniquity of the fathers ceases after the fourth generation, and we use four generations—one hundred forty years—as a foundation point, it's interesting to note that from the election of Harrison in 1840 to the election of Ronald Reagan in 1980 was exactly one hundred forty years. This would mean the biblical time span for this curse to end would have fallen during the administration of Ronald Reagan. This might explain how George W. Bush, who was also elected in a zero year (2000) was exempt from the curse, as he served eight years and left office without any major assassination attempt and in good health.

Israel and Harry Truman

Harry Truman was the US president when the United Nations voted to partition Palestine and to carve out a Jewish state for the Jews, for many who had come through the Holocaust. As a senator in a mass meeting in Chicago in 1943, Truman said "everything 'humanly possible' must be done to provide a haven for the Jewish survivors of the Nazis."[13] Truman knew that Palestine was the choice homeland of the Jewish survivors of Europe. It was noted by a Jew, David Niles, who served with Roosevelt, and in Truman's administration that Roosevelt did not have sympathy for the Jews and had he lived, things might not have turned out as they did. By reading the Bible and ancient history, Truman supported the idea of a Jewish homeland in Palestine. Truman's secretary of defense warned him that if he supported a Jewish state, he could impact the flow of Arab oil, to which Truman replied that he would handle the situation in the light of justice, and not oil.[14]

On Saturday, November 29, 1947, during a Thanksgiving weekend, the United Nations voted to partition Palestine for a Jewish homeland. Even the Soviet Union joined America and voted in favor of the partitioning. That day Jews at the United Nations headquarters began singing, "This Is the Day." At a Zionist rally over twenty thousand people showed up—at the same time Britain announced that they would pull out of Palestine in six months, on May 14, 1948.

A noted Jewish man, Chaim Weizmann, had assisted the British in winning World War I. He was partially responsible for the 1917 Balfour Declaration, giving the Jews access to Palestine. In failing health, Weizmann would live to see his dream of a Jewish state fulfilled, receiving the assurance of Truman's support at a secret meeting in March of 1948. Opposition to the UN partitioning was coming from the CIA who assessed that it would not work and would lead to Arab wars and Jewish deaths. One of the biggest objectors was George Marshall, who said the United States was "playing with fire while having nothing with which to put it out."[15] The State Department made attempts to prevent the partitioning from going forward, which, when the opposition was exposed, caused Truman to appear as a double crosser and a liar to many of the Jews.

On May 12, 1948, a meeting was held in the White House with five high-level administrative men. Some were in favor and others in disfavor of recognizing the coming Jewish state, once the British partitioning ended at midnight—May 14. Marshall and the State Department opposed it while White House Counsel Clark Clifford, quoted from Deuteronomy to verify the Jewish claims for a homeland.[16]

When May 14 arrived, to recognize the new state, Clifford called the State Department for paperwork. When it arrived at the White House, the name of the country was left blank as names such as Judah, Judea, and Zion were discussed, but the ancient biblical name was chosen instead, Israel! At the United Nations the American delegates were in shock, and some thought it was a joke as the entire delegation threatened to resign. However, in Brooklyn a new flag representing the nation was unfurled—blue and white with a star in the center. Even radio announcers commented that Americans would turn to the Bible to understand the significance of this day.[17]

Truman received a call from Chief Rabbi Israel Isaac Halevi Herzog to say, "God put you in your mother's womb so that you would be an instrument to bring the rebirth of Israel after two thousand years."[18] Tears ran down Truman's cheeks, according to David Niles. It was reported at one point that Truman even declared, "I am Cyrus," alluding to the Persian King that gave the Jews permission to return to Israel after their captivity in Babylon.[19] Truman's popularity before his decision was 37 percent, and despite every poll predicting he would lose in a landslide, he was reelected in November 1948, many believe because of his support of a Jewish homeland. God had blessed him for blessing Israel.

The Clintons and Old Testament Parallels

In 1992 with the election of Bill Clinton as president, many prophetic students were wondering if there were biblical parallels that would reveal coming events with the new Clinton administration. It was noted that his wife was the driving force in politics. Soon the comment was made that if he was elected, the nation would get "two for one."

In November of 1992, just a few days after the election, I stood in Pigeon Forge, Tennessee, and released a prediction that years later proved accurate. I already understood certain biblical events could repeat later in history, including in our own time. After reading a detailed account from the time of Elijah about a ruling king and queen named Ahab and Jezebel (1 Kings 18–22), I taught that those same patterns would be repeated during the presidency of Clinton and his wife, Hillary. I was not identifying them as Ahab or Jezebel, or disrespecting the office which Clinton represented, as the authority of the office must be respected. I was, however, simply showing how the events in this ancient king's life would reflect what was coming to America. Below are the parallels that came to pass.

King Ahab and Jezebel	Bill and Hillary Clinton
They lived in an "ivory house."	They lived in the White House.
Ahab led but Jezebel controlled behind the scenes.	Bill led but Hillary controlled behind the scenes.
They became involved in a land deal.	They were involved in the Whitewater land deal.
The land deal fell through.	Whitewater fell through.
An innocent man died (Nabaoth).	An innocent man died (Vince Foster).
Jezebel signed papers involving the deal.	Hillary signed papers (through the Rose Law Firm).
Walking in sin was a "light thing" to them.	Bill's sin was considered irrelevant to many.
An enemy was raised up against them.	Enemies were raised up against them.
A lying spirit deceived Ahab.	Bill lied under oath.
He eventually died.	Hillary remained in political office in Washington.

This pattern emerged, with the exception of the final one in the list. I said that I believed, after Bill left leadership, his wife, Hillary, would rise in politics and eventually make a run for the White House, which she did in 2008. Some suggest that President Obama placed Hillary Clinton in the State Department, knowing she would not run against him in 2012. However, she detected the handwriting on the wall with the assault on the

American Embassy in Libya and the health care confusion and after step-ping down from her administrative position, likely intends to make a bid for the White House in 2016.

I have met numerous individuals in Hot Springs, Arkansas, who were fellow students with Bill Clinton and friends in his teenage years. One woman said when Bill was a teenager he could make a memorable speech—with older town leaders whispering then that he would be a great leader one day. He did become governor at an early age but lost the position in 1981. Afterward he and his pastor traveled to Israel. When giving a speech at the Israeli Knesset and from a transcript dated October 27, 1984, Governor Clinton spoke of a word his pastor had given him:

> He thought I might one day become President....And he said, "If you abandon Israel, God will never forgive you." He said, "It is God's will that Israel, the biblical home of the people of Israel, con-tinue forever and ever."[20]

Believing this prophetic word, during the early Clinton years he served as a pro-Israel president.

Additionally, some of Clinton's closest friends were Pentecostal and charismatic ministers that he remained in contact with during his presi-dency. One of the lesser-known positive influences under Clinton was his dealing with Putin, the president of Russia. Putin was going to crack down on the growing Pentecostal groups rising up in Russia as he considered them a threat (Pentecostals were considered a threat and cult in the eyes of the Russian Orthodox Church, the traditional church in Russia). It was Bill Clinton who informed Putin some of his closest friends were Pentecostals, and they would not work against him but would be a valuable asset to him. Putin took Clinton's advice and later thanked Clinton for his suggestion.[21]

However, eventually the Clinton administration began pressuring Israel to give up land and compromise the areas of God's covenant. At the same time, a secret struggle was occurring as the president had a sexual encounter with a young intern, Monica Lewinsky. An Israeli reporter wrote in the *Jerusalem Post*, "Whenever Israel was threatened, women rose in defense of Israel. Such a woman was Deborah, such a woman was Queen Esther, such a woman is Monica Lewinsky."[22] Personally, I would not compare the

Clinton scandal to the godly women Esther and Deborah, but the writers point is that a woman was used in history to deal with Israel's "enemies." From a biblical perspective (Gen 12:3), Clinton forcing Israel to give up their covenant land opened a door to his personal difficulties, as God stands against those who divided His land (Joel 3).

The Bush Patterns

Another example of how history moves in a circle and what *has been in the past will repeat in the future* can be seen in the parallels of the 2000 presidential election of George W. Bush. The 2000 election was compared to the Rutherford Hayes election of 1876. In both elections a third-party candidate swung the vote to the Republicans.

The Election of 1876	The Election of 2000
Rutherford Hayes—Republican	George Bush—Republican
Samuel Tilden—Democrat	Albert Gore—Democrat
Peter Cooper—Greenback	Ralph Nader—Green Party
The Democrat won the popular vote.	The Democrat won the popular vote.
The Republican won by one electoral vote.	The Republican won by one electoral vote.
The election in Florida was disputed	The election in Florida disputed
The nation in a partisan split	The nation in a partisan split

The election controversy of 2000 unfolded on a Wednesday. The following vote count had been scrutinized by the media, politicians, and political students in universities. Some still question, "Was the election stolen from Gore?" or "What was the reason 'God' allowed Bush to win?" My Jewish friends in Israel may have a clue that explains this enigma. Before the 2000 election the majority of my Jewish friends in Israel wanted Gore to win, because Gore had selected a devout Jewish senator as his vice presidential running mate. This would almost guarantee a "pro-Israel" administration with Joe Lieberman, a Democratic senator from Connecticut on the ticket. When the Supreme Court gave Bush the state of Florida, giving the presidency to him, some of my Jewish friends were quite upset. That was before 9/11.

After 9/11 and the organized Muslim attack on America, I returned to Israel and asked my friends what they felt about Bush's response. They all replied they were glad Bush was president and not Gore. This made little sense to me as I recalled our former conversations. They all agreed when they replied, "If Gore had won, America would have a Jewish vice president, and it would have been virtually impossible to send troops into an Islamic nation. The Muslims would read this move as a 'Jewish led invasion' to conquer Islamic nations, since many Muslims believe there is a Western conspiracy to either occupy Islamic nations or to take over their countries and oil resources."[23] Only the Almighty knew the terror plots against America and prepared the right, strong leadership during that season to deal with this complex and dangerous issue.

Presidential Parallels

Perhaps the most stunning and bizarre historical patterns that America has ever witnessed is the list of uncanny parallels between presidents Abraham Lincoln and John F. Kennedy. This well-known and often publicized parallel is so precise, the probability of repeating is almost astronomical. Below are the parallels:

> » Lincoln was elected in 1860 and Kennedy in 1960—one hundred years apart.

> » Both vice presidents were named Johnson.

> » Andrew Johnson born in 1808 and Lyndon Johnson in 1908—one hundred years apart.

> » Lincoln and Kennedy both have seven letters in their name.

> » John Wilkes Booth and Lee Harvey Oswald have fifteen letters in their name.

» Andrew Johnson and Lyndon Johnson have thirteen letters in their name.

» Both vice presidents were southern Democratic senators before being elected.

» Both presidents had their elections contested.

» Both presidents were involved in the civil rights of the black community.

» Both presidents were congressmen (1846 and 1946) before becoming presidents.

» Both foresaw their deaths before they occurred.

» Both were shot on a Friday.

» Both were shot in the back of the head.

» Both were shot in the presence of their wives.

» Both assassins were killed (both shot) before going to trial.

» Both experienced the death of a child while in the White House.

» Both presidents were shot by a southerner.

» Lincoln was shot in a theater, and the assassin hid in a storage barn; Kennedy was shot from a book depository, and the assassin hid in a theater.

» Lincoln was shot in the Ford's Theatre, and Kennedy was shot in a Ford Lincoln Continental.

These parallels are quite eerie, revealing unmistakable evidence that history certainly does spin in repetitive cycles. This leads us to another president, Barack Obama, and the astonishing parallels his life and presidency carry with both Lincoln and Kennedy. The surprising rise of this rather unknown senator from Illinois carries some of the strongest patterns of two past presidents that none of the forty-four other presidents can match. Below are the mirror reflections of Obama and Kennedy:

» Both were sitting US senators when elected to office.

» Both were elected in their forties—considered young for the office.

» Both wrote popular books before their election.

» Both were Democrats.

» Both were former lawyers.

» Both went to Ivy League Schools.

» Both attended Harvard.

» Both worked for civil rights.

» Both worked on black/white relations.

» Both were athletic; Kennedy played football, and Obama played basketball.

» Both spoke of hope and used poetry in their speeches.

» Both made speeches in Berlin.

» Both gave their nomination speech outside (Denver and Los Angeles).

» Both had two children when they lived in the White House.

» Both had religious controversies—Kennedy being Catholic and Obama with his church in Chicago.

These parallels may not seem overly dramatic in nature, but they are quite intriguing. The more detailed parallels are the amazing connections with Barack Obama and Abraham Lincoln. Lincoln was the president accredited for breaking the back of slavery in America, and Obama felt he was the fulfillment of the dream for the black community when winning the vote to become America's first black president. Also, Abraham Lincoln is Obama's favorite US president.[24] The Obama-Lincoln parallels are as follows:

» Obama and Lincoln were both tall and skinny in appearance.

» Both were born outside of Illinois and both later moved to Illinois.

» Both served eight years—Lincoln in the House and Obama in the state Senate.

» Both spoke out against wars—Lincoln with the Mexican-American War and Obama with the Iraqi War.

» Both spent two years in Washington DC before running for president.

» Obama was born one hundred years after Lincoln became president (1861–1961).

» Obama was inaugurated president two hundred years after Abraham Lincoln's birth (1809–2009).

» Obama and Lincoln were both lawyers and practiced in the state of Illinois.

» Obama and Lincoln were both US senators representing the state of Illinois.

» Obama delivered a speech at the opening of the Lincoln Presidential Museum and Library in 2005.

» Obama announced his candidacy for president in Springfield, Illinois, the capital where Lincoln lived.

» Obama and his family took a late-night tour of the Lincoln Memorial.

» Obama took a one hundred thirty-seven mile train ride from Philadelphia to Washington, mirroring Lincoln's inaugural ride.

» Obama took his oath of office using the same Bible as Lincoln—called the Lincoln Bible.

» Obama's inaugural dinner was eaten on plates that were replicas of plates that Lincoln used.

> » Obama attended the grand reopening of the Ford's Theatre, February 11, 2009, where Lincoln was shot.

> » Obama's second term was filled with division over policy, just as Lincoln's.

The second half of Lincoln's administration was greatly criticized, and his popularity was in decline, just as President Obama experienced. Some said Mr. Lincoln's critics credited him with honesty and good intentions but indicted his judgment, his lack of system and his failure to act promptly. The death of Lincoln would follow. The Civil War was coming to a close, and the nation was divided down the middle, between the North and the South. It was Good Friday, and Lincoln wanted to attend a play being performed at Ford's Theatre in Washington DC. He was warned not to go but attended anyway. It was during the play that a political radical named John Wilkes Booth made his way into the Lincoln's private booth, shooting the president in the head. Lincoln's death came five days after Lee surrendered to Grant.

Sadly, every United States president receives death threats from individuals who disagree with their leadership or legislation. The Secret Service agency details and follows up on every threat the president receives. Months before the president travels to a major city, the Secret Service works behind the scenes on the president's flight schedule, driving routes, and speaking venues; they secure or remove everything—from manhole covers to mailboxes—on the streets. It is also their assignment to check out any threats made from individuals within a large radius in, and around, that particular location. This organization has masterfully done a thorough job to protect the leader of the free world.

I was in Washington DC talking with a retired military man who once flew in a helicopter, served as a sniper, and was assigned to protect several former presidents. I asked him about the threat levels against former presidents Bush and Obama. He said Obama of course, was given added security, because of numerous threats among hate groups and individuals. I assumed these "hate groups" were mostly white hate groups, angry about having a black president. He said, "The odd thing is there are, at times, as many blacks who are making threats as whites!" One suggested reason was

Obama had a black father and a white mother, which to some in the African community, is a strong negative. Those who dislike Obama are outspoken just as those who disliked President George W. Bush were vehemently outspoken. Freedom of speech is protected, until that speech reaches a certain level that borders on wishing danger to presidents and other elected officials.

Social networks such as Facebook are continuously monitored for negative comments made toward the president or his decisions. Federal agencies are tasked with tracking possible international and domestic terrorists. They monitor, track, and store any threats or even negative remarks made against Obama. If a person has, for example, ever made a negative comment using the word *Obama*, the *president*, the *White House*, or other "trigger words," his comments and entire conversation are examined to determine if there is any real threat.[25] In fact, as of this printing, the National Security Association (NSA) tracks and collects information on five billion cell phone locations a day. This is a stunning amount of data considering there are slightly over seven billion people on the earth.[26]

Is There a Dangerous Pattern?

Because history recycles in a circular motion and the things that have been are things that shall be (Eccles. 1:9–10), the parallels with Lincoln, Kennedy, and Obama should concern anyone understanding the rhythm of prophetic time and repetitive historical circles. The stunning links between the Lincoln and Kennedy assassinations and administrations weren't widely recognized until after the fact. However, with Obama clearly having the pattern of both former presidents who did not live out their assigned terms, there should be a *concern* and *watchfulness* among those surrounding Obama. Additional protection should be assigned to him, especially between now and the end of his term in 2016, to prevent two events from the past from becoming three of the same kind.

One concern is Lincoln and Kennedy were slain—both shot in the head—by radical Southerners: Oswald and Booth. I've observed that many of Obama's most outspoken critics are often from southern states, and on several occasions individuals have been arrested for making serious threats against him. I dare not imagine the uprisings and confusion as dangerous mob violence would be unleashed in America's major cities should this pattern of history circle again. The impact on the African American community would be devastating. Note that Lincoln dealt with freeing black slaves, Kennedy with the civil rights for blacks in America, and Obama is the first African American president whose biological father was from Kenya, Africa.

With such specific cyclical patterns, I am not personally predicting that Obama's term will be cut short, neither do I have a specific warning-word from the Holy Spirit, but historical cycles and patterns can certainly be repeated as with Lincoln and Kennedy.

Two interesting dates emerged in November 2013, as two significant anniversaries were celebrated. It was the fifty-year anniversary of the assassination of President John F. Kennedy (1963–2013) and the one-hundred-fifty-year anniversary of Abraham Lincoln's Gettysburg address (1863–2013). The number fifty is linked with the Jubilee cycle, and one hundred fifty days was the length of time the floodwaters were on the earth (Gen. 7:24). These numbers—fifty and one hundred fifty—are significant in Old Testament patterns and cycles, and it is interesting that in these two examples they are linked to Lincoln and Kennedy, and they occurred in the same month of Obama's presidency.

Someone asked, "Is there a way for a person to break these *personal* historical cycles?" In my view I believe there is.

The first is to be alerted of specific cyclical patterns, as Hosea 4:6 warned, "people are destroyed for lack of *knowledge*." The second emphasis is to pray for the repetitive cycle to be broken. In the time of Reagan there were several high-level administrative believers and Christians scattered throughout the nation who were aware of the "zero curse." They began to pray that these average twenty-year deaths of the presidents would be broken with Reagan, as he was the eighth president elected on a zero year (1980). Despite the March 1981 assassination attempt on Reagan at the Hilton Hotel in Washington DC, the fortieth president survived, serving double terms. He departed the office in good health, living an additional sixteen years past his retirement in 1988. The biblical number forty indicates trial, testing, and completion of a test or cycle. Thus, Reagan, the fortieth president, completed the cycle related to the zero curse. There may be particular, repetitive cycles that are providential and of sovereign design set to reappear during specific seasons to alter or change history, at times fulfilling prophecies.

However, prayer can interfere with man's evil plots, even releasing angelic messengers who can encircle protective hedges, preventing evil strategies from being enacted.

Following the Word of God

Secular America has a pressing emphasis on "spiritual tolerance"—accepting all religions as equal. Consequently, achievements of many leaders with a biblical worldview are written off as irrelevant by the "progressive" leaders in government; thus, they completely ignored the founders' faith as being outdated in need of a facelift.

Presidents from Harry Truman to George W. Bush inquired with America's pastor, Billy Graham, when making difficult decisions. Graham was with George Herbert Walker Bush the night the Gulf War began.[27] Bill Clinton, despite his moral weakness, understood biblical principles and converted to Christianity as a boy in a Billy Graham crusade. He stayed in touch with Billy throughout his administration.[28]

Reagan assigned "inner circle" administration officials to contact one of America's leading prophetic teachers. This was when the Berlin Wall was being smashed and communism was collapsing. Reagan wanted to inquire if the events carried prophetic implications.

Richard Nixon was known as a very stubborn, hardheaded president, often using profanity to get his point across, and the release of his presidential tapes reveals his tendency to be rather anti-Semitic. Certain taped conversations, now released, reveal Nixon's frustration with Israel during his administration. This was partially because the Arab oil nations were creating havoc with oil trading in the United States.[29]

On October 6, 1973, Egypt and Syria—backed by nine Arab states—initiated a war known as the Yom Kippur War with weapons supplied by the Soviet Union. Israel's enemies knew the nation was at a standstill as this day Jews fast, attend synagogue, and do not work. Even communications are normally cut off, as devout Jews spend the day in prayer. Syrian tanks, like a wall of steel, crossed the Syrian border into Israel. Prime Minister Golda Meir called Washington asking for military equipment, but US Secretary of State Henry Kissinger reportedly said, "Let Israel bleed a little." There was also fear of Arab oil retaliation against the United States.

At 3:00 a.m. Washington time, she awoke President Nixon and pleaded for his help.[30]

Nixon had been raised in the Quaker religion, and his mother was a devout Christian. As Nixon grew from a child to a young man, his mother taught him about the importance of faith and the Jewish people. That night it was said that Nixon could hear his mother's voice, behind the voice of Israel's nervous prime minister. It was reported:

> As a young boy growing up, his mother had told him that one day he would be in a powerful position, and a situation would arise where Israel and the Jews needed his help. When it did, he was to help them.[31]

Nixon ordered some of our top military transport planes, supplies, and firepower to be immediately sent to Israel. There were 815 total sorties flown dropping 27,900 tons of munitions with an additional 90,000 tons of material delivered by sea. Israel also received 56 combat aircraft.[32] Without this support, the war outcome would have changed, giving Syria and Egypt an advantage and giving Israel a loss of land, men, and military strength.

The price America paid for helping Israel win the war was revealed in October 1973 through March 1974, with an Arab sponsored oil embargo. Arabs raised the price of a barrel of oil and cut production, causing gas prices in America to increase and long lines at the gas stations. At the time we lived in Arlington, Virginia, and I recall the challenges and difficulties for drivers and businesses the embargo caused.

At times in history when American presidents worked in cooperation with world leaders, great prophetic events soon followed that altered the course of history.

Three Men and a Concrete Wall

For over seventy years the iron fist of communism gripped millions of souls in its cold, atheistic vice. This hold proved unrelenting, until the rise of three world leaders connected by divine providence. Together these leaders helped to melt the iron curtain between the East and West and initiate a season of religious, economic, and political freedom in communist nations.

The conclusion of World War I gave birth to the communist revolution in Russia. In 1917 the communist doctrine, penned and promoted by Karl Marx, would eventually spread like a cancer through Russia and create a Soviet Union, its national emblem the hammer and sickle. Westerners spoke of the Iron Curtain, a new system that held captive its population within its borders, restraining Westerners from entering. This new union of Russian states forbade freedom to express religious beliefs, controlled the people through government regulations, and prohibited disgruntled citizens from receiving visas to travel to the West.

Reports emerged that the "religion" of communists was atheism. Communistic doctrine forced religious faith out of the life of its population, oddly, in nations that were covered with historic churches and rich spiritual heritages. Soon the churches were closed, Bibles confiscated, countless ministers arrested, and many sent to the icy wasteland of Siberia. From an early age children were forced to study communist doctrine, and soon persecution against Christians cost the lives of millions of believers.[33] No one dared to speak of God or personal faith in public, and the true Christian church was forced underground.

As if this were not enough, within twenty years a new "ism" arose in Germany. Under the leadership of German chancellor Adolph Hitler, Nazism would compete against communism for the control of men, women, and children throughout much of Eastern Europe. Eventually World War II erupted, pitting communism against Nazism. From 1939 to 1945 seven years of destruction and division throughout Europe saw the extermination of six million Jews in the Nazi gas chambers, ovens, and death camps. The war concluded as Europe was divided between communism and democracy. Germany was also literally divided—between East and West—as the communists were rewarded half of the country for their involvement in the war.

For seventy years, from 1917 to 1987, the iron curtain nations held millions of souls in spiritual captivity. Suddenly and without warning, one chapter of history closed and a new chapter opened, as three world leaders set out with the same agenda—to challenge or to change the communist stronghold in Eastern Europe and the Soviet Union. Two of these men had personal prophecies from the Holy Spirit spoken over them many years before they took public office. Two of the men experienced assassination attempts that would change their life's purpose and destiny. These three men were Ronald Reagan, Mikhail Gorbachev, and Pope John Paul II.

The cardinals chose John Paul II as pope of the Roman Catholic Church on October 16, 1978. Ronald Reagan was elected in 1980 as the fortieth president of the United States, and Mikhail Gorbachev became the head of the Soviet Union in 1985.

These three world leaders formed what I termed, "a prophetic trio: the pope, the eagle, and the iron sickle." The trio helped alter the dominating plans of communism, becoming one of the greatest prophetic transformations to occur in the twentieth century. This change also initiated a new direction for the world, a direction which paved a road leading to the Last Days predicted by the biblical prophets. These three men—Ronald Reagan, Mikhail Gorbachev, and Karol Joseph Wojtyla (Pope John Paul II)—will go down as legends in world history. They were the "behind the scenes" trio that helped to bring about the greatest political changes in modern history—the collapse of communism in the Soviet Union and the Eastern bloc of Europe.

Few Americans are aware of a personal prophecy given to Ronald Reagan while he was governor in California, revealing his future destiny as president. According to the book *Reagan, Inside Out*, the story began in California on a beautiful October day in 1970.[34] Herbert E. Ellingwood, Governor Reagan's legal affairs secretary, had invited several guests to visit the governor. Among them were celebrity Pat Boone, Mr. Harald Bredesen, and a minister named George Otis. Boone was a longtime friend of the Reagans, and at the time the governor was running for reelection.

The conversations included a discussion on Bible prophecy and the Holy Spirit moving in the "Last Days." After a series of interesting discussions, Ellingwood led the group toward the front door as final good-byes were being said. One of the ministers spoke up and asked, "Governor, do you mind if we take a moment and pray for you and Mrs. Reagan?" Immediately Reagan replied, "We would appreciate that" and his countenance turned rather serious. Then the group joined hands forming a circle. Reagan bowed his head rather sharply, and the others tilted theirs a bit. Prayer was immediately offered to ask for God's blessings.

Suddenly in the middle of the prayer, the unexpected occurred. George Otis recalled what transpired:

> The Holy Spirit came upon me, and I knew it. In fact, I was embarrassed. There was this pulsing in my arm, and my hand—the one holding Governor Reagan's hand—was shaking. I didn't know what to do. I just didn't want this to be happening. I can remember that even as I was speaking, I was working…tensing my muscles and concentrating, and doing everything I could to stop that shaking.[35]

As this was transpiring the prayer of Otis changed completely, from the basic prayer of blessing to a more steady and intent word. The Holy Spirit inspired words coming from Otis's mouth directly to Reagan, addressing him as "My Son" and recognizing his role as leader in a state that was the size of many nations on earth. His "labor" was described as "pleasing." Suddenly, the following words were spoken, "If you walk uprightly before Me, you will reside at 1600 Pennsylvania Avenue."[36] Everyone knew that 1600 Pennsylvania Avenue was the address of the White House, the home of America's presidents.

Ten years passed. In 1980 Governor Reagan announced his run for the White House, being considered by the media at the bottom of ten other Republican candidates seeking the same high office. The major factor against him was his age, for near the time of the election he was approaching his seventieth birthday. Political analysts and critics prejudged him as being "too old to make correct decisions, believing he could die while in office." Others said he was incompetent and just an actor. Despite the objections, Reagan won and was reelected for a second term. He not only lived to be seventy-eight when he left the office, but he also lived on to age ninety-three.

In November 1980, upon hearing Reagan had been elected, Pat Boone telephoned the Reagans at their Pacific Palisades home to congratulate him. After speaking with Nancy, Reagan came to the phone. During the conversation, Boone inquired if Reagan remembered the prayer in Sacramento ten years earlier. Reagan said, "Of course I do."

Ten years before his election as president, God revealed His will for Ronald Reagan. Mr. Reagan was a dedicated Christian and loved the Bible. He was familiar with biblical prophecy, and at times privately consulted key ministers to ask for input on how certain world events would play into the prophetic scenarios of Scripture.

On the opposite end of the globe, behind the Iron Curtain of the Soviet Union, another divine "set up" was unfolding in the very strongholds of communism.

The Russian Prophecy of 1855

Sixty-two years before the rise of communism, a man named Dr. Hudson Taylor was ministering. Taylor was a missionary to China. It has been written concerning Taylor: "For forty years the sun never rose on China, but Hudson Taylor was on his knees praying for the salvation of the Chinese."[37]

In 1855, during one of his furloughs to England, Taylor was preaching when suddenly he stopped. He stood speechless for a time with his eyes closed. When he began to speak he explained:

> I have just seen a vision. I saw in this vision a great war that will encompass the whole world. I saw this war recess and then start again, actually being two wars. After this, I saw much unrest and revolts that will affect many nations. I saw in some places spiritual awakenings. In Russia, I saw there will come a general, all-encompassing spiritual awakening so great that there could never be another like it. From Russia, I saw the awakening spread to many European countries. Then I saw an all-out awakening followed by the coming of Christ.[38]

The war Taylor saw was World War I. Sixty-two years later, after Hudson's vision, the Russian Revolution birthed Communism following the war. The anti-God system grew like a poisonous vine, choking to death the belief in God. For almost seventy years the sword of godless Communism was dripping with the blood of Christian martyrs and Communist resisters. World War II was a continuation of the first war with Germany. However, in the late 1980s the Soviet Union began to break apart. To my knowledge, from 1917 to the mid-1980s, no Christian ministry in the West ever comprehended the possibility the Iron Curtain could melt, and a period of religious freedom would rise like steam from hot water. The "revolts and unrest," I believe, allude to the many uprisings among the common people in former Communist nations, such as Poland and East Germany. The predicted "awakening" did occur.

Since a true Communist must be a confessed atheist, Western Christians reasoned it impossible for the oppressed Soviet Christians to ever see the chains of oppression fall off. Yet, a few underground believers in the unregistered Pentecostal church were aware of a prophecy given in the 1930s revealing one day religious freedom would come! The leaders in the church guarded that prophetic word for over fifty years. Several years ago while visiting Russia, the old prophecy was told directly to Rev. Lovell Carey, former World Missions director for the Church of God in Cleveland, Tennessee.

1930 Prophecy Concerning "Mikhail"

Lovell was in Russia shortly after the fall of Communism. He met with one of the bishops of the unregistered Pentecostal Church, Bishop Fedatov. According to the bishop, in the 1930s a Christian woman gave an unusual prophetic word under the inspiration of the Holy Spirit. It said that in the future a person would arise in the Soviet Union whose name would be *Mikhail.* He would have a mark in his forehead. She continued to say that during his time, there would once again be freedom to worship and revival would come to the nation. However, this freedom would only be for a short time, then repression would begin.

About fifty years later (again, fifty being the number designated as Jubilee of freedom in Scripture), this prophecy would be fulfilled, when Mikhail Gorbachev became the leader of the Soviet Union! Words such as *glasnost* (a policy for transparency of the Soviet government) became globally recognized. A lesser-known part of the story about Mr. Gorbachev reveals the timing of the Almighty's hand in raising up men to rule.

Christian Mother Influences Mikhail

Lavon Riley was a tour operator from Texas. In the late 1980s Mr. Riley planned a trip to Russia, traveling with a planeload of Christians. Underneath their plane were thousands of Bibles. Upon his arrival, it was difficult to get clearance for the Bibles, but after a detailed visit with customs personnel and a special permit, the army came with trucks and delivered the Bibles directly to the churches.

Lavon personally told me this story, explaining that during this trip the KGB called him into their offices. Great fear of being arrested came upon him. The KGB proceeded to tell him they were aware of his every step. In fact, the man in charge said, "Let me show you your file." He proceeded to pull out a file, about four inches thick, that gave details of every time Lavon had ever traveled to Russia, this included the places he had spoken, hotels he had stayed, and restaurants where he had eaten. It turned out, the meeting was not to arrest nor interrogate, but to demonstrate to him that a "new Russia" existed that would allow more religious freedom. Lavon received his permit from the third man under Gorbachev to bring as many Bibles into Russia as Lavon desired.

It was at this time that Lavon learned that the mother of Mikhail Gorbachev was an Orthodox Christian. She had prayed for Mikhail for many years that he would become a leader in Russia. Lavon also learned that, during religious events, Mikhail's mother would make a special cake and at times place certain Scriptures on it. This was confirmed when Gorbachev appeared on *The Hour of Power* with Dr. Robert Schuller on October 15, 2000, and spoke about his mother's prayers and that "practically all" his family were Christians. During the interview, Mikhail said, "There can be no freedom without spiritual freedom, without human beings being able to choose."[39]

While Mikhail has kept close ties to the Russian Orthodox Church, none can deny that *perestroika* (the communist reform under Gorbachev) created an atmosphere of religious tolerance, opening the door to freedom of religious expression without repression, if at least for a season. Apparently, the predestined purpose of Gorbachev was twofold: to bring religious freedom to the Soviet Union (Russia) and to allow the Soviet Jews to migrate back to Israel. This action also was a direct fulfillment of ancient biblical prophecies concerning the return of the Jews from the north country back to Israel (Jer. 31:8).

In the Bible Israel was in captivity in Babylon for exactly seventy years (Jer. 25:11). God gave Israel Ten Commandments, and warned that if they disobeyed Him, the punishment would be seven times (Lev. 26:18). Ten multiplied seven times totals the number seventy. In 1917 communism took its hold in Russia and for seventy years held people captive until 1987, when the Iron Curtain began cracking.

While visiting Germany, President Reagan demanded that Gorbachev tear down the Berlin wall dividing Germany. Later Mr. Gorbachev did not prevent the wall from being demolished, but did help to unbolt the mighty

Iron Curtain over Russia and Eastern Europe. Both men rose to power at a pivotal season in history. The prophet Daniel tells us God "changes times and the seasons; He removes kings and sets up kings" (Dan. 2:21). As the hand of the Almighty was moving "pawns" into position on His chessboard, one more important move was needed to put Communism into "checkmate"!

Two Bullets That Charted Destiny

On May 18, 1920, Karol Joseph Wojtyla was born in Wadowice, Poland. During the Nazi occupation of Poland, Karol pursued his studies and worked as a stonecutter to hold a work permit, thus keeping him from being deported or imprisoned. He joined the UNIA, a Christian democratic underground group. Jewish organizations, such as B'nai B'rith, testified that he helped Jews find refuge from the Nazis. In 1942 he began to study for the priesthood and was ordained a priest on November 1, 1946. By 1967 he was elevated to cardinal, and on October 16, 1978, at age fifty-eight, Karol Wojtyla was elected pope and chose the title of John Paul II.

Oddly, both Reagan and Pope John Paul survived assassination attempts on their lives the same year! On May 13, 1981, the Pope was greeting the crowd at Vatican Square in Rome, Italy. As he leaned over to kiss the statue of the Virgin Mary, a Turkish terrorist fired a gun, and the pope was struck in the abdomen by the assassin's bullet. He slumped into the arms of his secretary as blood poured from the fresh wound. The world prayed and waited, concerned the pope would die. Despite losing six pints of blood, John Paul II survived. The pope realized he had been shot on the sixty-fourth anniversary of the famous Marion apparition known as "Our Lady of Fatima." This alleged apparition of the Virgin Mary had appeared to three children in Fatima, Portugal on May 13, 1917 (the same year as the Communist Revolution). Because of this strange coincidence, the pope credited Our Lady of Fatima (the Virgin Mary) with having spared his life and dedicated the remaining time of his papacy to her "immaculate heart."

It was also in 1981 that President Reagan was speaking at a luncheon at the Hilton Hotel in Washington DC. As he exited a side door, waving at reporters, a young man named John Hinckley fired six shots at the president. As secret service agent Jerry Parr hit Reagan in the stomach (to double him over into the limousine), both men realized the president had been shot. A single bullet had ricocheted off the limousine door and entered Reagan's chest. The X-rays at the hospital revealed the assassin's bullet had stopped one inch from Reagan's heart!

In his biography *An American Life* Reagan said, "I remember looking up from the gurney trying to focus my eyes on the ceiling tiles and praying." In the emergency room the president realized someone was holding his hand. The hand was touching his, holding on tight. He remembers a comforting, reassuring feeling. He asked several times who it was holding his hand, but received no response. He later tried to find out who held his hand, assuming it was a nurse. He was never able to locate the "person." Reagan said, "Someone was looking out for me that day." Reagan told several Secret Service agents he gave credit to God for protecting his life.[40]

These two assassination attempts helped to bond a special relationship between the president and the pope. In June of 1982 Ronald Reagan flew to the Vatican to have a personal meeting with Pope John Paul II. Years later their private discussion was made public. Both men discussed their assassination attempts and agreed that God had spared their lives for a special and specific reason. As they continued their discussion, they began to see a common thread of destiny. Both men discussed the terrible scourge of Communism and how the oppressive regimes had destroyed personal freedoms and faith in God from millions of people who desired to be delivered from the iron hold of this atheistic system. At that moment both men pledged to work together to help spread freedom throughout Communist nations. The pope knew all too well about Communism, since his homeland of Poland was a country gripped in the Communist vice.

Reagan did more than just talk about freedom. Three weeks after the meeting, he signed a secret National Security Directive to purchase and send into Poland the necessary equipment, including copy machines, fax machines, and other electronic equipment, to assist the Solidarity Movement working in Poland. This group would organize protests that would be aired via satellite around the world and would unite a large following of Polish workers.

The plan worked. Just as Communism had captured the minds of the common laborers during the 1917 revolution, it was the common workers of Poland who took the keys of freedom and unshackled the bands of iron. The impact of their uprising soon spread to Romania, Bulgaria, and Germany, where the world was stunned as the famous Berlin Wall was dismantled with sledgehammers by the German people.

Before Reagan departed from office, the Berlin Wall had crumbled, the Soviet Union had unraveled, and the icy cold war had melted. According to a report in *Time* magazine dated February 24, 1992, the coalition forged between Reagan and the Vatican consisted of a five-part strategy "that was aimed at bringing about the collapse of the Soviet economy, fraying the ties that bound the U.S.S.R. to its client states in the Warsaw Pact and forcing reform inside the Soviet empire."[41] Both Reagan and Gorbachev admitted the pope played a vital role in the collapse of Communism in Eastern Europe.

Few non-Catholics understand one of the unseen motivations of the pope's decision to become directly involved in liberating the Eastern Bloc Communist countries, especially the Soviet Union. His spiritual inspiration hinged on a prophecy that was given through an alleged apparition of the Virgin Mary in 1917.

The Fulfillment of Fatima

Pope John Paul II credited the Virgin Mary for sparing his life. One year after his near-death experience, the pope traveled to the famous Catholic shrine in Fatima, Portugal. He placed one of the bullets that was used in the attack in the crown of the statue of Our Lady of Fatima as a token of gratitude to her for saving his life. The pope pledged himself to Mary and gave himself to her message, especially the message of Fatima. His personal motto was *Totus tuus sum Maria*, meaning, "Mary, I am all yours." At the same time on May 13, 1982, the pope prayed before the statue of Our Lady of Fatima. In his prayer he consecrated the world to her, based on the promise from 1917, which said, "If my wishes are fulfilled...my immaculate heart will triumph; Russia will be converted, and there will be peace."[42]

From that moment, it became the goal of the pope to see Communism fall in the European Eastern Bloc including the Soviet Union, believing it would fulfill the word of the apparition. The pope received help from the "eagle of America" (Reagan) and a leader living under the "iron sickle," Mikhail Gorbachev.

The pope, along with most traditional European Catholics, was keenly aware of the prophecies given in Fatima, Portugal in 1917, about the future fall of communism. Because his life was spared on the anniversary of the Fatima visitation, the pope was compelled in his spirit to help fulfill the "wishes of the Virgin Mary," proclaiming at Fatima "Russia would be converted."[43]

This series of events shows how God uses men to change the course of history. It also demonstrates the power of a prophetic word and the altering impact of prayer.

The Prophetic Significance of 1917

In the year AD 1217 a Talmudic Rabbi from Germany, Rabbi Judah Ben Samuel prophesied the Ottoman Turks would take control over Jerusalem for eight Jubilees, or four hundred years (50 time 8 equals 400). Exactly three hundred years later, the Ottoman Turks took Jerusalem in 1517, and held control of Palestine and Jerusalem for four hundred years until 1917. During their four centuries of rule the Turks did a magnificent job of rebuilding the upper walls in Jerusalem and parts of the old city, which tourists can see to this day. In 1917 the British seized control of Palestine and Jerusalem, ending the Turkish control of the Holy Land. The year 1917 was one of the most important prophetic years for the world and the Jews, perhaps since the destruction of Jerusalem and the temple in AD 70. The following events occurred in 1917:

> » The Russian Revolution began in February 23, 1917, with the Tsar giving up his throne March 17.

> » Jews were expelled from Tel-Aviv and Jaffa by Turkish forces on March 28.

> » The United States declared war on Germany, entering World War I on April 6.

> » Three shepherd children allegedly saw the Virgin Mary in Fatima, Portugal on May 13.

> » A great fire destroyed 32 percent of Thessaloniki, Greece, leaving seventy thousand homeless.

» The signing of the Balfour Declaration giving Jews access to Palestine was on November 2.

» Lenin seized power in Russia—the beginning of communist and Soviet rule on November 7.

» British general Allenby took Jerusalem from four hundred years of Turkish control on Hanukkah, 1917.

» There were four solar (some partial) and three lunar eclipses in 1917.[44]

The same rabbi, Judah Ben Samuel, who predicted the eight Jubilees of Turkish rule over Jerusalem also predicted that on the ninth Jubilee (from his dating in 1217), Jerusalem would be a "no-man's" land. This would take us from 1917 to 1967, exactly fifty years (the time of complete Jubilee). Before the Six-Day War in June of 1967 Jerusalem was divided with a concrete wall and barbed wire, between Arab East (Jordan) and the Jewish Western section. The area where this barrier ran on both sides was called "no-man's land," meaning it was owned by neither side. The rabbi further stated that on the tenth Jubilee Jerusalem would be in the hands of Jews, then the Messianic times would begin. This requires adding fifty years to 1967, meaning the tenth Jubilee would fall on the year 2017. These "Messianic times" would mean the appearing of the Messiah or the Jewish people turning to the Messiah, both now occurring in Israel. There is a strong Messianic movement among both religious and secular Jews in which larger numbers believe that Christ fulfilled the Messianic prophecies in the Bible.[45] Clearly, 1917 was one of the most significant prophetic years since the first century, as events set a strong foundation for the biblical alignment of nations and the future reformation of Israel as a nation.

Raising Up and Removing Kings

American Christians have questioned just how much God is actually involved in the election of an American president, since the one running for office is selected by votes, implying *we do the choosing* and not God. Some believe there is an eternal creator, however, He has left the affairs of men in the hands of men. During the 2000 election, when Vice President Gore believed Bush had "stolen" the election, the body of Christ in America was divided in their opinions. I received e-mails and calls from Christians who were saying the election was rigged, Bush was a liar, and he would be an illegal president. I searched for a biblical response and found a scripture in Daniel, which I suggested could help settle the dueling taking place. It was a message Daniel gave to Nebuchadnezzar:

> Daniel answered and said: "Blessed be the name of God forever and ever, for wisdom and might are His. And He changes the times and the seasons; He removes kings and raises up kings; He gives wisdom to the wise."
>
> —DANIEL 2:20–21

Despite what some suggest, God can and does set up circumstances for the rise and fall of world leaders at specific seasons and times. This is not to say those raised up will listen to God or obey His instruction. At times in history a leader is appointed to enact a judgment from God. This happened when Babylonian King Nebuchadnezzar destroyed Jerusalem, taking the Jews captive. It was a tragedy for Israel, but the invasion was predicted one hundred fifty years prior by Isaiah (2 Kings 20:17–18), long before the birth of Nebuchadnezzar.

Even US presidents whose decisions are morally bad and biblically forbidden can be permitted to take power as an act of selective judgment on America for allowing abominations. In the Scripture the Almighty will judge the god of the nation first; in America's case it is the love for money—or the spirit of mammon. Following this judgment, there is often a crash in the economic security. Ancient Israel depended on rain and a good harvest as their life source. Without the rain, the harvest ceased, and the economy eventually crashed.

Israel flowed in a rhythmic cycle of righteous kings, followed by evil kings. The increase of the unrighteous kings brought spiritual oppression, economic disasters, and opened the door to outside enemies entering the land and taking possession of what belonged to God's covenant people. The purpose for allowing bad leaders was to break the pride of the people, humbling them to turn back to the Lord, repenting of their iniquities, and restoring their covenant. Christians can either curse the darkness and complain about how bad things are or humble themselves and pray. Darkness does not depart by cursing it, but by bringing light where there is none.

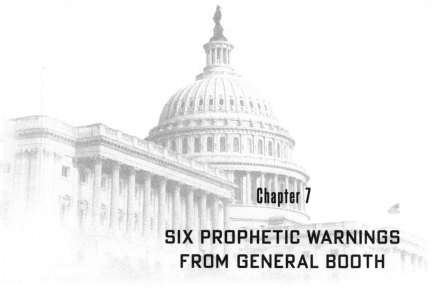

Chapter 7

SIX PROPHETIC WARNINGS
FROM GENERAL BOOTH

OST AMERICANS HAVE heard of the Salvation Army, but few have heard the name General William Booth (1829–1912). When the Christmas holiday arrives, Salvation Army volunteers are often seen standing outside stores. Usually a ringing bell serves as an invitation for people to drop some change in the slot of a red pot. The donations are used to help clothe and feed the poor. So, why a "Salvation Army"?

In the same year the Civil War came to an end, General Booth declared war on the powers of darkness by establishing the Salvation Army in 1865.[1] At that time the local churches refused to allow the poor into their ornate buildings, so Booth, who was pastoring a church but seeing the needs of the poor, left his church and began ministering on the streets. The Christian Revival Society, as it was first called, began in the slums of East London, but soon they were expanding to other countries, including America in 1880, then Israel, and eventually to fifty-eight countries by 1912.[2]

Chains of missions were born as the power of God was made manifest in meeting after meeting. Booth's favorite weapon was the power of prayer. It was a common event for the general to lead an "all night of prayer" when preaching the Word of God, where "people were frequently, struck down, overwhelmed with a sense of the presence and power of God."[3]

When Booth died in 1912, up to one hundred fifty thousand people visited as his body lay in state. His funeral drew more than forty thousand, including the queen, who sat next to an ex-prostitute—a convert of General Booth's.[4]

However, before his passing, he received a significant vision for what was to come. As the twentieth century began, he was asked what he saw as the greatest dangers in the next one hundred years.[5] Booth gave six warnings about the dangers he saw on the horizon in his vision.

> The chief danger that confronts the coming century will be religion without the Holy Ghost, Christianity without Christ, forgiveness without repentance, salvation without regeneration, politics without God, heaven without hell.[6]

Warning Number 1—Religion Without the Holy Spirit

Booth's first warning of religion without the Holy Spirit echoes a warning Paul gave in 2 Timothy 3:5 that the time would come when men would have a form of godliness, but deny the power thereof. I believe that if the Holy Spirit's presence ever simply departed from our churches, 90 percent of the music, teaching, and activity of many churches would continue unhindered, and a majority of people would never miss His presence—as long as things just continued as "normal" and the monthly expenses were paid.

Religion without the Holy Spirit is dry, formal, and boring. Without the Holy Spirit, Christianity is reduced to the same level as any other world religion. General Booth's wife, Catherine, preached when called on; this is what she said about the need of the Holy Spirit in one of her sermons:

> What can we do without it? This is the reason of the effeteness [weakness] of so much professed Christianity; there is no Holy Ghost in it. It is all rotten. It is like a very pretty corpse…it is a perfect form, but dead. It is like a good galvanic battery. It is all right—perfect in all its parts—but, when you touch it there is no effect—there, is no fire or shock. What is the matter? It only wants the fire—the power. Oh friends, we want the power that we may be able to go and stretch ourselves upon the dead in trespasses and sins, and breathe into him the breath of spiritual life. We want to go and touch his eyes that he may see, and speak to the dead and deaf with the voice of God and make them hear. This is what we want—POWER.[7]

Warning Number 2—Christianity Without Christ

The Christian faith is connected to the Cross, as Christ's sufferings are the road that leads to eternal life. I know of a minister who purchased a large facility for his church from two businessmen of another religion. Both requested that if the minister purchased the facility, he should never preach that other religions cannot go to heaven. This is a Christianity without a cross and without Christ.

This compromise of truth is seen when the secular media asks megachurch ministers if they believe Jesus is the only way to heaven. Instead of boasting on the finished work of Christ, these ministers compromise and make it appear there are many possible ways to heaven, that Jesus works for them—implying He may not be effective for anyone else.

Warning Number 3—Forgiveness Without Repentance

This warning may seem odd, considering the first foundation of the Christian faith is the call to repent. From the biblical prophets to John the Baptist and the apostles, *repentance* is required to inherit eternal life (Luke 13:3–5). Repentance means to be regretful for your evil or carnal way, changing your mind and direction by completely turning to Christ as Savior and Lord.

Sadly, I have observed people who come to the altar and ask God for forgiveness, yet afterward continue living in their same lifestyle, holding on to the same mind-set that led them into the spiritual sin cycle in the first place. Asking for forgiveness must be the fruit of repentance and not just mental ascent without a transformation.

Warning Number 4—Salvation Without Regeneration

Booth felt there would be numerous people claiming salvation but not being transformed into new creations in Christ Jesus. Today's more formal churches seldom give an altar invitation to repent and turn to God; instead, they replace tears of godly sorrow with "sign this card," or "shake the minister's hand."

Salvation must be more than making a mental "deal" between you and God. There must be a change that leads to a new life—a change in thinking, lifestyle, and desires. The old things must pass away, and new things must emerge (2 Cor. 5:17).

When Christians practice the same lifestyle as the unsaved, then we are in danger of a toothless Christianity that reduces salvation to another club membership, this time at some local church.

Warning Number 5—Politics Without God

The fifth warning was politics without God. It was five years after Booth's death when the Russian Revolution (1917) produced the first government without God. The new regime was one emphasizing atheism and persecuting Christians. This form of an anti-God government eventually spread to many nations and today (as of this printing) remains in power in China, Laos, Vietnam, Cuba, and North Korea. Since 1917 Communism has sent millions of Christians into the martyr's paradise in heaven (Rev. 6:9).

In America political hopefuls once sought out Christian pastors and their members to help unite votes for their election. But with over 50 percent of professing Christians either not registered or having never voted, the American church is now seen as weak and anemic. Thus, most politicians, with the exception of some Southern states that maintain a higher number of Christian voters, see no need to express publicly or practice the Christian faith.

In my lifetime I have never witnessed such a lack of interest among elected officials, especially in Washington DC concerning pure faith and spirituality. These men and women seldom, if ever, attend church, and if they claim to be Christians, we are reminded that they don't "wear their faith on their shirtsleeves." Obviously it's not in their hearts either.

Booth accurately perceived that a day was coming when Western governments would have no fear of God nor would they follow biblical principles. In Isaiah 33:22 we are told the Lord is our judge, our lawgiver, and our king. As judge, He judges between righteousness and unrighteousness. As our lawgiver, His laws are superior and must be followed to receive His covenant blessings. As king, He alone is the King of kings, set to rule over all nations.

Warning Number 6—Heaven Without Hell

Booth foresaw a time in which there would be preaching that included heaven but omitted hell. Western preaching today tends to emphasize prosperity, blessing, and favor. It is void of anything considered "negative," with hell being at the top of the list—even though hell is mentioned fifty-four times in the King James Version.

Now, a new wave of ministers is exempting themselves from this troubling and frightening teaching of eternal punishment, careful not to offend the unbelieving and unrepentant. These smiling ministers can say glowing words about heaven, but willfully ignore the Scriptures on hell. Alleged Christian authors publish popular books, omitting and rejecting the idea of life separated from God.

This is a dangerous, deceptive teaching that if believed could destroy souls for eternity. The subject may not be pleasant, but it was Christ who gave the firmest warnings against the dangers of hell (Matt. 5:22–30; 10:28).

General Booth's warnings were for both the church in America and Christians in general. Believers living in the Unites States can hear thunder over Washington DC, and the knowledgeable ones are expressing concern for not just spiritual storms but also for the political and economic hurricanes that are forming.

Will Tax Increases Bring Another Revolt?

Two wars that have begun on American soil have been linked to tariffs and high taxes: the Revolutionary War and the Civil War. In case you're a little rusty on your American history, let me refresh your memory.

In the 1700s the French and Indians were trading with the British and Americans. However, the French alone desired the trade deals. This resulted in the seven-year French and Indian War, as the Americans and British united in fighting the French. The foundation for the Revolutionary War was paved when the British felt the American colonies should foot the bulk of the war debt. Since America was a British colony, the British chose to raise revenue through new taxes, compiling a list with sugar, paper, and tea. The colonists repealed the tax with the Stamp Act. The colonists believed they were being taxed without any legal representation (taxation without representation), igniting the Boston Tea Party, where colonists dumped British tea in the Boston Harbor.

This event was the trigger that would build anger and cause colonists to demand separation from the British, leading to the Revolutionary War. The fire of war was sparked over tax increases and who would control the tariffs in trade and maintain control over the land deeds, many of which were mandated by the kings of England.

The most divisive war was the Civil War. A simple explanation as to what inspired the Civil War was the South wanted slavery and the North didn't, so an internal war between the North and South broke out to settle the issue. In reality the war was much more complicated than that.

Before the war the majority of manufacturing was in the North, as about 90 percent of US workers lived there, and labor costs—in that day—were becoming expensive. High import tariffs were viewed as good, since it raised prices on imported goods, and goods from the North could be purchased instead of goods from Europe.

In the South a strong movement of state's rights clashing with federal government control had been brewing, and the South's slave labor was cheap as cash was pouring into the larger plantations with the combined invention of the cotton gin and cheap labor. The southern farms were covered in cotton and indigo (dye) for cotton yarn. Soon the government began placing high tariffs on cotton in the South. The Southerners perceived this was being done to give the North money and fill the coffers of the northern banks.

The state of South Carolina decided to secede from the Union of states, with the issue of its "Declaration of the Causes of Secession." Before Lincoln was elected, seven states had already seceded from the Union. On April 12–14, 1861, the Civil War began with an attack on Fort Sumter. Eventually the southern states, united in a confederacy of eleven states, printed their own money and developed their own banking system. However, during the war the southern confederacy lost two-thirds of their men, with thousands of farms and homes burned.

After the war 4.5 million slaves were free. However, without work on the plantations—many which were in complete ruins—there was a disruption in work. Unless former slaves chose to remain in the region and find work, or chose to stay on the plantation, they would move northward.

The wealth of the southern plantations in some areas was almost totally destroyed. While it is true the issue of slavery became the primary issue of the Civil War, the center of the struggle was over high tariffs that the South resisted.

There were three senators, expressing the three main opinions surfacing in the slavery debate at the time of the Civil War. One desired to send the blacks back to their own country, Africa. A second wanted the land prices to collapse so large chunks of southern land could be bought up at cheap prices. A third senator truly believed that slavery was wrong. These three opinions were shared by different politicians and completely divided the leadership in Washington DC and the nation.

America and Ancient Rome Parallels

The reason for pointing out the tariffs that led to two wars within America is that the demise of the Roman Empire was partially the result of Rome's need of money to feed their armies, rebuild bridges, and prepare roads. So many of the citizens lost jobs and quit working after realizing that a steady income and food could be received through the government welfare, and was much easier as these benefits required no work or remuneration. Many people began depending on government doles, similar to our welfare system, that taxes were increased until the middle class was squeezed out of existence.

Early in the empire the Roman currency was brass and silver coins. However, as inflation spread, the silver eventually was mixed with other metals, reducing the true value of the Roman currency. America's monetary policy was once backed by gold and silver, called the gold standard. After 1964 the silver content was removed from our coins and replaced with cheaper forms of metal. Historians note the Roman tax burden became so great that revenues dwindled, eventually leading to the collapse of the Roman government.

The early founding fathers and others since then have understood the economic history of past democracies and gave warning for future generations. In a letter dated May 23, 1857, Lord Macaulay wrote a letter to Henry S. Randall, Esq., in which Macaulay made predictions of America's future troubles:

Your Republic will be as fearfully plundered and laid waste by bar-
barians in the twentieth century as the Roman Empire was in the
fifth; with this difference, that the Huns and Vandals, who ravaged
the Roman Empire, came from without, and that your Huns and
Vandals will have been engendered within your country by your
own institutions.[8]

America's national debt is a nuclear time bomb that will eventually
explode. It is futile to print the national debt in this book, knowing by the
time it goes to press the numbers will be higher—as the expenditures of the
nation rise by each minute that passes. The federal government only knows
of one way to bring income into government coffers: to tax everyone and
everything in sight. Men and women sit behind closed doors discussing
how to increase tax revenue without offending too many people from their
states, especially those who would rise up in anger as a voting majority,
sending them home without a job.

Americans tend to be extremely passive with any political decision as
long as it does not affect their wallets. Politicians have learned that the bait
that draws voters, inspiring their fingers to press their names on a voting
machine, is to guarantee as much "free stuff" to as many voters as possible. Politicians have also baited voters by intimidating them with the fear
of possible losses if they do not keep them as their state representatives
in the marble halls of Congress or the White House. Over 50 percent of
Americans are now receiving some form of government entitlement. In
a few years a massive number of Americans will retire, requiring more
money from federal resources. Eventually a nation runs out of other people's money and can't finance the promises made. Just look at Greece for a
possible example of what is coming.

All six of William Booth's warnings are rooted in the despairing and
dark spiritual condition of America. The powerful preaching voices of the
past that once pierced the darkness are, perhaps, viewing from heaven,
watching a new generation of powerless preachers echoing empty words
bouncing off church walls as robed choirs anticipate the final "amen," so
they may rush to the local restaurant to beat the rest of the church crowd.

Progressive theologians in America's new progressive Christianity have a
new false revelation: there is no hell, everyone is going to heaven anyway, so

don't sweat the possible heat. The unregenerate are made comfortable, and the Holy Spirit is expected to leave His ability to convict sin at the front door before entering the worship service.

There is one promise in Scripture that, in times such as these, resonates with concerned believers. When Ronald Reagan was sworn in as president, he placed his hand on his mother's Bible. A certain page from that Bible was later photographed—one of Reagan's favorites. It worked in Reagan's time and will work again. The Scripture blessings from the ancient past are also cyclical and can release repetitive blessings, if the same faith is exercised today as in the past. The verse that was marked in the Reagan Inaugural Bible read:

> If My people who are called by My name will humble themselves, and pray and seek My face, and turn from their wicked ways, then I will hear from heaven, and will forgive their sin and heal their land.
> —2 CHRONICLES 7:14

The responsibility to repent is on those who are called by the name of the Lord. Part of our repentance should be apologizing to God for compromising His Word for our own benefits, and trusting in a man-made system for our provision instead of God. Too many alleged Christians have tied their souls to the wrong places, people, and leaders. William Booth's predictions have all occurred, and only the true church can reverse these trends.

Chapter 8

DANGEROUS SOUL TIES
TO POLITICAL SPIRITS

I N THE TIME of Israel's judges every man did what he considered right in his own eyes (Judg. 17:6). This freedom to choose your own absolutes led to idolatry and captivity surrounding the tribes. God, Himself, established priests and prophets to instruct in the law and in righteousness. Israel was a theocracy, a religious nation whose king was God. Later in the time of Samuel Israel demanded a monarchy and a physical king, setting up a kingdom mirroring the surrounding nations (1 Sam. 8:6–19). By the time of Christ Rome began controlling the Jewish religion where it had become political. Even certain Jewish leaders had mingled the Holy Scriptures to please the emperors and governors, forging a dangerous soul tie to a political spirit.

Politicians pass *secular* laws and ministers preach and practice *God's* laws, which especially clash with the liberal and social opinions of today. We find there is always a conflict between powers of two: the kingdom of God and Satan, light and darkness, man's legislation and God's legislation. Within this battle, there are two social issues that have turned into political issues: abortion and same-sex relationships, or same-sex marriage, which in reality are spiritual issues. To the politicians, these controversial issues garner needed votes, but to informed believers they garner future judgments.

Regional judgment struck the twin cities of Sodom and Gomorrah, burning the buildings into ash heaps, for practicing and permitting six sins. One of these sins was "same-sex relations" and was called "abominations." (See Ezekiel 16:49–50.) In AD 70 the city of Jerusalem eventually was overtaken by its enemies, the temple lying in ruins, and the Jewish population either slain or taken captive, because of their shedding of innocent blood. (See Matthew 23:34–35.) The two "social-political issues" were truly spiritual.

It is the responsibility of God-fearing, covenant-keeping believers to be the *salt* and *light* in a morally tasteless and dark culture. If our understanding is darkened, and our salt loses it flavor, Jesus said it is good for nothing (Matt. 5:13). The enigma is this: How could a Bible-believing, Spirit-filled believer place their approval on politicians who allow and promote abortion (shedding innocent blood) and publicly promote and affirm marriage between a man and man or woman and woman? Knowing the biblical warnings, historic examples of individuals, nations, and empires being destroyed for both sins, believers still excuse themselves by saying, "Morally I don't agree with them, but…" The "but" is said only to ease their conscience. The three possible explanations for supporting these politicians are a believer's total biblical ignorance, unbelief in the possibilities of judgment, or a *soul tie to a political spirit*.

When Prophets and Politicians Clash

In the time of Elijah Israel was in a spiritual, economic, and governmental crisis. A forty-two-month drought had decreased their food supplies, and Ahab and his wife, Jezebel, were leading a corrupt government, confiscating land for their own selfish purposes. The violent beheadings against righteous prophets had sent thousands to hide in caves. Ahab and Jezebel had, however, offered *their supporters* free government entitlements during the crisis, including food for eight hundred fifty prophets.

These were men who rejected Israel's God, instead accepting an invitation at Jezebel's table. These alleged "prophets" bonded with workers of iniquity by mentally agreeing with political spirits. It is sad to see similar parallel patterns with present-day America. Out of the eight hundred fifty compromising prophets, four hundred fifty were called "prophets of Baal." The followers of Baal believed their god presided over the weather and the environment. Thus, these *environmentalist "prophets"* were happy to align with Ahab's administration, as they wanted their idol-groves and high places in the mountains secured to protect their "environmental god." It reminds me of the extreme environmentalist whose "mother" is the earth and whose "gods" are the spirits dwelling in the trees and rocks.

On the peak of Mount Carmel the showdown between the righteous remnant and the counterfeit prophets came to a climax. The Baal followers stacked stones, making an altar, picking up the same type of rocks from the same dirt that true prophets would use, forming a sacrificial altar to the Almighty. In the narrative the prophets of Baal were dancing around the altar, looking like an emotional Hebrew worship festival. These false prophets were shouting and placing their "offerings" on the altar, whooping and hollering until noon. If a Hebrew follower of the Almighty had been at the base of the mountain, unaware of *who* was doing the shouting, they may have interpreted it as an Israelite prayer meeting. What looked "real," was in reality, a counterfeit.

This illustrates a danger in Pentecostal-charismatic circles of believers shouting, dancing, and throwing their offerings on the altar but aligning themselves with a wrong spirit and a counterfeit fire. Their actions outside the church contradict what they do inside the church. Clearly, unholy noise may be acknowledged by a committee of dancing prophets, but not by God. Malachi said:

> "Who is there even among you who would shut the doors, so that you would not kindle fire on My altar in vain? I have no pleasure in you," says the LORD of hosts, "Nor will I accept an offering from your hands."
>
> —MALACHI 1:10

It is possible for church members to accept the religious form of Christianity, but God has turned a deaf ear and a blind eye, withdrawing His heavenly blessings. Elijah later rebuilt the altar and began pouring water on the sacrifice, making it difficult for anyone to light a man-made fire on wet wood! He prayed a sixty-three-word prayer and the fire of God fell consuming everything it touched.

America needs a rekindling of God's fire in the pulpit and in the pew. Using the Elijah analogy, I have said that God's fire will fall when the wood is wet on the tear-soaked altars from a repentant church. Like Elijah on

Mount Carmel back in the days of old, wet wood on the altar means the fire will fall! The showdown on Mount Carmel demonstrates the clash between a prophet (Elijah) and a politician (Ahab), and how the prayer life of Elijah broke the back of the spirit of drought (James 5:17–18). This also demonstrates that corrupt governments can give rise to true prophets!

> » Pharaoh plotted to abort the lives of the Hebrew infants at birth. Baby Moses was securely hidden in an ark in the bulrushes but grew up to become the *basket case* that eventually crushed the Egyptian Empire.

> » In the days of Ahab and Jezebel God countered government and spiritual corruption by raising up two prophets: Elijah and Elisha.

> » When Babylonian laws were passed forbidding prayer, furnaces awaited the resisters. A supernatural, fourth man showed up in the flames; God proved Himself to the king through three Hebrew men that He alone was God.

> » The uncompromising voice of John the Baptist shook the inner-circle of King Herod. Christ Himself was a threat to the entire Roman Empire and to the corrupt temple priesthood of His day.

> » Paul the Apostle dealt with civic governments in Roman provinces and Greek cities, many dominated by idols, gods, and their temples. Yet, Paul's apostolic anointing penetrated the counterfeit, broke the *soul ties to pagan gods*, and released multitudes from the pagan superstitions that held them captive.

Since corrupt leaders give rise to prophetic voices, I would say that America is overdue for a visitation.

The Digression of American Leadership

From 1776 to today there has been a digression in the *character* of elected leaders. Recently the popularity of the US Congress sunk to a septic tank low—a 14 percent approval rate.[1] In retrospect, America's early politicians began as *statesmen* who attended a local church out of their love for God. These men, connected with the founding government, believed their decision-making would make a positive change. They believed they were building a strong foundation that would provide a moral-spiritual compass for the colonies.

Eventually our statesmen became *elected leaders*, who continued attending church out of a love for God or giving the *appearance* of having a love for God. These were gifted individuals who passed laws that benefited the nation rather than just ensuring a reelection.

The spiritual digression is evident today, as elected leaders have evolved into *professional politicians.* On election cycles you see them attend church for support and "photo ops," but only after surveying the number of church attendees who show up at the voting booths in their district or state. These slick, media-marketed lawmakers have learned how to make promises they can't keep, spend money they don't have, and at times lie about their opponents, anemically apologizing for "misinformation," but only after their swearing-in ceremony.

Thankfully there are still a handful of dedicated, godly leaders who are the *remnant* on Capitol Hill in Washington DC. They have roots in a biblically based faith, refusing to be intimidated when expressing America's need for faith. To this remnant, faith is the compass for the ship of our republic, now lost in a typhoon surrounded by the fog of uncertainty.

The saddest commentary on a nation in moral and spiritual decline is when, with a straight face, an official lies and breaks the laws while no one pins them to the wall with the arrows of accountability. In fact, lying is now part of the strategy. When we breathe the stink of corruption without choking and gagging, and when political lies are expected instead of exposed, then deception has already rotted the soul of the nation, setting up for the final state of gangrene.

If you think that political corruption is a new phenomenon, consider the comments made by famous individuals concerning politics:

Crime does not pay as well as politics.[2]

—Alfred Newman

Politics is the art of looking for trouble, finding it whether it exists or not, diagnosing it incorrectly, and applying the wrong remedy.[3]

—Earnest Benn

The problem with political jokes is they get elected.[4]

—Henry Cart VII

The word politics is derived from the word *poly* meaning "many" and the word *ticks* meaning "blood sucking parasites."[5]

—Larry Hardiman

Politics is not a bad profession. If you succeed there are many rewards, if you disgrace yourself you can always write a book.[6]

—Ronald Reagan

Politics is supposed to be the second-oldest profession. I have come to realize that it bears a very close resemblance to the first.[7]

—Ronald Reagan

Now I know what a statesman is; he's a dead politician. We need more statesmen.[8]

—Bob Edwards

Since a politician never believes what he says, he is quite surprised to be taken at his word.[9]

—Charles De Gaulle

Get all the fools on your side and you can be elected to anything.[10]

—Frank Dane

If God had wanted us to vote he would have given us candidates.[11]

—Jay Leno

The purpose for exposing the soul ties to political spirits is found in Scripture. The strongest spirits in the kingdom of darkness are called "principalities" (Eph. 6:12), one of four levels of powerful spirits that can impact cities and nations. The word *principalities* at times is translated as "governments." These spirits are linked to manipulating, wicked leaders who attempt to hinder the righteous or pass legislation that persecutes believers.

The authoritative strength of principalities is demonstrated in Daniel 10, where a prince controlling the Persian leaders was dominating the atmosphere over the city of Babylon. This "principality prince" was hindering an angel of the Lord for three weeks from bringing a message to Daniel. These stronger spirits in the kingdom of darkness are assigned to prevent any godly influence or to keep righteous leaders from taking higher positions of authority in the nation.

Unless there is a kingdom of wicked-spirit entities in the earth, how does one explain the destructive desires of numerous dictators to slay multitudes without any remorse? How do you explain Joseph Stalin (Russia), Adolph Hitler (Germany), Mao Zedong (China), Nicolae Ceausescu (Romania), Gamal Nasser (Egypt), Saddam Hussein (Iraq), and the numerous others from smaller nations whose hands were dripping with the blood of the slain?

Years ago I conducted an evangelistic meeting in Uganda. While staying at a hotel in Kampala, the nation's capital, I could see another hotel across from where we were. Day after day many vultures would circle or perch on trees and at times would land on the ground. I inquired of the local host pastor if he knew anything about this strange happening.

He told me this was the place where the former dictator, Idi Amin Dada (1971–1979) had slain hundreds of his own people, scattering their bloodied bodies on the ground to be fed to the vultures. These birds would return to the same site, even though the dictator no longer ruled. The locals genuinely believed some of these birds were controlled by demons because of strange activities occurring when they were present. They presumed this from the biblical story where evil spirits took possession of the swine (Mark 5:11–13).

The desire to slay the innocent and to shed blood is difficult to explain, unless one believes there exists a satanic kingdom operating on earth, attempting to dominate the decisions of wicked men.

Exposing Lying Spirits

At times a spirit of lying is assigned to a high-level leader. According to a powerful, biblical narrative, King Ahab was strategizing a battle, looking for a coalition to join his strategy of expected victory. The prophet Micah experienced a vision in which he saw angelic armies positioned in God's heavenly throne room, discussing a plot on how to end Ahab's life in the war. The true prophet saw a *lying spirit* sent to deceive Ahab's false prophets. The false prophets were deceived into predicting Ahab's victory in the coming battle. In reality, one true prophet knew Ahab would go into battle never to return (2 Chron. 18:18–22).

This story indicates world decisions are strategized first in heaven, before being performed on earth's stage. Spirits can plant a seed of lies and thoughts in a leader's mind, inducing deceptions that lead to a damaging decision, setting the person up for failure instead of success. As an example, we read where Satan provoked David to number Israel, without collecting the required half-shekel tax. By ignoring God's law, he brought a terrible plague from the Almighty against Israel (Exod. 30:12; 1 Chron. 21:1).

From the Ahab account, we also see that it is possible for a lying spirit to influence a noted leader and set him up for a major fall or even a premature death. When Richard Nixon publicly denied that his administration had anything to do with the Watergate break-in, the truth surfaced, leading to his impeachment and resignation. The same occurred with Bill Clinton, when under oath he denied having relations "with that woman," Monica Lewinsky.

America and Babylon Parallels

Some prophetic teachers try to connect the American empire with Jeremiah 51–52 and Revelation 17–18, since both speak of Babylon. I will not debate the theological points in favor of or against these interpretations. However, I will point out that ancient Babylon parallels the same controlling government that is challenging America's freedoms.

The Babylonians invaded Jerusalem to seize the highly prized and valued gold vessels from the temple. Taking this wealth back to Babylon increased Babylon's economic assets, as King Nebuchadnezzar was expanding the city and building pagan temples, increasing the government debt. The Babylonian system sought total control over every area of the people's lives. In Daniel 1 the Hebrews were told what type of *foods* to eat (including meat sacrificed to idols); later, they were forbidden *to pray* to their God (Dan. 6:1–13). On another occasion, the king commanded three Hebrew men to *bow to an idol* or face death (Dan. 3:1–25).

These three regulations were totally contrary to the convictions and beliefs of the Hebrews. These three parallels are similar to governmental regulations that certain liberal influencers in Washington demand. By law, they regulate the type of hybrid-seed farmers use, they control the amount of food, milk, and eggs made available, and now they are working to regulate the types of food we eat.[12] Christians no longer have the freedom to pray in public schools. They are prohibited from expressing thanks to God in many public venues, and when they do, it is not without criticism or threats of lawsuits. Evangelicals are taunted by critics who scream "intolerance," especially when we proclaim that Jesus is the only the way to eternal life.

Just like the three Hebrew men in Babylon, we are told to bow down and honor counterfeit religions. We are pressured never to confess that Christ is the only way to God, but to be tolerant and accept all religions as a way to eternal life. Four Hebrew men in Babylon (Daniel, Hananiah, Mishael, and Azariah in Dan. 1:7) refused to compromise their moral and spiritual values, despite the *heat* of a fiery furnace or a den of wild lions that awaited them (Dan. 3:6).

Now back to the question: Why are so many Christians comfortable electing men or women who will pass laws contrary to Scripture? It is ignorance and peer-pressure. Many Christians are ignorant of God's Word, of historic judgments, and of cycles and patterns in prophecy. There is also the Babylonian pressure—in many Christians' case, their unsaved or carnal family members place pressure on them to ignore their convictions to keep a specific political party in control.

Those identifying themselves as Christians must make the same decision that Elijah demanded of the Israelites on Mount Carmel. He said, "How long will you halt between two opinions?" (1 Kings 18:21, KJV). The word *halt* in this passage means to *hesitate*, but it also means to *limp*.

The church has been weakened with limp believers who cannot decide whose side they are on. Each Sunday they ascend to the top of "Mount Carmel church," where they will cry aloud, dance around the altar, shout, and lay their offerings down, yet they return to the table of compromise with the Ahabs and Jezebels. Their souls are connected to a deceptive system, believing the lie that as long as they personally don't believe in abortion or same-sex marriage, they are justified and God will never place any responsibility on them at the heavenly judgment.

Believers are instructed not to be unequally yoked with unbelievers

(2 Cor. 6:14). I was taught this verse was Paul reprimanding believers from marrying unbelievers, yet marriage is not alluded to in the text. Paul is dealing with believers associating and fellowshipping with workers of darkness.

Notice to whom God tells you to be joined: "You shall fear the Lord your God; you shall serve Him, and to Him you shall hold fast" (Deut. 10:20); "He who is joined to the Lord is one spirit with Him" (1 Cor. 6:17); "They have addicted themselves to the ministry of the saints" (1 Cor. 16:15, KJV; "We have many members in one body" (Rom. 12:4).

The controlling spirit the Jews encountered in Babylon is facing America today. Attempting to change the populace's diet, personal spiritual beliefs, and passing laws to impact their religious practices in public, are all fundamental changes liberals have made in America. Many prophetic teachers attempt to discover America in prophecy by comparing the United States to the Scriptures in Jeremiah and Revelation that allude to Babylon; however, there is no doubt, the events in ancient Babylon paint a picture of religious oppression toward those who differ with the Babylonian system.

The Stone and the Bricks

In Genesis 11 Moses gives a historical account of the world's first global kingdom called Babel. It is a city constructed under Nimrod, Noah's great-grandson through his son Ham. Josephus, the Jewish historian, describes events that followed Noah's flood, as men repopulated the earth remaining on mountains but eventually moving toward the lower plains:

> These first of all descended from the mountains into the plains, and fixed their habitation there; and persuaded others who were greatly afraid of the lower grounds on account of the flood, and so were very loath to come down from the higher places, to venture to follow their examples.[13]

It appears many men eventually became united in one location, instead of in colonies, and they all spoke one language (Gen. 11:1). Nimrod was admired by the people, yet was a rebel against God. His plans to build a tower so high that no floodwaters would ever reach the top were in defiance. Josephus again comments:

He (Nimrod) said he would be revenged on God, if he should have a mind to drown the world again; for he would build a tower too high for water to be able to reach, and that he would avenge himself on God for destroying their forefathers.[14]

The strength of Babylon was simple: they all spoke one language uniting them with one leader (actually a dictator) who reigned over them. It is believed they had one main religion, which was based on mother-son worship. They viewed their kingdom to be so strong that nothing could defeat them (Gen. 11:1–4). However, through a supernatural act of God Himself, the tower fell, and the unity of the kingdom, with the people, scattered to the four winds.

The Brick and the Stone—A New World Order

One often overlooked part of the Babel narrative is the "brick" and the "stone." This segment of Scripture gives us a prophetic parallel for man's present attempt to reform this ancient Babylonian Order into a New World Order.

And they said one to another, Come, let us make bricks and burn them thoroughly. So they had brick for stone, and slime (bitumen) for mortar.

—GENESIS 11:3, AMP

The kingdom of God and the return of Messiah are compared to a stone cut out without hands that will, at the time of the end, emerge, crashing down on the kingdoms of this world (Dan. 2:34–35). Jesus is identified as the "chief cornerstone" (Eph. 2:20) and believers in the church are called "lively stones" (1 Pet. 2:5, KJV). Even John the Baptist used the metaphor of a new worshipper as being "stones" raised up from the children of Abraham (Matt. 3:9).

Globally there have been increased discussions of nations forming a New World Order. This coalition would unite all the countries of the world into ten divisions, yet would be under the control of a select unit of men, chosen to represent each division. This new government would have one currency, remove religious barriers, and unite the masses through international laws. This repeat Babylonian group desires to make "bricks" out of humanity.

However, there is a difference between a *brick* and a *stone*. Bricks are all formed from the same mold; they look the same, and you cannot tell the difference in one from the other. This was the concept of Communism: to put every citizen on the same political and economic level, building a kingdom of bricks. The people wore the same type of shoes, clothes, and coats, and they lived in the same type of government housing. They were given one job to do for the well-being of the system, and even were paid equally.

When the European Union (EU) promoted their slogan with twelve nations, one of their symbols of unity was the Tower of Babel. An artist named Pieter Bruegel[15] did three oil renditions of paintings in the 1500s, and all were of the ancient Tower of Babel. The round base is in the form of the Roman Coliseum. The EU Parliament building in Strasbourg, France—the capital of Europe—is also in the shape of the Tower of Babel, looking unfinished; thus, the Tower of Babel became a new symbol of a new unity among the EU nations.

The EU used the painting the *Venusian version*, and underneath were the words "Europe: Many Tongues, One Voice."[16] With the same Bruegel painting, a poster was made showing numerous people assembled at the Tower of Babel; however, they all are in the form of Legos, the plastic toys children play with. Their heads are all square, with the exception of one baby in the picture whose head is round, being held by its mother. The implication is that infants are born free but as they grow they will eventually become a part of the new order.

God's intent remains to have a kingdom of stone. Stones come forth from the dust of the earth and are different shapes, sizes, weights, and even colors. There are white, black, red, and tan colored stones, just as people from the seven continents are different sizes and colors! God gives each "stone" a different position and purpose when building His church on the foundation of Christ and the Apostles. When He spoke of Himself as being the Son of God, Christ announced, "Upon this rock I will build my church" (Matt. 16:18, KJV).

The Tower of Babel was brick, held together by *slime* (Gen 11:3, KJV). The word *mortar* (Gen. 11:3) refers to a dark, tar like substance found in areas of ancient Babel (modern Iraq) where oil is underground. Slime is underground, but under pressure it rises to the surface. It seems today "slime," or men, are holding the systems together—established by men—and the motivating force underneath its surface is greed, lust, and power. Corrupt leaders are becoming a *reflection of the people* who keep voting them into their positions. Liars love other liars, crooks connect with crooks, and deceivers relate to other deceivers. Perhaps those who lead us are not influencing us as much as reflecting us.

Consider how the leaders in Washington have changed: leaders knowingly lie by making promises they know cannot be kept, just to maintain the status quo and to hold onto their positions. Laws and bills are now passed behind closed doors, after the approval of uninformed voters (such as the Affordable Healthcare Act). Evidence is often ignored, which proves those voting for their favorite candidates are later rewarded with positions and jobs. If you pay, you can play.

Both Babel and Egypt reveal a preview of America moving toward a type of European socialism. In Babel bricks replaced stones; in Egypt the Hebrew slaves were commanded to make bricks and build treasured cities. Each morning the Hebrews went to work under Egyptian supervision, doing the same four things: collecting straw, mixing mud, pouring water into pits where the bricks were made, and then baking them in ovens. It was the same routine over and over every day. However, the Egyptian government provided food and housing for those brick makers.

Just as in Israel, until a prophet with divine authority rises up supernaturally with signs and wonders, challenging the Pharaoh's iron dictatorship, the people will simply be the brick-makers. Brick-makers whose daily struggle, like Israel in Egypt, will bring on more oppression, discouragement, and debt as the treasured city of Washington keeps the money pouring in.

I am convinced the greatest fear some American leaders have is citizens of this nation breaking the brick stronghold, and turning back into what God created them to be: an individual stone that is dependent upon God for their source instead of Uncle Sam and his siblings. For many years in America liberal professors have promoted the concept of a socialist society, including the redistribution of wealth. After years of promoting this idea, in 2008 America willingly elected a leader who made it clear this was his chief motivation—to fundamentally change America. He has fulfilled this vision.

The world's way of thinking is a *brick mentality*, while the church's should be a *stone mentality*. From coast to coast conservative believers are considered narrow-minded and intolerant. To some in the federal government, key members of the Tea Party or certain conservative political groups are even labeled as being part of possible "domestic terror groups."

Liberals brag on their tolerance, which is clearly expressed when you think as they do. You will receive a smile and warm embrace from them if you convert from a "moral-spiritual" way of thinking to a more "open-minded" and "progressive" belief system. To them, you have "seen the light" and are received with incredible tolerance.

However, the spirit of intolerance is released in rage when liberal hypocrisy is exposed, and individuals disagree with their ideas. If you warn of the dangers of sin, you are being judgmental and have no right to tell others how to live. If you defend traditional marriage, you are a homophobe. If you believe there are dangerous Islamic terrorists that must be captured, you are tagged as anti-Islam. If you disagree with the decisions of a person of a different skin color, it's because you are a racist.

The spirit of Babel and the control of Nimrod are being repeated in modern history. Notice the Book of Revelation chapters 17 and 18; these Scriptures deal with a system called "Mystery Babylon" (Rev. 17:5). The *cycle of history* comes full circle, as Babel appears in Genesis 11; then centuries later King Nebuchadnezzar builds Babylon, and at the time of the end an economic and religious Babylon comes to its completed cycle. In all three biblical examples (Babel, Babylon, and Mystery Babylon) there were, and will be, global influence.

The New BRICS Coalition

The word BRIC is an acronym referring to the countries of Brazil, Russia, India, and China, which are merging under a new economic development strategy. In 2010 the four nations added South Africa, making the acronym BRICS—the "S" representing South Africa. This coalition may not seem important to other nations; however, these five nations make up one-fourth of the world's land mass and 43 percent of the world's population. At this printing, they also generate nearly one-fourth of the world's income. This political and economic union of nations called BRICS was formed collectively, so individually it would raise their national status and transform their growing economies into influential powers on the global stage. The four original countries now have the world's fastest-growing economies.[17]

On a recent trip to Israel several individuals from South Africa joined the group I was traveling with. This was when I was made aware of BRICS and the goals reported in South Africa.

Since America continues to borrow money, and the national debt is enlarging, there is a belief among global economies that the dollar will not be the global currency of the future, and a new global currency should overtake the dollar. According to this belief, this coalition of powers would determine the future economic stability of the world, and eventually become the leader to replace America's economic dominance.

China and India are both the leading suppliers of manufactured goods as America closes factories and becomes a purchaser instead of a producer. Some believe the BRICS coalition eventually desires to create their own currency that will overtake the dollar. All five emerging economies acknowledge what the American administration refuses to admit—it is impossible to pay off the national debt, even if we tax the rich at a 100 percent rate.

The Tower of Babel was a sign of the unity and economic power of the east after the flood. Using bricks for stone, the ancient tower became the modern symbol of the European Union. To emphasize the unity of the coalition, the lower half of the headquarters in Brussels, Belgium, is shaped in the form of the tower. Now, the latest unity of BRICS becomes the latest of global coalitions—perhaps one that will compete with the future system of the beast's ten kings, led by the Antichrist.

Babel tries to unite the world through economic power, military strength, and political influence. God struck down the first tower, overthrew the kingdom of Babylon after seventy years of controlling the Jews, and will burn a future Babylon in one hour. Man's attempt to unite the world into a global unit will fail when the Antichrist and his ten kings rise with their own weapons of mass destruction.

The church and individual believers must make a choice. Will they allow the "slime and mud" to stick to them, becoming puppets to the "puppet masters" in the future global system or will they remain free by joining with other stones in laying a strong foundation, refusing to compromise biblical truths? After all, the kingdom of God is the stone kingdom and in the end the "stones" will rule.

Uniting to Control the Masses

I am very grateful for a nation that encourages the support of the poor. It is good we have been a country who has helped those who are physically disabled and unable to work. However, after many generations living on the dole and receiving government assistance, it has created a codependency on the system, making slaves of the people. The support is now suppressing their potential to exit the cycle of poverty to move on to a better life for themselves and their children. I have learned that many individuals—especially single mothers—find it difficult, if not impossible, to move from government support to a job. They find the moment they get a job making minimum wage, most aid is cut off. They receive more aid by not working than by working, which holds them hostage to a "Babylonian system" of control.

I was born in Parsons, West Virginia. My mom, dad, and both sets of grandparents were also from West Virginia. In the early years the economy of West Virginia centered on the coal mines. The strongest political influence in the state was the United Mine Workers (UMW) organization. Many years ago when the various rural and small-town mines were established, bosses and owners at times mistreated the miners. Eventually miners sought to form a *union* of miners to voice complaints, set good wages, and provide health protection, as the mines can be (and still are) dangerous workplaces. Resistance came from owners to the union forming, not among coal miners. At times violent clashes resulted between the two. Miners who wanted a union began wearing a *red bandana* around their necks, and soon became known as "rednecks." Eventually the unions were formed and wielded great power over decisions, including politics in West Virginia.

Opposition came from the wealthy and from independent miners; however, one political party supported the miners union. Thus, the UMW consistently pushed all miners in West Virginia to vote only for that party, especially in their gubernatorial, senatorial, and US presidential elections. As a child, I can remember my granddad in his mining days, talking about how it was impossible to find someone voting for the opposing party in the coal mines, or for that matter in the entire state. Being born in and having family in West Virginia, I do not exaggerate when saying that growing up in the rural towns, you could be in physical danger if you ever confessed voting for anyone other than the party behind the unions.

West Virginians still tend to vote for the party in support of the unions in their local elections. The trend remains that way since most local candidates are conservative, and the majority of the elderly are conservative in their moral and social issues.

Nonetheless, in the presidential elections the state has changed in recent years, often voting for the party the unions have opposed. One reason is many of the older West Virginians see America falling into a pit of extreme liberalism. They remember a President-elect Obama in 2008 speaking to liberal, pro-environmental groups in California. These liberal groups were making negative comments toward the coal industry, which did not settle well with the sons and daughters of miners. According to miners in West Virginia, Obama's new environmental regulations have made it difficult, if not impossible, to open new mines. The new rules have even proven arduous in keeping older mines performing, as many have closed. The coal industry has suffered a deathblow in some communities throughout the state.

The UMW was very good to their workers, even the older retired miners. They covered medical expenses for my granddad and grandmother in their later years and upon their passing, their total funeral expenses were paid. However, today in many cases, certain unions are spending hundreds of millions of dollars that could be set aside to help workers and their families. Instead, it is poured into advertising and checks are cut during voting seasons to keep extreme liberals in power in many places. We're seeing union dollars funding many who encourage legislation that is not only dangerous economically, but also promotes legalizing abominations, which would result in selective judgment from the Almighty.

In the time of the judges the Israelites chose their own direction as to what was right or wrong:

> You shall not at all do as we are doing here today—every man doing whatever is right in his own eyes.
>
> —DEUTERONOMY 12:8

When Israel did what was right in their own eyes without a king, no spiritual leader, and no voice of influence, look at what emerged: the people turned to false gods and idols. Their souls became tied to idolatrous spirits. Another biblical account found in Judges reveals an alternative parallel in America today.

> When these went into Micah's house and took the carved image, the ephod, the household idols, and the molded image, the priest said to them, "What are you doing?"
>
> And they said to him, "Be quiet, put your hand over your mouth, and come with us; be a father and a priest to us. Is it better for you to be a priest to the household of one man, or that you be a priest to a tribe and a family in Israel?" So the priest's heart was glad; and he took the ephod, the household idols, and the carved image, and took his place among the people.
>
> —JUDGES 18:18–20

> And the children of Dan said to him, "Do not let your voice be heard among us, lest angry men fall upon you, and you lose your life, with the lives of your household!"
>
> —JUDGES 18:25

In the story the tribe of Dan had turned to idols under the eyes of compromising priests. Notice, they commanded the priest to put his hand over his mouth. (We would say to "shut up" or "be quiet.") And later the children of Dan said, "Do not let the people hear your voice." The truth emitting from a God-appointed priest, assigned to speak on behalf of God, could stir up anger among an idolatrous people (Judg. 18:25).

There was such a fear to please people that spiritual leaders, whose words should carry authority, were too fearful to speak up. Consequently, intimidation watered down their spiritual authority to the point of becoming empty voices. However, the Bible gives us plenty of examples among our spiritual ancestors who did not have the word *intimidation* in their vocabularies.

> » Can you imagine Joshua at Jericho saying, "Everyone get out a white handkerchief and wave it on a stick to let these Canaanites know that we are coming in peace and not war?"

» What about seeing Moses standing before Pharaoh and handing his miracle rod over as a gift to Egypt's king; after all, wouldn't protocol teach to respect a visitor, to honor the leader with a great gift?

» Picture David approaching Goliath, offering to give up his five smooth stones, if Goliath would only hand over his sword as a token that Israel and the Philistines could all live together in peace.

» Then there is always John the Baptist, who could host a private dinner with leading Pharisees to discuss doctrinal disagreements, so both could better understand one another's differences.

» I cannot imagine Peter receiving money from Simon, the sorcerer for purchasing spiritual gifts, and Peter suddenly declaring, "The wealth of the wicked is laid up for the just, and God has used a sorcerer to finance my crusade in Samaria!" Since it is the truth that sets you free (John 8:32), compromising the truth could tighten the chains of bondage, holding down those who seek freedom.

To the person "who knows to do good and does it not, to him it is sin" (James 4:17). How would early believers Peter, Paul, James, and others view the spiritual compromisers of today? What would they say to those who claim to know right from wrong, yet support and give approval to men and women by keeping them in high positions, knowing they will pass legislation that angers God and has proven to bring judgment on nations?

To me, this would be like the Jews at Christ's birth voting in Herod after he killed infants under the age of two, using the excuse, "We support him because he is a great builder expanding the temple in Jerusalem and is helping us economically; although I don't believe in his social activity." *When your support of people overrides your biblical convictions, you have a soul tie to a political spirit.*

The Molech Spirit

Many Christians are comfortable with individuals who support legalized abortion. So where is the harm in that?

Ancient Israel fell into the same sins being practiced among the pagan tribes living among them. The Canaanites worshipped an idol called Molech, in the Valley of Hinnom, located outside the southwestern walls of Jerusalem. Molech was man-made from hammered brass—a calf from the waist up and human from the waist down—and rested on a brass pedestal. Wood was laid and lit in the belly where a hole was cut, causing the metal frame to become hot, as fire burned inside the idol.

The pagan custom was to pass an infant between the arms of the idol, called in Scripture "passing children through the fire" (Lev. 18:21, 2 Kings 23:10). Some scholars suggest that infants may have been cast into the burning belly of the idol as an offering to this pagan deity. The modern parallel of Molech worship is the aborting of an infant, when a medical procedure reaches into the belly extracting the fetus from its protective womb. The Lord warned Israel:

> And you shall not let any of your descendants pass through the fire to Molech, nor shall you profane the name of your God: I am the LORD. You shall not lie with a male as with a woman. It is an abomination.
>
> —LEVITICUS 18:21–22

The two national sins of America are mentioned in these two verses (abortion and men having relations with men). Both are abominations, and both legalized by the Supreme Court in America and supported by liberal politicians. Notice the penalty for Molech worship was strict, a death penalty:

> Then the LORD spoke to Moses, saying, "Again, you shall say to the children of Israel: 'Whoever of the children of Israel, or of the strangers who dwell in Israel, who gives any of his descendants to Molech, he shall surely be put to death. The people of the land shall stone him with stones. I will set My face against that man, and will cut him off from his people, because he has given some of his descendants to Molech to defile My sanctuary and profane

My holy name. And if the people of the land should in any way hide their eyes from the man, when he gives some of his descendants to Molech, and they do not kill him, then I will set My face against that man and against his family; and I will cut him off from his people, and all who prostitute themselves with him to commit harlotry with Molech."

—LEVITICUS 20:1–5

Under the new covenant, we do not kill those who break God's law or stone individuals for their sins. We see how Jesus refused to stone the woman in adultery, as God will judge each person either in this life or in the life to come. Instead, the way a democratic nation prevents legalized abortion is by "killing the bill," or putting pressure on lawmakers to protect the unborn. The danger is, if believers, including ministers, are not careful, we will shut our mouths, hide our eyes, and our silence will bring in clouds of ignorance and darkness. We should be reminded of Peter's admonition:

Yet if anyone suffers as a Christian, let him not be ashamed, but let him glorify God in this matter. For the time has come for judgment to begin at the house of God; and if it begins with us first, what will be the end of those who do not obey the gospel of God? Now "If the righteous one is scarcely saved, where will the ungodly and the sinner appear?"

—1 PETER 4:16–18

Believers must break soul ties to political and idolatrous spirits. They must act on the convictions planted in their spirits with the knowledge of God's Word, supporting men and women whose ideas and character line up with the Scriptures—the same Scriptures from which we will all be judged. Forget the political parties and look at their platforms. Any "platform" built on the wrong foundation will never stand.

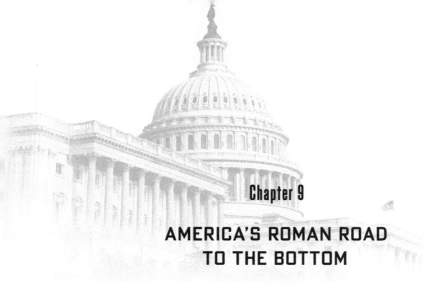

Chapter 9

AMERICA'S ROMAN ROAD
TO THE BOTTOM

Y EARS BEFORE 9/11 several pastors were invited to have dinner with a renowned pastor, David Wilkerson, at his church, located in the heart of Times Square in New York City. That evening the ministers met at a restaurant atop a skyscraper in downtown Manhattan. From the restaurant, the view was spectacular, surrounded by windows, and the city shimmered with lights as far as the eye could see. Wilkerson asked the men to look carefully around at all the buildings. He wanted them to tell him what they thought was the common thread. Numerous comments ensued, but none had given Wilkerson the answer for which he was fishing.

He eventually asked, "Can't you see? This American city is now owned by foreign investors and foreign nations." He pointed out that among the curses of the law is a warning. If God's people break His statutes, commandments, and judgments, the Almighty would allow the stranger, or foreigner, to rise higher in the land, eventually bringing His own people lower (Deut. 28:43). It was pointed out that the warning also says the foreigner would lend, and we would borrow, making the foreigner the head and God's own people the tail (v. 44).[1]

Is it possible that America, the single greatest nation-building experiment in world history—beginning with thirteen colonies and expanding into fifty states—is on the brink of economic, moral, and spiritual decline? Are we moving down the same economic road as the ancient Imperial

Roman Empire to have the same spiritual apostasy as ancient Israel? In a previous generation, when the seven-lettered word *America* was spoken, nations worldwide identified our country as the world's greatest military, the strongest economy, best job market, and the highest standard of living in the world. The freedoms provided to Americans were the envy of the world as millions from foreign nations dreamed of obtaining permanent visas to the United States.

For many years sociologists, historians, and professors in Ivy League universities have conducted research, hosted seminars, and held classes attempting to explain the mystery of America's economic success. It is often explained with two phrases: capitalistic ventures and democratic ideas. In summary it is the liberty to think, create, build, and make your dreams come true through hard work and creative ideas.

However, when looking below the surface as a believer, the true key unlocking generations of economic prosperity is more than a well-organized industrial machine. It is greater than venture capitalism whose monetary success is rooted in stock market investments. The secret is another "c" word called "covenant."

America has been blessed because it was built on a covenant foundation birthed by spiritually minded men who understood what this generation has ignored or lost. They knew America must be founded on principles and ideas rooted in the ancient laws of the Holy Scriptures and the colonies must be favored by divine providence. This is why our founders applied the instructions and principles given to ancient Israel. Consequently, America and Israel have interwoven their foundational threads.

"Progressive" is another name for liberal. The progressives' or liberals' blind assessment of America's spiritual heritage is opposite from the average patriotic American who has spiritual understanding. Conservatives believe our early founders came to America seeking freedom—but liberals willfully ignore this freedom being sought.

The historical answer is they came to find freedom from religious oppression. The ships traveling from England were not seeking democracy. They were escaping a tyrant king who was forcing them to participate in something they rejected. The early pilgrims were not seeking freedom *from* religion, they were seeking freedom *to practice* their religion.

In the year 1607 about one hundred pilgrims journeyed by sea from

England, arriving at the shores of a nonexisting community they eventually built and named Jamestown. They constructed a cross and dedicated the new land to God. The harsh winter killed off half the original clan; however, with determination the survivors built forts, set up trade, and eventually learned to coexist with the natives in the region. In 1620 the Mayflower Pilgrims arrived in what is now Provincetown Harbor near Cape Cod, Massachusetts, and penned a written decree called The Mayflower Compact. It read:

> In the name of God, Amen. We, whose names are underwritten, the loyal subjects of our dread sovereigne Lord, King James, by the grace of God, of Great Britaine, France, and Ireland king, defender of the faith, etc., having undertaken, for the glory of God, and advancement of the Christian faith, and honour of our king and country, a voyage to plant the first colony.[2]

If a United States senator or president today spoke of America being a place "to advance the Christian faith," the progressives who brag on their open-mindedness would immediately demand the resignation of such a "religious fanatic." The secular news media bigots would force a public apology for such a historically inaccurate perception of America—the melting pot. The fear of offending one atheist is presently far more important than offending tens of millions of believers. This is the case even in American classrooms where the phrase "and advancement of the Christian faith" is replaced in government school textbooks with an ellipses ("…").

The Christian fabric continued to be woven in America, as in the year 1734 when about two hundred Lutherans came from Austria to Georgia. The truth is America's first citizens were religious, and the majority were Christians.

The Founding of States

Not only were Protestants from Europe seeking refuge in the new colonies, the nation was also open to receive others from different religious beliefs. George Calvert, also known as Lord Baltimore, set up a state for those who were Catholic. George followed the Catholic faith; in England, only the "Church of England," the recognized and practiced religion was accepted.

George and his wife lived in Virginia and had not been accepted because their faith traditions were different from the Virginians. Calvert went north of Virginia, forming a settlement he called "Mary land," named after the wife of the king of England.

After Calvert's death, two hundred fifty Catholics journeyed by sea from England, arriving in "Mary land" on ships called the Ark and the Dove. The ships found their way up the Potomac River to a place called Saint Mary's, named after Mary the mother of Christ. A cross was erected in the area dedicating the land to Christ. The entire land became known as Maryland, and their first settlers were called Redemptioners. In 1649 a law known as An Act Concerning Religion was issued, stating, "No person or persons whatsoever within this province … professing to believe in Jesus Christ shall from henceforth be in any ways troubled, molested, or discountenanced for or in respect of his or her religion, nor in the free exercise thereof."[3]

The name William Penn is synonymous with early America. Penn desired to conduct what he called a "Holy Experiment,"[4] by forming a colony of his own in the Northeast. Penn was quoted as saying, "If I had a colony of my own, I would make it a place of true Christian and civil liberty."[5] England's King Charles owed the Penn family a large sum of money. William suggested the king pay the debt by giving him land in America. The region chosen by the king was the land between Maryland and New York. Penn was of the Quaker faith, and wanted to call the new territory Sylvania, meaning "forest land." King Charles, however, had another idea and added Penn's father's last name to the new charter, calling it Pennsylvania, meaning Penn's Woods, or Penn's Forest. William Penn was a very religious man, a strong Christian, and promoted the Christian faith in his new territory. The main city in Pennsylvania was Philadelphia, meaning "brotherly love," a name of one of the seven churches in the Book of Revelation (Rev. 3:7).

America Founded on Biblical Principles

President Harry Truman made some interesting observations concerning the link between America's founding documents and the Holy Scriptures. According to Truman:

> If we don't have the proper fundamental moral background, we
> will finally wind up with a totalitarian government which does not
> believe in rights for anybody except the state.[6]
> —President Harry S. Truman
> Addressing Law Enforcement Problems

> The fundamental basis of this nation's ideals was given to Moses
> on Mount Sinai. The fundamental basis of the Bill of Rights in our
> Constitution comes from the teachings, which we get from Exodus,
> St. Matthew, Isaiah and St. Paul. The Sermon on the Mount gives
> us a way of life, and maybe some day men will understand it is the
> real way of life.[7]
> —President Harry S. Truman,
> 29th Annual Convention of
> the Columbia Scholastic Press Association

The three main documents of our Founding Fathers: the Declaration of
Independence, the Constitution, and Bill of Rights, were based on God's
laws in the Torah, portions of Isaiah, and principles in the four Gospels.
Our Christian connection was also prominent in the founding of America's
institutions of higher learning. A minister, Reverend Witherspoon, founded
Princeton University. Dartmouth College was initiated as a mission effort
for training Indians. Yale and Harvard were both originally Christian universities and were the early training grounds for ministers of the gospel.

One United States president was also a minister. When he was sixteen
he left home to work on a ship and six weeks later returned home sick.
His mother took seventeen dollars and sent him to a Baptist academy. He
was converted and baptized in the Disciples of Christ Church and taught
Bible in the church. He began preaching every Sunday in nearby churches,
also attending Williams College, a Christian college in Massachusetts.
He believed sometimes Christians needed to be involved in politics. He
became a professor of Greek and Latin and at age twenty-six became president of Williams College. He began preaching every Sunday and even conducted revivals debating religion and science. He eventually ran for senator
in Ohio and won, becoming a general in the Civil War. In 1880 he gave
a speech at the Republican convention, where the delegates dumped their

candidates and elected him to run for United States president. Thus, in March of 1881, James Garfield became the twentieth president.

Can you imagine the kickback and resistance today if a minister of the gospel ran for president? It did happen in America in 1988, when the founder of a popular Christian talk show *The 700 Club*, Pat Robertson, threw his hat into the ring as one of many Republican candidates. Robertson placed high in several "straw polls," shocking the Republican establishment. Immediately opponents surfaced, painting Robertson as a religious fanatic, incompetent, and even as a danger to the nation as they charged he would start a world war to bring in Armageddon to fulfill prophecy and help bring Jesus back. I was touring in Israel in 1988 when a well-known, extreme liberal business-media kingpin from America made a statement. He said that he would do whatever was necessary to stop or destroy Robertson if he thought he was headed for the party nomination; not because he was incompetent, but because he was a minister and a devout Christian.

Seeking to Silence Ministries

In the late 1940s when Billy Graham began his evangelistic ministry, the American patriotic spirit was strong. Having witnessed victories over Japan and Germany in World War II, the population was cemented together by solid moral standards as the majority were religious—most either Protestant or Catholic. Graham's famous Los Angeles revival continued for eight weeks in 1949, winning thousands to Christ. During the revival, media mogul William Randolph Hearst, a newspaper owner, gave the instruction to "puff Graham"[8]—meaning to write positive articles, pushing his ministry and meetings to the readers. Within months his notoriety spread throughout North America and eventually the world.

Graham had a captivating speaking gift and huge crowds, making him like a magnet to political leaders, especially American presidents. They often sought to align themselves with Graham, using what I term "influence by association," meaning, association with Graham was viewed positively, and those who liked Graham automatically would approve of a politician who was seen with him. This association in turn could be an effective method of increasing a larger Christian voting bloc for the candidate. Other presidents were not as open in their relationships, but respected Graham and occasionally called him to the White House for advice or private prayer.

Nixon appeared in May of 1970 at a Billy Graham Crusade. Thereafter, the IRS audited Graham. On the Nixon tapes the president expressed anger that the IRS was "going after Billy Graham tooth and nail."[9] This was completely unnecessary as the Billy Graham Evangelistic Association had from the beginning kept impeccable books and followed every IRS, not-for-profit rule. However, Nixon believed it was a conspiracy among some of the wealthy men in America to retaliate against Graham's support for him. It was during the Nixon administration that the Department of Justice began monitoring the movement, messages, and income of the top media ministers in radio and television. These included Rex Humbard, Oral Roberts, Demos Shakarian, and Jimmy Swaggart. The reason for my knowing this is, at that time, a pastor friend from Baton Rouge was informed of the monitoring from a Christian inside the Department of Justice.

With emerging technology in the 1970s and 1980s more evangelists and megachurch pastors took to radio and television, vastly expanding their messages and influence. This expansive influence caught the attention of various US government agencies, which became concerned that conservative ministries were gaining millions of adherents and "followers." The following story illustrates the efforts to disrupt that influence.

I heard that many years ago a major media ministry was impacting the nation with a large daily audience. The ministry had two main sources of income: resource materials and donations. Offices were set up on the ministry grounds where numerous employees were hired by the ministry. The employees were sitting in booths, sorting, and opening the mail, entering data for both orders and contributions, and processing trays of mail. At the conclusion of each day, the cash and checks were collected, orders were filled, donations were checked, and bank deposits were made.

After many months and following income reports, a ministry executive noticed one woman working data entry was always "falling short," of the average amount of income. When compared to other entries being received daily through the mail, hers was significantly lower. The ministry executive and the vice president set up hidden cameras and found the woman had been removing the cash and placing the money in her Bible, which she daily carried to and from work. They called her in privately, telling her,

"We know what you are doing," meaning stealing the money. However, the woman immediately broke down and said it was not "her" idea—it was "their idea." She began confessing a plot, stating government agents had approached her. They secretly set her up, prompting her to steal the cash to bring to her apartment, where it was stored in boxes. This would give the appearance that the ministry was stealing donations. If the accusation proved reasonable, it would open the door for a federal investigation with the IRS. Obviously this would make national news, which would cause the faucet of giving from his supporters to shut off. Thus, the false allegations would dry up their resources to preach the gospel, and their income would stop, eventually causing great damage to the televangelist's reputation, silencing his voice.

According to some in Washington, the television minister wielded too much influence over multitudes of Americans through his media empire. This was causing a "concern," since he could influence voters in numerous states. Without further details, her story was proven true; the cash was retrieved and placed back into the ministry.

The wicked concept behind this secretive plot was if "followers" gave cash but at the end of the year never received a tax receipt, there would be no record of their giving in the ministry's computers; thus, the allegation could be made that thousands of dollars were secretly being siphoned off by the minister (although he never opened the mail)! Without records of the cash, he would be unable to prove where the money went; thus, he could be charged with mail fraud or some other crime. Thankfully this was exposed but to this day, the minister himself has never spoken of this.

It may come as no surprise, but some media ministries are being targeted to this day. While visiting overseas, I met with a man whom I have known for years. His father was once well connected with the international global intelligence community. In 2013 an American with skills in computers and tracking, who worked for a US agency, was in my friend's Israeli home. He told my friend, "We are tracking and compiling information on all of the major ministries in the United States." When asked why, the answer was, "If we decide they are doing something we don't like, then we can release any negative information we have in our systems to destroy their influence." To prove his point, the man named a world known television minister and said to my friend, "Do you want to talk to him on his personal cell phone?"

My friend replied, "Sure I would like to talk to him." The American went to his computer, and in a brief moment released a private, personal phone number. He dialed the number, and to my friend's surprise, the minister answered. Although the preacher knew the man calling, he was stunned and said, "How did you get this number? It is a special phone, and my wife doesn't even have this number!" These individuals can tap into any number, even private or restricted lines.

As the man revealed, the idea behind data collection is if agencies feel it necessary, they can release what is compiled against any individual publicly in an attempt to ruin their reputations. If you believe the press releases stating the US intelligence agencies *only* use their resources to track and collect national security information on possible domestic or international terrorists, you are ignorant of the facts.

Tapping phones, listening in on conversations, and compiling information are not anything new. It was happening in the days of John F. Kennedy by the FBI under J. Edgar Hoover, who knew of Kennedy's surreptitious relations with women. Martin Luther King Jr. (1929–1968) was building a massive black following for many years, climaxing in a march on Washington DC, where from the steps of the Lincoln Memorial, King's "I Have a Dream" speech electrified the crowd and initiated a pivotal point in the civil rights movement. King was being watched by the NSA, and his phones were tapped.[10] One of King's friends present the day of his assassination in Memphis believed there was a great fear among many people in Washington that King could eventually run for president. With the black votes in the major metropolitan cities, King could, in the future, win the election.

This is not to say his slaying was a conspiracy since it appears the public evidence points to one lone gunman, James Earl Ray. However, in a nation that prides itself of free speech, why would certain heads of agencies want to listen in on King? One of the ideas was, eventually, to accuse him of some type of moral failure that if proven, could publicly destroy his integrity. Of course, by today's standards those wielding power who detest or despise an influential individual might be willing to tell a story, disproportionately, if the lie fulfills their intent.

How would America's history and destiny have changed if ministers of the gospel were silent? The ragtag militia who formed the soldiers of the

American Revolution were recruited out of many churches in the northeast with the inspired messages of their pastors speaking about freedom. During the Civil War, ministers in the northeast and other regions of the nation were speaking out against slavery. Look at the civil rights movement and the leadership of Martin Luther King Jr. and hundreds of other black ministers who, from their pulpits, spread the message of civil rights. *Powerless pulpits produce nations in bondage.*

Are We Not a Christian Nation?

If the Puritans were still living they would be labeled "Christian radicals," in every sense of the term. They called themselves Jewish fellow travelers, comparing themselves to Israel when the Hebrews returned to their Promised Land. In England Puritan banners were inscribed with the phrase "Lion of Judah"—as they rode into battle singing Psalms. In 1649 Puritan settlers made a motion in the House of Commons to celebrate the Lord's Day on Saturday, the Jewish Sabbath, and not Sunday. There was a discussion to make the Mosaic Code incorporated into English law. In the early colonies in a Puritan church service, men and women sat apart, even as they do today in a Jewish Synagogue. The historical, spiritual connection is unmistakable, even with the biblical names given to American cities: Jericho, Jordan, Salem, Bethlehem, Babylon, and so forth.

Even the nation's capital is covered with biblical symbolism. The Washington Monument has engraved on the metal capstone the words *"Praise Be to God."* The monument also has Scriptures engraved in the blocks, including Luke 18:16, and the phrase "Holiness to the Lord."

The Thomas Jefferson memorial has many God centered quotes of his from principles engraved in it, "God who gave us life gave us liberty. Can the liberties of a nation be secure when we have removed a conviction that these liberties are the gift of God? Indeed I tremble for my country when I reflect that God is just, that his justice cannot sleep forever."[11]

The writings carved inside the Lincoln memorial use both the name of God and also verses from the Bible. At the US Senate is a plaque *In God We Trust.*

Moses with the Ten Commandments is in the Library of Congress and it

also holds *The Giant Bible of Mainz* and *The Gutenberg Bible* on prominent permanent display. Bible verses chiseled into the walls include:

> The light shineth in darkness; and the darkness comprehendeth it not.
> —JOHN 1:5, KJV

> Wisdom is the principal thing; therefore, get wisdom: and with all
> thy getting get understanding.
> —PROVERBS 4:7, KJV

> What doth the LORD require of thee, but to do justly, and to love
> mercy, and to walk humbly with thy God.
> —MICAH 6:8, KJV

> The heavens declare the glory of God; and the firmament sheweth
> His handywork.
> —PSALM 19:1, KJV

Moses and the Ten Commandments are on the face of the Supreme
Court and at the chapel of the US Capitol. At the chapel is a beautiful
stained glass window of George Washington kneeling in prayer!

Additionally, fifty-two of the fifty-five signers of the United States
Constitution attended churches. "In God We Trust" was printed on the
paper currency and coins and has been since 1864, adopting the same
phrase as its official motto since 1956. The pledge of allegiance added the
words "under God," in 1954. These are just a few examples of scripture and
references to God in America's foundation, for there are many more!

Some have suggested America is not a Christian nation. This statement
is one of three things: an attempt to cover up, willful lying, or complete historical ignorance. America's spiritual (Christian) heritage from 1607 to the
present could fill a library. Our birth was providential and our assignment
clear. America has been the leading voice for the message of the gospel to
the nations of the world.

Americans have financed missionaries and cared for the poor, the
orphans, and the needy, always being the relief in disasters, and on its
own shores saying, "Give me your tired, your poor, your huddled masses
yearning to breathe free"[12] (a phrase on the Statue of Liberty, taken from a
poem written and donated by a Jewish girl who worked with Jewish refu-
gees coming from the "Russian Pale of Settlement" to New York). What

makes us different is the compassion believers have for others because of our Christian values. Until recently we have been guardians of the Christian faith.

Another assignment has been America's strong support for the nation of Israel, since 1948 until recently. Most American presidents have been supportive of the Jewish state. Since 1948 Israel has been involved in about six wars with surrounding nations, defeating their enemies using the weapons provided by the US administrations. Years ago I met with the future Israeli prime minister Benjamin Netanyahu, who said that when he visits the United States, he is amazed at the large number of evangelical Christians who tell him they are praying for Israel and him personally. He said, "I have discovered that some of Israel's best friends are in the evangelical Christian community."

Another point must be made that America has restrained the spread of evil on the earth. Some countries view the United States as an aggressive nation whose desire is to rule over people and nations, seizing their land or resources through military occupation. However, consider our involvement in World War I and II, and how the loss of hundreds of thousands of America's soldiers prevented the rise of dictators and spread of murderous regimes.

For example, today northern Iraq has a large population of Kurds, who are pro-American and are very appreciative of being released from the bloody clutches of Saddam Hussein. If America had sat back passively, then Communism would have swept over Europe and atheism would rule, with spiritual darkness and depression joining as twins. Without American intervention, Hitler could have completed his dream of destroying the Jewish race in Europe. Time would fail to explain our intervention in Japan, Korea, and other nations. Without both the first and second invasion in Iraq, Saddam Hussein could have continued to use chemical weapons against his own people. With his invasion into Kuwait, had we not intervened, we could have been buying oil from this dictator. Nations can complain, but without America, the world would be a dark, depressing place!

The American Shift

The spiritual shift from *faith* to *unbelief* began in the early 1960s. In 1962 the Supreme Court banned official prayers and Bible reading was banned in 1963.[13] Nine years later (1973), a national tragedy was legalized when abortion was passed as a legal option for a pregnant woman. As the years have passed, the marriage covenant has been assaulted as outdated, and the new norm is same-sex relations. In some western states home Bible studies have been banned or hindered by newly imposed zoning laws. In public schools Christian youth are told to remove their crosses and never wear Christian T-shirts while Christmas carols or nativity scenes in public schools invite lawsuits from the ACLU.

Anger toward biblical warnings spreads like a tidal wave when any type of national disaster strikes an American city and a minister warns that the act may be a judgment from God. For example, I once picked up a secular book in an antique store, written in 1907 and documenting the deadly April 18, 1906, San Francisco earthquake. The introduction described the event, where fires burned for three days as the "judgment of God" against the iniquities of the city.

Fast-forward to the Northridge California earthquake that struck in the heart of the porno district, and read the comments from the citizens in newspapers, saying such things as, "I am sure some religious fanatics will say this is God's judgment, but I don't want to hear what those nuts have to say." In the past United States presidents would call a day of fasting and prayer for the nation to turn to God in humility. Today prayer is only the last resort and often for a photo op on election years if it benefits the vote count.

What Will Happen to Us?

There is now concern about how America is paralleling Imperial Rome, before its economic and political demise. Books, articles, and commentaries have been written, attempting to decode the mystery of the specific triggers that brought down the Imperial Roman Empire. Interest in this subject has grown in recent years, as the American empire is on the same downward spiral. This short list explains the parallels between the Roman and American "empires."

Because these parallels are so similar, Americans should pay attention to the root causes of why Rome economically collapsed and was overrun by pagan tribes. One of the more well-known reasons for Rome's decline was their military; this once strong and feared unit became spread too thin and too far to keep the peace. The cost of upkeep for the empire, including protecting the borders, occupying other lands, and the cost of roads and infrastructure repairs added up to an unsustainable debt.

Farming in the empire was once a prosperous occupation, until the government of Rome began heavy taxation on the farmlands. The Roman government had to pay numerous debts, including a welfare system that led them to become the headquarters of a welfare state. With so many living off the government dole, those who had jobs were making less money than those receiving government assistance. The high taxes led to countless farmers giving up their farms, and becoming bankrupt. A bankrupt farmer could choose to go on the government aid program, join the Roman army, or move from Rome to other countries to colonize new lands. The decline was evident when it was cheaper and more attractive to live off the government than to work a job and pay the high taxes. The cry of the empire's leaders was to tax the rich. However, eventually the middle class were squeezed out, and a person was either rich or on the lower level of the economic ladder.

Those discerning the times can clearly see how America is now at the same economic, moral, and spiritual condition as Imperial Rome. Now, 49.2 percent of Americans are dependent on some form of government dole,[14] and recent reports show that more people are receiving help than are working.[15]

Another observation is the declining birthrate. When families lived on farms, more children were born to assist in the labor force of milking cows, feeding the animals, plowing, harvesting, and general work. My father's own family had ten children. If families grew their own food on their farms, larger families were more affordable. As couples moved from the rural lands to the cities with both parents working, there was a major decline in the birthrate, with the average couple having two children.

In America alone, as of this printing, there have been over fifty-five million infants aborted.[16] Not only is this a terrible moral and spiritual tragedy, but an American tragedy. From a purely national perspective, over fifty-five million American individuals who would have solved problems and created inventions to become a workforce to sustain the economic needs of the nation, were killed.

I say this because of the declining birthrate in the Roman Empire. Toward the time of the collapse, the tax burden was so high that a couple would quit having children, as they could not sustain the financial weight.

In the time of Nero, four hundred senators' families lost their heritage because they had no children. The Roman Empire collapsed internally, like cancer slowly eating the organs in the human body.

There are twenty-four parallels between America and Rome:

> » Both had been the leading superpowers of the world
>
> » Both had the greatest military in the world
>
> » Both had their soldiers keep the peace
>
> » Both occupied the Middle East
>
> » Both had dealt directly with Israel and the Jewish people
>
> » Both had a "Capitol Hill"
>
> » Both had a "Statue of Liberty:" Romans had the goddess of Libertas and America's Statue of Liberty
>
> » Both had a senate
>
> » Both had the same style architecture in their government buildings
>
> » Both had a main leader (a caesar and a president)
>
> » Both had the eagle as its emblem
>
> » Both allowed the killing of infants
>
> » Both allowed freedom and practice of homosexuality
>
> » Both had stadiums for sports events
>
> » Both had high-paid athletes loved by the empire
>
> » Both emphasized competitive races in sports (for example, chariot races and car races)

» Both had a national anthem, which was sung at sporting events

» Both of their people stood when the anthem was sung at the stadiums

» Both had a flag and pledged their allegiance to the flag

» Both had slaves and slavery, which was later outlawed

» Both saw the middle class squeezed out of their lands and home

» Both had half their population dependent upon government money for assistance

» At the end of the Roman Empire, the senators were godless and had no religious affiliation. All religions were accepted, but Christians were persecuted for being intolerant.

The western division of the Roman Empire experienced great prosperity for hundreds of years; however, laziness and dependency on the government for provisions overtook most of its citizens. Rome never fell because of a war or from a competing, rising empire, as did the previous empires of prophecy. Rome slowly deteriorated from within, through bad leadership and bad decisions, leading to economic, spiritual, and moral bankruptcy. The business regulations from the Roman Senate began to destroy private initiative, making it too expensive to live. Roman cities created to sustain a higher standard of living decayed through economic woes. The numerous economic and social reforms, intended to make life easier and better, only increased the number of government employees and bureaucrats, further burdening the taxpayers. The farmers in Italy began giving up their land, unable to bear the increasing taxes. Eventually they gave up their homes, packing up and moving to other areas outside of Rome's control. Researchers have pointed out the excessive tax burdens of the citizens and its terrible impact:

By the third century the burden of taxation had become so heavy that it had begun to consume the capital resources of the taxpayer. This was due to the increasing costs of the imperial administration without any corresponding increase in production on the part of the population of the empire....The increases in taxation coincided with a falling off in production and in manpower. The result was bound to be a heavier weight of taxation for the survivors, and their gradual impoverishment, which, in turn, would cause a decrease in the public revenues.[17]

When the Republic of Rome was nearing its end, domestic issues divided the population. With excessive taxes from the rich being doled out to the nonworking lower class, the conflict between the rich and poor intensified. The wealthy senators became more concerned with maintaining their voting power and position than they did with actually solving the problems. The common people were willing and ready to follow any leader who promised them food and entertainment. It was the Romans who used the word *dictator* when giving their emperor the authority for total control in a time of a crisis. However, his dictatorial power was limited to six months. During the announcement of dictatorial powers, emperors often used the occasion to come after many or all of their enemies, or anyone who opposed their legislation. If this doesn't sound familiar to you, then you have been living in a cave.

In 49 BC the senate gave Pompey political power. He ordered Caesar's expulsion to his home. Instead, Caesar organized his army and crossed a forbidden invisible line called the Rubicon, causing a civil war. After defeating Pompey, Caesar returned to Rome to cheering crowds. One of his actions was to open the borders of Italy and grant foreigners citizenship, similar to the discussions today to open our southern borders and allow millions citizenship in America. Eventually the senate began fearing the unrestrained power of Caesar and his ambition, and hard-core popularity among certain groups began to be seen as dangerous to the empire, as Caesar wanted to be king. Five years after the clash with Pompey, in March 15, 44 BC, two Roman nobles plotted an assassination and were successful, stabbing Caesar to death on the floor of the senate. It was an inside job and Rome's own politicians that eventually brought his demise.

The death of Caesar plunged Rome into a terrible civil war. Eventually Caesar Augustus rose to power. He was the Caesar at the time of the birth of Christ (Luke 2:1). Augustus ruled for forty-one years, dying in AD 14.

During his rule, he initiated Pax-Romana, or "the Roman Peace," in which Roman military force was assigned to keep the peace and squelch any uprisings in the Empire. From the time Rome became an Empire under Augustus in 27 BC until its fall to Germanic tribes in AD 476, Rome had domination as an empire for 503 years.

The Amazing Insight of Lactantius

There were spiritually discerning individuals in the fourth century that began predicting the fall of Rome. Lactantius lived from AD 240 to AD 320, serving as an adviser to Emperor Constantine. Considered to be one of the church fathers, Lactantius wrote an apologetic, called *Divine Institutions*. Under a heading called, "Devastation of the World and Change of Empires," he begins by using Egypt's fall that led to the release of the children of Israel in the opening paragraph:

> Since at that time the people of God were one, and in one nation only, Egypt only was smitten. But now, because the people of God are collected out of all languages, and dwell among the nations, and are oppressed by those bearing rule over them, it must come to pass that all nations, that is the whole world, be beaten with heavenly stripes, and the righteous people, who are the worshipper of God may be set free.[18]

He indicated that as the signs were given to Egypt, revealing their coming destruction, in the last times wonderful prodigies will also take place. (A prodigy is a sign preceding something astonishing that is predicted to happen.) He wrote that as the end of the world approaches, human affairs must undergo a change. He predicted that righteousness will decrease and impiety (lack of reverence), avarice (greed for wealth), and lust will increase, and that good men will be a prey to the wicked and harassed on all sides by the unrighteous. He penned that all justice will be confounded, and laws will be destroyed. There will be no security, government, or any rest from evil wars that will be raging everywhere, including neighboring states who will carry on conflicts.

These warning signs are evident in our time. Morality and righteousness have declined without any protest from the righteous. Financial greed is seeded, bringing a harvest of major banking and housing market crises lasting for years. The guilty are freed, and the innocent suffer ridicule while the courts pass laws contrary to biblical principles. Nations rise against nations—such as North Korea against South Korea, India in conflict with Pakistan, and China engaged in verbal wars against Taiwan.

Lactantius's most noted warning given in the time of Emperor Constantine was the prediction of the fall of the Roman Empire, and how the rule will switch from West to East:

> The Roman name, by which the world is now ruled, will be taken away from the earth, and the government return to Asia; and the East will again bear rule, and the West be reduced to servitude.[19]

It is believed, based on his prediction of Rome's soon collapse, Emperor Constantine divided the empire and went eastward to Asia Minor, building a new "Rome in the East" that he named Constantinople, which today is Istanbul, Turkey. Later this city would become the seat of a new Christian centered empire, called the Byzantine Empire. Eventually Rome and all of Italy fell into the control of pagan tribal hordes, as eventually the empire was divided into ten different sections controlled by ten different tribes. The Byzantines entered the Holy Land and began constructing elaborate churches to mark holy places and Christ's ministry. This eastern branch continued for about one thousand years until Constantinople was overrun and seized by the Muslims in the fifteenth century. Oddly, this division was a fulfillment of Daniel chapter 2, the dream of the metallic image with two legs of iron—East and West—identifying the two divisions of the Roman Empire. It was noted:

> The fall of Rome spelt the fall of the empire; it even meant the end of the world. A century before Lactantius had written: "The fall and ruin of the world will soon take place, but it seems that nothing of the kind is to be feared as long as the city of Rome stands intact. But when the capital of the world has fallen…who can doubt that the end will have come for the affairs of men and for the whole world? It is that city which sustains all things.[20]

Using Crisis for Change

National economic woes often lead to change. At times the change comes naturally, such as with the Industrial Revolution or the tech explosion in the 1990s. At other times change became a smoke screen: a crisis is generated to seize control or to make changes. The communist revolution in Russia used the discontent of the common people in the workplace to expel the Tsars and introduce a manifesto that looked good on the surface but put millions into terrible poverty and oppression.

For hundreds of years world leaders have used a crisis in the economy for their political benefit. Dictators have also used the lower income masses, or nonworking masses, to rise up against a corrupt government, promising to change it. Then seeds are planted, blaming the rich (Wall Street, the bankers, business owners) for the crisis, and they must "pay" for their evils. All dictators have one theme: "I promise to redistribute the wealth of the rich to those less fortunate and put everyone on the same playing field."

It is done all in the name of opportunity. In every uprising, revolution, or mass anti-government gathering, it is the youth who play the most important role. Even Hitler had his own youth movement, which he used to indoctrinate the younger generation.

There are several well-known world leaders who used this strategy effectively and took control of every aspect of their government to introduce change for the worse! They are:

> » Lenin, who produced Communism, lead multitudes into poverty and death.

> » Hitler produced Nazism, leading to World War II and six million Jewish deaths.

> » Mussolini became a dictator of Italy and joined the war with Hitler.

> » Castro became a dictator, leading rich Cuba into poverty and depression.

To put it another way, the economic crisis in France led to the rise of Napoleon, and a worker's crisis in Russia led to the Russian Revolution.

A terrible collapse of Germany's fiat currency, called the mark, gave the opportunity to the rise of Adolph Hitler, the Third Reich, and Nazism. Economic woes in Venezuela gave rise to the promises of Victor Chávez. With America's unsustainable debt, where will this leave us in the future?

The American Tax Code

If you have ever questioned what is or is not deductible on your taxes, it is possible you can seek out different tax specialist's opinions and sometimes get different answers. This may be because the tax code is rather confusing.

The Bible has roughly 774,746 words when combining both the Old and New Testaments. How long would it take you to read through the Bible? Many believers take one year to read several chapters a day to complete a reading of the entire Bible.

Now, how many words are in the United States tax code? According to the Government Printing Office, the complete set of title 26 of the US code of Federal Regulations has twenty volumes, and you can order them for $974.00.[21] The Government Printing Office says it has 13,458 pages. Including an additional part written by congress (3,387 page count), the total page count is 16,845.[22] My average study Bible has 1,500 pages. Thus, the Federal regulations are nearly nine times larger than an average Bible! Perhaps every politician in Washington is a lawyer, since it would take a lawyer to interpret this mish-mash of bogged down legislation.

During tax season, many Americans are frustrated when IRS agents are asked a question, and in response give three different answers. Don't blame them. If it takes one year to read the Bible a few chapters at a time, it would take a person nine years to read the federal regulations a few paragraphs at a time!

You may have never considered the number of taxes you actually pay. Working Americans, and those who have money to spend, pay all the following or numerous taxes listed:

» State sales tax for everything you purchase, including food, clothes, and daily living supplies

» Property tax

» Tax for each gallon of gas

» Tax on public utilities

» Taxes taken from your paycheck (payroll tax)

» Taxes taken when you purchase a car

» Taxes on any capital gains

» Taxes on your profit on savings and investments

» Taxes on your outside additional income

» Taxes on your inheritance

» Taxes on your estate

» Taxes collected on toll roads

» Taxes (VAT) from purchases overseas

» Taxes on technology or services (cell phones, Internet, cable, etc.)

» Penalties in the new health care bill if you don't have health insurance

It is clear we are in the same cycle as the Roman Empire years before its collapse. However, our political problems are only the surface of an underlying spiritual problem. The nation has willfully moved away from the principles that laid our foundation—the principles of the Scriptures.

When Faith and Government Clash

Why did dedicated Christians and the Christian faith eventually clash with the leaders of the Roman Empire? First, from a religious perspective, Rome allowed all forms of idols to be worshipped and temples to be built in the name of tolerance. This also provided a source of income from thousands of visitors providing offerings and purchasing idols. Christians, however, believed in only one true God and one way to heaven, Jesus Christ. This stirred violent opposition among the Greek-Roman citizens whose income was often linked to the temple visitors and the pagan rituals they provided (including temple prostitutes). Christians were thus viewed as intolerant.

Second, they did not look to the Roman government or emperors for entitlements, as believers developed a method of caring for people within their community, especially the poor and widows, through offerings that were collected and distributed (Acts 6:1; 1 Tim. 5:16). This distribution to the needy took the influence of the Roman dole out of the hands of the government and into the hands of local churches caring for their own. God intended the church to be a station of provision for those in need within the body. In America, however, the church has too often allowed government entitlements to replace the compassion and helping hands of His body on earth, the church.

Third, there was a special day set aside where Christians did not work. In the beginning both Jews and Christians kept the Saturday Sabbath as Christianity came out of the Jewish faith tradition. As more Gentiles became believers, a conflict arose between devout law keeping Jews and Jewish Messianic believers. In Acts we see conflicts at the temple and later in synagogues, forcing Gentiles to start home churches. Sunday was a normal workday for the Roman Empire, and Christians began meeting the "first day of the week"—Sunday (1 Cor. 16:2). This practice could have served as a conflict with a Christian's personal work time required by the Roman work system.

The Greek-Roman culture was steeped in myths and idolatry, including god and goddess worship. Also, as mentioned, it was an income maker for locals who molded and carved idols for visitors. Conversion to Christ meant a rejection of all idols and other "gods" to serve the true creator. These converts ceased giving offerings at their favorite temple and refused to purchase small idols or other religious trinkets, bringing income and tax revenue in Roman controlled cities to an all-time low. Thus, conversion to Christ in pagan Roman cities was "a negative" economically to the income base of the cities. (See Acts 19:19; 19:24–41).

Compare these facts with the neo-Roman Empire, America. In our politically correct society we are instructed that all religions are a path to heaven and must be treated equal—Christianity is no different than Islam or Hinduism. As Christians we proclaim Christ is the way, the truth, and the life. When we declare He is the only path to eternal life, you hear a cry, "Narrow-minded—right-wing intolerance!" shouted in response from the lips of the media elite. We are "hate mongers" if we accept only one God and one road that leads to eternity. It is considered unethical or socially unacceptable to criticize the idol gods, or other religions in America; however, it is always "open season" on Christians for any arrows shot in their direction.

The original plan of God was for His people to support the poor and needy, not a government. It began with the law of not permitting gleaning the corners of the field and leaving grapes on the vine for the stranger and the poor to have access to grain and grapes (Lev. 19:9–10). A third tithe was collected from all Israelite farmers, used to support the Levite, stranger, fatherless, and widow that "they may eat…and be filled" (Deut. 26:12). If a fellow Jew lent money to a poor person, they were forbidden to charge interest (Exod. 22:25). Under the law, if the poor needed income and sold his possessions, a near of kin could redeem what was sold and return it to the poor family (Lev. 25:25). If a fellow Jewish brother "fell into decay," then the other Jewish men were to assist and relieve him (v. 35).

Often in the ancient culture if a man (or a woman) could not meet their financial obligations, either they or their children were sold into slavery, and the money from their purchase was placed on their payment. Among the Hebrew people, others were to "relieve" the man who fell into such terrible economic circumstances. If the man was sold to a fellow Hebrew, the buyer could not make the man a permanent bond servant because slaves could return to their homes or families every seventh year or Jubilee year (Lev. 25:39; Deut. 15:12). Once a poor servant was released, his brothers were to provide as it is written:

> And when you send him away free from you, you shall not let him go away empty-handed; you shall supply him liberally from your flock, from your threshing floor, and from your winepress. From what the LORD God has blessed you with, you shall give to him.
> —DEUTERONOMY 15:13–15

God does honor those who assist the poor, and I am grateful that America does use a portion of its tax revenue to assist those who are truly in need and often unable to do physical work. One can never go wrong when helping the poor and needy, as our actions are called "lending unto the Lord," and the Lord will repay those whose charity assists the least among us (Prov. 19:17). America has continued to be a blessed nation through our benevolence outreaches in providing food, clothes, and housing to a segment of our society that could starve or freeze to death or suffer greatly without the assistance.

However, during the past several years, it has been revealed that hundreds of thousands of able-bodied people in America are simply "milking the system," staying home and collecting the government doles. In the final chapter of the Roman Empire the need for taxes to pay for the free entitlements hit a crisis as more people were living off the free handouts than were working. Today half of America now depends on some form of federal government aid. The government brings in $2.5 trillion of revenue a year. One percent of Americans pay $1 trillion in tax revenue, while only 40 percent of the population actually pays any type of taxes. When the working class retires, the demand for social benefits will go up, even while the workforce is not being replaced, meaning more people will pay higher taxes to care for more people who will eventually not be working. What began sincerely as an important benefit to assist people, even to provide for their retirement, has become a beast rising up, preparing to devour the middle class.

Many local churches provide food, clothes, and other basic necessities through special outreaches in the community. There are over four hundred fifty thousand churches in America. It is estimated that 118 million people attend church on a Sunday (or about 40 percent). While both testaments instruct on the tithe (10 percent of the income or agricultural increase), only about 9 percent to 14 percent of church attendees in America tithe to their local churches or ministries on a consistent basis. The largest tithers were evangelicals at 23 percent. If all believers tithed, it would be possible to assist the truly needy in our communities.

America's spiritual and religious patterns are parallel to Israel, and their federal government patterns are mirrored with the Roman Empire. Note how Israel had thirteen tribes, Rome had thirteen provinces toward the time of its collapse, and America's original colonies totaled thirteen:

13 Tribes of Israel	13 Provinces of Rome	13 Colonies in America
1. Tribe of Reuben	1. Province of Spain	1. Massachusetts
2. Tribe of Simeon	2. Province of Britain	2. New Hampshire

13 Tribes of Israel	13 Provinces of Rome	13 Colonies in America
3. Tribe of Levi	3. Province of Africa	3. Connecticut
4. Tribe of Judah	4. Province of Gaul	4. Rhode Island
5. Tribe of Gad	5. Province of the city of Rome	5. Pennsylvania
6. Tribe of Dan	6. Province of Italy	6. New Jersey
7. Tribe of Ephraim	7. Province of Egypt	7. Delaware
8. Tribe of Manasseh	8. Province of Macedonia	8. Maryland
9. Tribe of Naphtali	9. Province of Pontus	9. Virginia
10. Tribe of Asher	10. Province of Thrace	10. Georgia
11. Tribe of Issachar	11. Province of the East	11. North Carolina
12. Tribe of Benjamin	12. Province of Dacia	12. South Carolina
13. Tribe of Zebulun	13. Province of Asia	13. New York

When breaking down the details of operation and activities of the Roman emperors, senate, armies, and people, the parallels with America are uncanny. Repeating them is almost impossible, unless there is a providential design linking what was (Rome) with what would be (America). I listed them earlier, but allow me to elaborate more on each point here.

Rome and America as superpowers

No nation of its time could match the influence and prestige of Rome at the peak of its imperial status. In the twentieth century the Soviet Union and America were viewed as dueling superpowers. With the collapse of Communism in the Soviet Union and Eastern Europe, America, with Russia's economic quagmire, has emerged as the single world power, especially in economic and military domination.

Rome and America's military powers

The Roman soldiers and legions covered the civilized world like swarming locusts, being feared and respected as the greatest military unit on earth. At the peak of their success soldiers were well trained and equipped with the best weapons of their time. Nations were in awe of the Roman legions and no country could stand against the Roman soldiers when they gathered en masse against their enemies. For many years soldiers were scattered throughout the empire to keep the peace.

America has organized coalitions in two Iraqi wars plus Afghanistan, and our four branches of military—Marines, Army, Navy, and Air Force—are recognized globally as superior to other nations. China and Russia are steadfast in attempts to steal and duplicate military technology. When Rome began its decline, the military was one of the primary branches of government that was weakened, and eventually ten different tribes divided the Empire.

Both occupied the Middle East

The Roman military occupied many nations in the Middle East, including Israel. Roman soldiers were assigned to slay infants in Bethlehem. Roman soldiers formed a six-hundred-person "band" of men (John 18:3, KJV). Just as with Rome, American military troops are presently "occupying" the nations of Afghanistan and Iraq and have built military bases in Israel, Germany, the Philippines, and other nations. In the Roman time the Romans called Israel Palestine. Oddly, America recognizes Israel by the name Israel, but the Arab world uses the name Palestine.

Both dealt directly with Israel and the Jewish people

The Roman Empire was influential in the religious and governmental matters in Israel, controlling the appointments of regional governors and even the priesthood at the temple. The modern nation of Israel never makes major political decisions without the consent and support of United States administrations.

Both had a Capitol Hill

In the city of Rome was a large hill called in Latin Capitolina. From this hill, the Roman senate met to forge laws and pass legislation impacting the Roman citizens. In Washington DC is the US Capitol, from which Congress initiates legislation that impacts the lives of the citizens of America. The Capitol is known as "Capitol Hill"!

Both had a senate

The legal and national laws of Rome were discussed and passed through the halls of the Roman senate. These laws required obedience from the citizens, but were often omitted or ignored by certain emperors whose love for power, and narcissistic style of rule prevented them from obeying their own laws. In America Congress pens our federal laws at Capitol Hill. However, they have become masters at passing legislation that American citizens must follow, while exempting themselves from their own laws.

Both had a main leader (caesar and president)

The Romans called their highest official, an emperor ruling the empire from Rome, a caesar. During the time of Paul's ministry, the caesar was named Nero. He was one of the great persecutors of Christians. Every leader appointed over Rome was called a caesar. America appoints one main leader called the "President of the United States."

Both had the eagle as its emblem

One amazing link is the national emblem. The Roman Empire selected the eagle as their national emblem. The eagle sat atop the military standards of the Roman legions. The United States also selected the eagle as our nation's emblem. The eagle appears on the presidential seal and all US military seals.

Rome experienced slave wars

Slavery was common throughout the world in the time of the Roman Empire. Eventually there were several revolts among slaves, which led to slave wars. America once allowed the purchasing and owning of slaves, until the time of a "revolt" called the Civil War, which freed slaves and changed national laws.

Both allow the killing of infants

At the time of Christ's birth, King Herod instructed the Roman soldiers to enter areas called Ramah and Bethlehem. They were to slay all male children who were under two years old. The heathen king heard that a king of the Jews had been born. America has taken the same spirit of Rome by allowing infants in the wombs of their mothers to be aborted. Just like Rome, American legislators and courts pass laws that disregard life in the womb.

Freedom to homosexuals

During the time of the apostle Paul, the sin of homosexuality was actively practiced, especially in the ranks of the Roman Empire. History reveals that Nero was a homosexual and that homosexuality was accepted as a normal lifestyle among many of the Roman citizens.

In America the "gay lifestyle" is called an "alternative lifestyle." This lifestyle is not only acceptable in Western culture, but it is also growing at a rapid rate.

Both had stadiums for sports events

The Greek and Roman citizens were captivated by sports events. This included running, wrestling, and chariot races. These events were often conducted in large stadiums, built to accommodate thousands of spectators. America is also a nation filled with stadiums where thousands gather to watch their favorite teams compete.

The wrestling industry has become a popular form of aggressive entertainment in America, and the car races have replaced the once popular chariot races enjoyed by the citizens of the Roman Empire.

Both of its people stood when the national anthem was sung on the stadiums

Rome had a national anthem and America has a national anthem. In Rome the anthem was sung in the stadiums and coliseums. Today it is common for the national anthem to be sung in major sporting events prior to the opening of the games.

Both had a flag and pledged their allegiance to the flag

In another strange twist Rome had a special flag, which represented the nation. Those who were faithful to the empire would stand and pledge their allegiance to the national flag. During certain national events, including special military events, it is a tradition for Americans to pledge allegiance to the flag.

Rome eventually turned to eastern cults and religions

Foreign religions found it easy to become established in the empire because Rome had no chief religion but welcomed all religions (except Christianity). The people of Rome filled in their spiritual gap by turning to Eastern cults. Rome had a mixture of spiritual ideas but did not consider religion as a spiritual experience. Today Americans are filling their spiritual voids by turning to Eastern mysticism, Kabala, Hinduism, and Buddhism, all Eastern religions.

Rome became obsessed with luxuries

The citizens living in Rome became obsessed with Roman glass, jewelry, and expensive luxuries. It was fashionable to attempt to outdo your neighbor with fancy clothes and "stuff." The same is true with Americans. People will pay twice as much just to be seen in name-brand shoes, clothes, and "stuff."

Rome conducted a census every five years

Rome conducted a census every five years and every man had to report the number and names of his family and slaves. The United States also conducts a national census in which information is recorded concerning family members. Both Rome and America had a place known as the suburbs, where families lived on the outskirts of the city.

The decline and fall of the Imperial Roman Empire cannot be penned upon one negative, but a combination of political and spiritual choices that collided at once, weakened Rome, and eventually brought it to a collapse from within.

The political and economic parallels of the Imperial Roman Empire are clearly reflected again in modern American history.

Chapter 10

IS IT 1933 ALL OVER AGAIN?

REPEATED CYCLES OF history are best understood by those who lived in the initial cycle. Clearly they can see the parallel patterns repeated in their lifetimes. If cycles are prophetic, they often match significant biblical years, such as forty years, fifty years, seventy years, and one hundred years. These important numbers are found in both testaments, triggering prophetic cycles in biblical history.

For example, Christ predicted the destruction of the temple in about AD 30 (Matt. 24:1–3), and forty years later in AD 70, the Roman tenth legion destroyed Jerusalem and the temple. In 1898 the Zionist movement predicted the Jews would have a homeland in Palestine within fifty years, which did occur exactly fifty years later in 1948. In 1917 after four hundred years of Turkish rule, Jerusalem exchanged hands and was taken by the British. It was exactly fifty years later, following the Six-Day War, that Jerusalem was reunited as the capital of Israel. In Russia the 1917 Revolution introduced Communism to the entire nation, causing Russian Jews to become enslaved in a system that forbid personal expression or freedoms. This bondage continued from 1917 to 1987, for seventy years—the same number of years the Jews were in Babylonian captivity (Jer. 25:11). However, in 1987, under Mikhail Gorbachev, the Jews began returning to Israel, and today there are 1.2 million Russian-speaking Jews in Israel, fulfilling Jeremiah's prediction:

"Therefore behold, the days are coming," says the LORD, "that it shall no more be said, 'The LORD lives who brought up the children of Israel from the land of Egypt,' but, 'The LORD lives who brought up the children of Israel from the land of the north and from all the lands where He had driven them.' For I will bring them back into their land which I gave to their fathers."

—JEREMIAH 16:14–15

Throughout history, empires, invading armies, and regional tribes have targeted the Jews for persecution; however, their greatest persecution came under the Nazi regime. In 1938 an event happened that foreshadowed the Holocaust when persecution struck the Jews living in Germany: "Kristallnacht," The Night of Broken Glass.[1] A thousand synagogues were burned, and numerous homes and seven thousand Jewish-owned stores were ransacked by Germans. The Nazis held the Jews responsible for the damage and imposed a fine of four hundred million dollars (in 1938 rates). Hate-filled, negative words were painted on the walls of Jewish buildings, and nearly one hundred people were killed. More than thirty thousand Jews were sent to concentration camps.[2]

It was the introduction to a seven-year Holocaust that concluded with the death of six million Jews. It was a preview of the future tribulation, a seven-year time frame predicted in Daniel 9:27, Matthew 24:21 and Revelation 7:14. The terrible birth pains of the Holocaust gave birth to the nation of Israel. At the conclusion of the seven-year tribulation, its birth pains will produce the kingdom of the Messiah, ruling from Israel. (See Zechariah 14.)

As stated, those living through previous cycles are the first to be aware of a repetitive pattern. I was unaware of a possible repeat of history until three different occasions. The first one was in Orange County, California, and the second happened in Hixson, Tennessee. The third time was during another major conference, where I met three different Jewish women who were all in their eighties, who lived in Germany as children in 1933. One had personally met the newly elected chancellor that had enamored the nation, Adolph Hitler. All three, who had never met one another, expressed the same opinion to me. Displaying great distress on their faces and tears forming in their eyes, they uttered to me that they were witnessing the same dynamics in the land of the free as what they experienced in Germany. With deep emotion, they recounted exact patterns and changes occurring in America that are all parallel in the German government, years prior to the persecution against the Jews. The dangerous cycle is repeating in America.

The pivotal date was 1933. At that time America and the entire world was entering a transitional season both economically and militarily. The Great Depression and stock market crash had caused severe economic depression in America. Below is a quote from 1933:

> Finally, in our progress toward a resumption of work we require two safeguards against a return of the evils of the old order; there must be strict supervisions of all banking and credits and investments, so that there will be an end to speculation with other people's money; and there must be provision for an adequate but sound currency.[3]
>
> —Franklin D. Roosevelt
> March 4, 1933

In 1933 the domestic and international economies were falling into chaos. Today consider America's unsustainable debts and note the monetary crisis overseas. In Greece, Spain, Italy, and Portugal, high unemployment and an inability to meet the demands of their people is rampant. By 1933 there had been thousands of bank failures with "runs" on the banks—depositors demanding their cash to be withdrawn. World trade was falling, and long soup and unemployment lines were seen in all major American cities. Today, for the first time in modern history, American cities, such as Detroit, have filed bankruptcy, unable to meet their obligations.

Events from 1933 to 1939 led to World War II to prevent a German dictator from rolling over Europe with his Nazi war machine, invading nations and destabilizing Europe. Today America has prevented the increase of dictatorship powers by engaging in wars inside foreign lands. By going to war, America, with its allies, has removed Saddam Hussein and worked behind the scenes to support uprisings leading to the removing of both Hosni Mubarak in Egypt, and Muammar Gaddafi in Libya.

In 1933 the federal government added massive new government programs—as poverty was at an all-time high. Now Americans living in poverty and dependent on government entitlements are at record highs. Just as in 1933 Franklin Roosevelt used his popularity among the media elite to promote his programs, the present administration uses the liberal media. Today it is used to verbally attack those opposing the administration's opinions or agenda, and to support any project, unconditionally, coming from their agenda. The economic challenges of recent years have been compared to those in the Roosevelt years, especially during the 1930s. Roosevelt and his administration were socialists, and today we have come full circle as socialists ideas mold the new laws being written and passed.

Perhaps the strangest and concerning parallel of our present time comes from this series of questions. Read carefully, and see if you can guess who this is speaking of.

Who Am I?

- My nation was a democracy.
- My nation had spent billions during war before his election.
- Before being elected I was relatively unknown.
- Before my election, many did not know what I believed or stood for.
- I became famous for my charisma and my speeches.
- I wrote a best-selling book that was read across the nation.
- Women would often scream, people would cry, and some would pass out when I spoke.
- Large crowds followed me and people waited for hours just to see me.
- The people of my country wanted a major political change.
- My country at the time was in an economic crisis.
- I promised to restore the economy, bring jobs, and rebuild the infrastructure.
- When elected I was considered a messiah or savior to many people.
- I was accused by some of having thugs in my life and background.

- It was the youth vote that got me into power.
- I made a famous speech in Berlin.
- I made my speeches in huge outdoor stadiums.
- Certain records about my past were hidden from the public.
- People were bullied and harassed if they spoke against me.
- I was called the man of the common people.
- My secret was my charismatic speeches that impressed the masses.

Who do those statements apply to? The answer is Adolph Hitler. The world knows him as the terrible dictator who tried to destroy the Jews, but the Germans in 1933 knew him as an economic messiah that worked and restored the pride in German nationalism. They saw him as one who had helped their economy to recover—after the German economy had collapsed.

If you read the list carefully, you will be amazed to learn, every aspect of this list was repeated by another man who was elected president in 2008, Barack Obama. Again, this is a repetitive pattern of the past and election of the German chancellor does not in any way indicate the latter events in Germany will be repeated in America.

It is the eyewitnesses living today who were children living in Germany that express the concern of our government taking over an industry, including health care. According to Germans who lived in that time, the government began monitoring everything the people did. Now, we are learning in America the National Security Agency (NSA) and other federal groups have been surveying Facebook, Twitter, phone calls, e-mails, and all forms of social and electronic communication of Americans. In Germany the government began raising taxes to give out as much free stuff as possible, keeping the masses dependent on the government for help. Nearly 50 percent of America works while the other 50 percent must receive various entitlements to eat, live, and function.

[In Germany] Newlyweds immediately received a $1,000 loan from the government to establish a household. We had big programs for families. All day care and education were free. High Schools were taken over by the government and college tuitions were subsidized. Everyone was entitled to free handouts, such as food stamps, clothing and housing.[4]

Actually nothing was "free," as the working class paid for it all. The German government raised the tax rates of 80 percent of their people. Adding up all the different forms of taxes that working Americans pay, up to 50 percent of our income is taxed. The German government became the government of regulations including regulating such things as the shapes of tables in restaurants and what you could use or buy for a local business. The German government was a socialist government and wanted the destruction of the capitalistic system. The Nazis used class warfare, the rich versus the poor, to win over the mass populace to their causes.

> We Nationalist Socialists are enemies, deadly enemies, of the present capitalist system and its exploitation of the economically weak…and we are resolved under all circumstances to destroy this system.[5]
>
> —GREGOR STRASSER,
> NATIONAL SOCIALIST THEOLOGIAN

Those who lived in Germany recall when the health care system was taken over by the government:

> Before Hitler, we had a very good medical care. Many American doctors trained at the University of Vienna. After Hitler, health care was socialized, free for everyone. Doctors were salaried by the government. The problem was, since it was free; the people were going to the doctors for everything. When the good doctor arrived at his office at 8 a.m., 40 people were already waiting on him and, at the same time, the hospitals were full. If you needed elective surgery, you had to wait a year or two for your turn. There was no money for research as it was poured into socialized medicine. Research at the medical schools literally stopped, so the best doctors left Austria and immigrated to other countries.[6]
>
> —TESTIMONY OF EYEWITNESS KITTY WERTHMANN

Just as in America today, in Germany God was removed out of the public schools and pushed out of public life. Germany began implementing gun control laws, passing legislation to confiscate guns.

> Next came gun registration. People were getting injured by guns. Hitler said that the real way to catch criminals...was by matching serial numbers on guns. Most citizens were law abiding and dutifully marched to the police station to register their firearms. Not long after-wards, the police said that it was best for everyone to turn in their guns. The authorities already knew who had them, so it was futile not to comply voluntarily.[7]

Without guns, it became impossible for individuals to defend themselves. When massive numbers of Jews were forced away from their jobs and homes to life in ghettos, eventually carted in trains like cattle to consecration camps meeting untimely deaths, there was no defense. While Americans still have rights to bear arms, the federal government has been buying up millions of rounds of ammo, causing shortages in some areas. There were even 174,000 rounds bought up by the Social Security Administration[8], leaving gun owners questioning why that administration needed bullets when dealing with older, retired Americans.

Survivors of the Nazi regime also remember how a speech on the radio was monitored. This helped them determine who was being too outspoken against the government. Now, all forms of communication are monitored, and people are placed on four different levels, represented by colors. If you are a person considered to be passive and nonthreatening, then you are flagged one color. If you are political or a religious believer, you are classified as negative. If you are outspoken about policies or of the administration, or you disagree with the president, and you are a believer, then you are flagged a different color and can be tagged a possible domestic terrorist. Monitoring has increased since entire departments have been assigned to the task.

According to my sources about the monitoring process, here is a list of what might qualify you as a possible domestic terrorist[9]:

» People who are fiercely nationalistic (extreme patriotic Americans)

» People who are anti-global who speak against a global government and New World Order

» People suspicious of centralized federal authority

» People who are reverent of liberty

» People believing their way of life is under attack

» People who believe in preparing for survival and are stockpiling food, gold, or other items

» People inserting religion into the political sphere

It should be noted that most people groups having these traits live in the Southeast to the Midwest of the United States. The question has been posed to individuals entering the military, if they would be willing to "fire" on United States citizens. This type of question makes conspiracy theories that the government is planning martial law, or dealing with mass riots, more believable to the general public.

You often hear reports of hundreds of thousands of coffins made of plastic being produced in refurbished army bases. These are not rumors but facts, although denied by agencies. More recently hundreds of thousands of black plastic baby coffins were produced. I have seen with my own eyes a yellow plastic coffin for an infant that has a small pillow and a blanket to wrap the corpse. Inside there is a roll of tape with printed instructions on how properly to seal the coffin. Underneath it has ridges from one side to the other, as if to place on a conveyer belt. My first question was, "Why were so many made?" and second, "Why infant coffins? Were they being prepared for foreign or national disasters, such as a major tsunami or earthquake?" Being plastic, they were defiantly made for a mass, quick burial, without a funeral. After researching, some believe they are prepared for an expected plague that would take countless lives of infants, or a chemical or biological attack with tens of thousands of deaths at once.[10]

In Germany the people had little concern for the unjust control placed on them, as long as the terrible economy was recovering, the value of the German Mark recovered, and the spirit of the German people was revived. One German noted:

As long as the economy was strong, people didn't care whether they had freedom of speech, freedom of travel, or freedom of elections. Under the Republic, people were starving in the big cities; bread on the table was more important than a ballot at a voting booth....In Nazi Germany, as in every era, it was the economy that was the key to the political fortunes of a particular party or dictator. Even the Antichrist will count on the premise that most of us act as if our body is worth more than our souls.[11]

The German Pastors

When asked, "Who was to blame for the death of six million Jews?" some older survivors say, "The German church did little to prevent the rise of its dictator, or paid little to no attention to the Jewish persecution—as long as the persecution did not personally impact their daily lives." When speaking of Christianity in Germany, Hitler stated:

Do you really believe the masses will be Christian again? Nonsense! Never again. That tale is finished. No one will listen to it again. But we can hasten matters. The parsons [ministers] will dig their own graves. They will betray their God to us. They will betray anything for the sake of their miserable jobs and incomes.[12]

Most of the German pastors were supportive of a political platform that was, at times, in contradiction to biblical principles. About 95 percent of the German pastors were either Protestant or Catholic. Even the Nazi symbol of the Swastika was placed on flags with a Christian cross in the middle and hung in some churches, demonstrating support for the Third Reich. In 1933 Hitler knew all the right trigger words to gain support of the ministers and their members. He invoked God's name, spoke of Christ's teachings, and when he won the election, he was hailed a hero-messianic figure to the Germans. Years ago, when Lester Sumrall was a young minister, he traveled to Germany just after the election of Hitler. The Christians were so enamored with Hitler that the pastor where Lester was speaking asked if Lester would be all right collecting an offering from the people to give to Hitler's cause. Remember, this was six years before the Holocaust would begin.[13]

One German minister, Dietrich Bonhoeffer, who was a German Lutheran, became recognized as an anti-Nazi resister. He was part of the Confessing

Church, true Christians who held to the truth of God's Word. Two days after Hitler was elected, Bonhoeffer warned on the radio of Germans slipping into the cult of the Führer (leader) who could well turn out to be a miss-leader and seducer.

The radio station cut him off in mid-sentence. Over time Hitler imposed church control and the elections of officials, and Nazis were given the main leadership in German churches. At one point Hitler feared losing an election, and he gathered thousands of pastors in a stadium and claimed he would give freedom to the churches and ministers that would support him. Thousands refused and were eventually arrested.

In the small yet powerful book *How Do You Kill 11 Million People?* Andy Andrews speaks about the power of the lie. Adolph Eichmann went to a Jewish ghetto with unarmed men, telling a total lie to the Jews, who willingly followed his instructions to board trains. On pages 24–25 we read:

> Jews: At last, it can be reported to you that the Russians are advancing on our eastern front. I apologize for the hasty way we brought you into our protection. Unfortunately, there was little time to explain. You have nothing to worry about. We want only the best for you. You will leave here shortly to be sent to very fine places indeed. You will work there, your wives will stay at home, and your children will go to school. You will have wonderful lives. We will all be terribly crowded on the trains, but the journey is short. Men? Please keep your families together and board the railcars in an orderly manner. Quickly now, my friends, we must hurry![14]

Train cars that usually held an average of eight cows in each car, now held one hundred Jews headed unknowingly to concentration camps. There were an estimated fifteen thousand different camps in Nazi-occupied countries, and eleven hundred were accessible by rail. Train tracks ran through towns where during Sunday services the church members could actually hear screams coming from the trains.

The passing trains and screaming people became so common that instead of investigating and rising up against the government, once the people knew the train was coming they began to sing louder. Louder they sang to drown out the uncomfortable and frightening sounds of Jews heading to the camps where they would meet their untimely and premature death in gas and torture chambers.[15]

Now, let me go back to the three Jewish women, all from three different states, having never conversed with one another. All three made the same types of statements to me about the events they have seen with the bank and auto bailout, the new health care laws, and the parallels of the actions and events in 1933 to today. Their words are, "It is happening again, and no one realizes it. Americans are like the German people. They can't see it until it is too late…history is repeating itself again." To these women, when they see the media bias against the conservatives and Christians, and the extreme liberal's agenda supported, they are literally afraid. It is sobering for them, as again, they observe the preplanned takeover of our freedoms, where we are given no choice but to follow the leader's own agendas to change the nation.

The Holocaust represents eleven million lives that suddenly ended; people executed for what they were, not who they were. Groups such as the disabled, Catholics, Poles, Soviet prisoners of war, political dissidents, and others were persecuted by the Nazis because of their religious and political beliefs, physical defects, or failure to fall into the Aryan ideal.

Keep in mind, there were six million Jews killed, but also an estimated seven million killed across Europe were Christians. There were godly believers, such as Oskar Schindler who saved the lives of thousands of Jews. Common families, such as Corrie ten Boom, whose family was Dutch, provided a hiding place for Jews in their own home and clock business. Four of the ten Booms died to save the Jews, only Corrie made it out of the death camp alive to share God's forgiveness with over sixty nations, telling them, "Jesus is victor!"[16]

In the United States ministers speak about faith, unity, and the body of Christ; yet, the Christian church is the most divided as it has ever been between liberals and conservatives, Democrats and Republicans, ethnic groups, and right and wrong.

1943 to 2013: the US and Tehran Connection

November 1943 to November 2013 is seventy years. Another odd cycle may be in its beginning—decisions made with evil men, promising a hope they are not capable of delivering. On November 28, 1943, "The Declaration of the Three Powers" happened in Tehran, Iran with Britain's Prime Minister Winston Churchill, US President Franklin D. Roosevelt, and the Soviet Union's Marshal Joseph Stalin. Churchill and Roosevelt were reaching out to Stalin, not understanding fully what he truly believed. This is what historian professor David Reynolds says,

> They have no idea how Kremlin politics work, but they gradually come to the view that Stalin is a kind of moderate, somebody willing to reach out to the West, and around him there are these shadowy figures, they don't quite know who they are, but they're the hard-liners, they're the Mr. Nasties. Molotov's probably one of them and they have this amazing belief that Molotov is an independent figure, whereas in fact we know that he's basically under Stalin's thumb all the time…It's very hard for 21st Century people to imagine how little we knew about Russia in the Second World War, but it's against that background of ignorance that we have to understand the way Churchill and Roosevelt both reach out to Stalin as…something human in an insane, dark, and in human country…They're completely wrong. But that's what they are putting their money on.[17]

After Stalin agreed to help in our D-Day efforts and successfully defeat Hitler, Stalin wished to have the borders of Poland, claiming East Poland, an agreement the Poles never got to vote on; and after 220,000 deaths (200,000 of them civilians), Stalin got East Poland and the land divided from the German Nazis. He then began to enlarge his labor camps for all who disagreed with him. In speaking of these negotiations Sir Max Hastings said, "Roosevelt also displayed a pretty cynical indifference to the fate of Eastern Europe, that Eastern Europe was to be liberated from one tyranny in order to be surrendered to another."[18]

Seventy years later, the P5+1 and Iran reached an agreement about Iran's nuclear program that may be possibly producing an atomic bomb, located in Tehran. (P5+1 is made up of the five permanent members of the UN Security Council—the United States, the United Kingdom, France, Russia, and China—plus Germany.) However, instead of its goal being to set free the Jews from the gas chambers, this agreement threatens the very existence of the nation of Israel.

Using centrifuges, which are machines that purify uranium to a high level, this uranium is used for nuclear weapons. Iran has more centrifuges than there are Starbucks, and under this new agreement they cannot install new ones, with the exception of upgrades from "wear and tear." Iran is already testing several different, new, and more efficient centrifuge models at its Natanz research facility, according to the UN nuclear watchdog.[19] Speaking in terms the West can quickly identify with, using the word "our right," a senior Iranian government official said, "We have to make sure *our right* to research and development is respected."[20]

Again, it is seventy years later, and America and the West naively trust an evil ruler who will stop at nothing to get what he wants. Media accounts claim the new leader of Iran is a "moderate." However the new leader is being controlled behind the scenes by Ayatollah Ali Khamenei, the same religious "supreme leader" who controlled the last Iranian president. However, this time, there is no D-Day to be won, and Americans are not the focus of these negotiations. The focus is the agenda of America's leaders who chase a false legacy of "peace" at the cost of its and Israel's freedoms. We say we stand with Israel while we hand its most brutal enemies billions of dollars to build nuclear weapons to be used against it.

While Iran's leaders confidently tweet, "World powers surrendered to Iranian nation's will" (Hassan Rouhani, January 14, 2014)[21] they continue with their advanced centrifuge program, developing a new nuclear facility.

Obama threatens to veto new sanctions, currently under consideration by Congress, as a risk to the nuclear deal—many times. He claims if it doesn't work, we can set the clock back. Once nuclear bombs deploy, they cannot be put back nicely into the box.

Americans must be persistent with their prayers for the peace of Jerusalem and make their voices heard to their congressional representatives. We must refuse to sing louder while the train of freedom passes us by.

Where Does It Go From Here?

In years past I stated the issue of abortion is now so ingrained in our culture that without some miracle it will be a lost issue in the future. The next political nightmare will be legalizing same-sex relationships and even gay marriage.

Christ compared His return to the day of Lot. In the biblical narrative in Genesis 19 the old and young men in the city were corrupted by sexual perversion. They wanted to have sexual encounters with the two men who came to Sodom to warn Lot of the coming destruction. One part of the story, often overlooked, is the extreme oppression and violent threats made against those who disagreed with the lifestyle of the Sodomites. Peter wrote about God's faithfulness to deliver Lot:

> And delivered just Lot, vexed with the filthy conversation of the wicked: (For that righteous man dwelling among them, in seeing and hearing, vexed his righteous soul from day to day with their unlawful deeds;)
>
> —2 PETER 2:7–8, KJV

When a person is vexed they are worn down with toil or mentally worn down with what they see and hear. Notice he heard and saw things that troubled him. The English says it was the "filthy conversation" of the wicked. The Greek word for *conversation* is not just words spoken, but actually refers to behavior or a lifestyle—referring to the lifestyle of men with men.

There are also two different Greek words for *vex*. In verse seven he was vexed daily, meaning, mentally worn down by seeing the behavior of the men in the city. In verse eight his soul was vexed. This Greek word means to torture. It is the same word used in Matthew 8:29, when the demons were tormenting a man who was possessed. Thus, the immoral condition of the city was so terrible that Lot was mentally tormented living among these Sodomites.

The Book of Jasher, a book of sacred Jewish history, shows four out of four judges, of the five cities, passed laws stating that beds could be placed in the streets, and strangers could be tied to those beds and molested. Perhaps this is why Lot refused to allow the two men (angelic messengers) that came into his home to go out into the streets at night.

The second important observation is the violent threats made against Lot. When Lot refused the demands by the mob to bring the men outside so they could be molested, they screamed at Lot. Notice this comment from evil men in the city:

> But they said, Stand back! And they said, This fellow came in to live here temporarily, and now he presumes to be [our] judge! Now we will deal worse with you than with them. So they rushed at and pressed violently against Lot and came close to breaking down the door.
>
> —Genesis 19:9, AMP

The sinful men were violently angry for a righteous man telling them they were wrong, telling him they had no right to judge him for their actions. They told Lot, in plain terms, if he resisted their desires, they would make it very difficult on Lot and deal worse with him—which would imply gang raping him or even killing him to get their way.

This same type of spirit was evident with a vote that supported marriage between a man and woman. A northeastern state voted in favor of traditional marriage, and an organization obtained the names of the voters and began making threats to their families and children. When the unrighteous become violent against the righteous, and when speaking out against iniquity is considered threatening, then God Himself will take notice, and both the nation and individuals will be judged.

Notice the level of immorality in Sodom. Strangers were threatened with gang rape as reprobates were gone wild. Lot was being threatened if he interfered with their perverted desires. Lot was willing to offer his two virgin daughters to these wild men to protect the two men from their perversion. This seemed very troubling to me, until I realized the men were so twisted in their emotions that Lot knew they had no desire for women, only men.

When Men No Longer Repent

In the narratives of Noah and Lot both men warned their generations, and neither were able to convert anyone with their warnings, only family. Eight people, all family, were in the ark, and in Lot's situation only he and his two daughters survived. Noah's message was destruction by water, and the angels warning to Lot was destruction by fire. Lot had daughters and sons-in-law who mocked him, refusing to flee the wrath to come, and dying in the cities destruction. Based in biblical numbers, Noah had one hundred years to prepare the ark before the flood, but Lot only had a twenty-four-hour window to gather his entire family—and was unsuccessful.

As the nation enters the time of the end, it becomes apparent humanity is becoming harder in their hearts and is not responding to the message of repentance. They don't believe they have done any wrong, and they teach sin is only based on the opinion of the person, since nothing is absolute. In Revelation 9:20, 16:9, and 16:11, in the coming tribulation men will no longer repent of their wickedness.

There is a false security in the minds of the unbelievers and sinners. Peter spoke of Lot's day and how Lot was rescued before the destruction came:

> The Lord knows how to deliver the godly out of temptations and to reserve the unjust under punishment for the day of judgment.
>
> —2 PETER 2:9

The Greek word here for *reserve* means to keep an eye out to prevent from escaping, meaning, in the end the ungodly will not escape the wrath to come. Peter compares the unrighteous to the fallen angels that are presently bound in chains of darkness, "reserved" to the day of judgment (2 Pet. 2:4; Jude 6).

At the time of the end the hardness of men's heart will cause a separation between light and darkness, righteousness and unrighteousness. In 1930s Germany there were two groups clearly divided. One group blindly followed their leadership by the masses in the well-marketed media to their own demise. The other group was a small righteous remnant who saw through the facade; they spoke up against the spiritual powers manipulating their nation's leaders, and yet were persecuted—many suffering death for their stand.

I certainly hope, in America, it never comes to the latter part. However, if history repeats itself, the cyclical patterns are evident in where the nation is headed. We could be in for some turbulent, troubling times in our near future. We must remain firm in our faith.

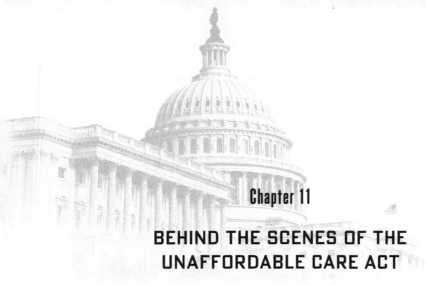

Chapter 11

BEHIND THE SCENES OF THE
UNAFFORDABLE CARE ACT

EFORE THE AFFORDABLE Care Act (often tagged "ObamaCare") became law, the liberals in Congress, the media, the administration, and the president himself made the following quotes:

> "Don't believe the noise about not being able to keep your health care plan."

> "If you like your healthcare plan, you can keep your healthcare plan."

> "You seniors are going to like ObamaCare."

> "If only [the] stupid public realized how great ObamaCare is."

> "ObamaCare will reduce the deficit."

> "Once morons 'understand' ObamaCare, they'll be thrilled."

> "Ignore Republican lies: ObamaCare is [the] best thing in fifty years."[1]

The famous quote by California senator Nancy Pelosi has proven prophetic, "We have to pass the bill so that you can find out what's in it."[2] So, what was so difficult about reading a health care bill and debating the details within it? Perhaps it was the size of the new law as the initial law was

2,409 pages. So who came up with the details of this so-called Affordable Care Act?

The architect of the plan was Dr. Jonathan Gruber.

From the beginning I had total reservations about the public statements and the media marketing of this new social program. While the sound bites were appetizing, "You can keep your doctors and your present plan." "You can keep your hospital." "Prices of health insurance will go down." "Those without insurance will now have it." "Your child can stay on your policy until age 26." "You cannot remove a person who has a preexisting condition." All this sounded too good to be true. The problem? It *was* too good to be true—especially the part where health care is affordable and you can keep your doctor, your policy, and your hospital.

The more I researched, the more concern I felt. For example:

> » How can you add millions of new people, pay for their coverage, save money, and bring costs down? Nothing of this magnitude is ever free, as someone is paying for the "free stuff."

> » How can you add millions of new people and maintain the quality of care and the freedom to get up and just go to your doctor when you choose? There are not enough doctors, nurses, and hospitals to cover the millions of the newly insured.

> » What about the doctors who said they would rather close their family businesses and retire than deal with the overrun of patients, the penalties, and the regulations required under the new law?

Americans were paying little attention to the fact that if you choose not to have coverage, you will be penalized each year and be required to pay a penalty to the IRS that will go into the government coffers. No one saw that the forty-hour work week would be cut for millions of workers to twenty-nine hours, to prevent businesses from paying the higher cost for the coverage. Neither did they realize the government reimbursements to doctors for Medicare patients would be cut, and many doctors would cut back the number of people they see. Then there was the totally unexpected result of private family physicians and rural hospitals closing their doors.

One physician from Kentucky, who has been in business for twenty-years, is closing his doors for good. At age sixty-five he feels he is unable to continue in business with all the new regulations, one of which would require all hospitals to move from paper records to electronic records. Changing the format would require tens of thousands of dollars in man-power to physically transfer the records over. So instead of spending the money and the many weeks of work required to comply with the new law, he is closing his doors. This is only one example.

In Hamilton, Alabama, the only hospital in the town is closing its doors. For many years, they treated people at no cost; as a result, they went into the red by millions of dollars. One doctor told of performing a surgery that cost $35,000 and was reimbursed by the government about $350. When asked what would happen if a person was in an accident, he said the emergency services would still operate as they are private, but the person would have to be taken across state lines into Mississippi to be treated. The doctor said, "There will definitely be people who will die unnecessarily because the city has no life-saving medical equipment required to treat urgent care."

President Obama's mother and other members of his family were socialists. He and his inner circle desires socialized medicine for every American. It sounds great in speeches, but look at the nations that have this form of "care." Often Canada is used as a successful example of socialized medicine. However, why do so many Canadians cross the border and come to America for their major surgeries?

I ministered in central Canada and asked the people how they enjoyed their health care. The answer was, "It's free, but not free. Each working Canadian is taxed, and it is estimated that the government gets our income from January through August and we keep the rest from September through December." In the church where I ministered, the pastor said two of his church members were sent to the hospital recently. One was an older woman who busted her knee in a fall. She sat in the emergency room for over forty hours in pain, without pain medication, just waiting to see a doctor. The man, who also had an emergency, waited hours before receiving any care. It was pointed out, depending upon your medical needs and your age, people have to wait for surgeries, at times up to five months. And the Canadian population is only 10 percent of America's population.

During a Mediterranean cruise, my Italian tour guide and I were discussing socialized medicine in Italy. He was a professor of history and was sharing with me that he believed America was an empire and was moving in the same direction as the ancient Roman Empire. When asked about socialized medicine, he said, "This is what your government wants. It was sold as 'free health care,' but it is certainly not free. I am taxed 60 percent of my income just to cover the numerous taxes the government requires, including out of health care coverage. He also pointed out that it can be difficult to schedule an appointment to see a doctor. He also said, America (at that time) has the best health care system, doctors, and hospitals in the world, and the new system would change everything.

Building a Legacy?

Every American president enters the Oval Office with the intent of doing something substantial to build a historical legacy that will go down in the annals of time with their name forever attached to it. For Harry Truman, it was supporting a new homeland for the Jewish State of Israel. For Carter, it was the peace agreement between Egypt and Israel. For Reagan, it was the collapse of Communism in Europe and the demise of the Iron Curtain. For George Herbert Walker Bush, it was the liberation of Kuwait from the invasion of Saddam Hussein. For Clinton, it was the recovery of the economy and balancing the budget. For George W. Bush, it was his war on terror and his stand to defeat our enemies on their own soil instead of fighting them in America. During his administration, numerous terror attacks were stopped on our soil, which were never reported.

Based on a conversation I had with a former US congressmen who personally met Barack Obama, he has chosen that health care for all Americans become his legacy. This former congressman told me that prior to the Affordable Care Act being passed, two Republican senators requested a personal meeting at the White House to bring up concerns they had over parts of the health care bill. After being brought in, Obama came in and made two statements. The first was, "I won and you lost, so get over it." The second statement emerging in the brief conversation was, "Health care will be my legacy, so don't mess with it."[3] Years ago, Obama reportedly made a similar statement to the administration of Israeli Prime Minister Benjamin Netanyahu, "We are going to change the world so don't get in our way."[4]

If you will recall, before becoming president, Obama stated many times that he planned to "fundamentally change America." Only one journalist, to my knowledge, has ever asked the question, "Why do you feel it's necessary to fundamentally transform the nation that has afforded you so much opportunity and success?"[5] President Obama deflected the question and gave another answer to a question that he preferred, which wasn't asked. He did, however, make it clear in a confrontation with "Joe the Plumber" in Toledo, Ohio, that he wanted to redistribute the wealth of the country. It has also been made clear that he desires a twofold legacy:

> » First, to be recognized in the history books as America's first black president.

> » Second, to make history as the man who gave government controlled health care to all.

Why was it so important to pass this bill as soon as possible, even before it was read, without debate? I suggest that Obama was uncertain he would be elected for a second term and wanted it passed into legislation before 2012. Thus, the reason is not the administration "cares," but rather, the administration wants to "fundamentally change America." The changes in the health care system are not just fundamental changes, but are drastically dangerous and, if left unchallenged, they will bring in unexpected economic disasters for individuals, businesses, and the nation as a whole.

It is now obvious that there are liberals in government—on the federal and state levels—who want to take complete control of the health care system. There are billions of dollars made in the development and sales of pharmaceuticals, and there are specific diseases that cost billions of dollars to treat. Standard and traditional medicine and doctors are often skeptical of newer natural health practices, if they have not been tested and proven.

I was informed that the medical teams and researchers in Israel have actually found treatments for certain diseases that are global, especially prominent in America, but the FDA will never approve the "cures." If they did, it would hinder the profits needed for doctors, medical equipment, and hospitals to survive. In my part of the country there was a tradition that the Cherokee Indian medicine men had found a combination of herbs and roots that could treat certain diseases, but over time their combinations were lost. I just wonder, if they were ever rediscovered, if they would be permitted on the market, especially if they cured a problem and didn't just treat or cover the symptoms.

The Unseen Part of the System

In the Book of Revelation, at the time of the end, a system that John describes as a "Beast" economic system will control all buying and selling. It will be done through one of three methods: a mark on the right hand or forehead, a name of the beast, and the number of his name. Before the Affordable Care Act was passed, I was made aware of an electronic RFID chip. It was part of the plan and personally concerned myself and others who were aware of the "mark" of buying and selling. There is another part of this plan that came to my attention two years before the legislation was passed. Unless changed, this part of the plan will impact every American now and those who will be born in the future. It involves a tiny health care chip implant.

The RFID Chip

I was one of the first prophetic ministers (in the early 1990s) to be interviewed on Christian station CTN in Tampa, Florida, and show a small chip the size of a grain of rice, encased in a clear plastic case that held a miniature tracking device. A major tech company produced the chip for tracking pets and expensive farm animals. If the pet was lost or stolen, a small implant, just under the skin, could be tracked and located by computers, discovering the location of the lost animal.

Several years later I was in Florida ministering, when a church member informed me of an implantable device being researched by the government, where in the future it would be implanted in the entire population. To confirm this, I was personally invited to visit a man living in the area. He was involved in micro-welding parts for satellites and could literally go online and speak to astronauts inside the space shuttle. I went to his home and spent about three hours gleaning astonishing insight.

During our conversation, he told me about a special chip that was, at that time, with the astronauts on the space shuttle. This man could follow the movements of the shuttle from his office, and I could even watch him carry on a brief conversation with one of the astronauts in the shuttle. He told me in the future a special chip would be implanted in the right hand or just below the hair line of every person. These two locations were important, as the *body heat* from these two areas would keep the tiny battery operative. This of course was an older form of technology.

Before the health care overhaul, I was told the selling points to convince the public for the imbedded chip. Americans will be persuaded to accept the chip, to protect children from kidnappers (a tracking device), to tag illegals in the country, to separate legitimate citizens (having the chip) from possible terrorists (without the chip) and to take health care for personal information data storage. While in Texas, I was told that about 2.5 million individuals already have this chip implanted. It is called an RFID chip.

While ministering near Cincinnati, Ohio, the pastor related to me that a couple in their church had a son working for a major barge-shipping company out of Missouri. Homeland Security contacted the company. They were told every employee was required to have a chip implanted in their right hand. Those with the chip would be the only ones allowed on the barges. The son of this Christian couple felt that any implant in the right hand was too much like the warning mentioned in Revelation 13:17–18. He told his boss he would not receive this device. They threatened to terminate him from his job. They finally reached a compromise, and he was permitted to carry a card. The card cost him $800 and had a small, gold, square foil "chip" holding information on the back of the card.

The Chinese Powder Tag

Hitachi invented the Chinese Powder Tags. Measuring at only 0.05 by 0.05 millimeters, they are so tiny that they almost get lost on the fingertips. They are called "Powder Tags," and are sixty times smaller than any previous tags. The most amazing fact is these tiny chips have the ability for a 128-bit-ROM for storing a thirty-eight-digit number. An article in *TechNewsDaily* reported that an agency had spent $50,000 in setting up a system for Head Start to use these tags in tracking children in school.[6] To place data on the tag, electronic beams are used and they are inserted like powder on the hand. The tags can easily be used to track individuals. They are so small that people would be unaware they were being monitored. These tags can be inserted in paper, gift certificates, and even money. As tiny as they are, a scanner from ten inches away can read the tags.

Wired Magazine and *WorldNetDaily* reported that a California school used $115,000 in stimulus to have children embedded with RFID chips to track their movements. The selling point was that it would save teachers three thousand hours of dealing with attendance records. They would be used either on lanyards worn by the child every morning, or inserted in their clothes.[7] In the state of Missouri special devices were put on one hundred forty-seven school buses.[8] The selling point among the Western nations, like America, for developing and implementing such a system will be because it will save time and money.

The Indian Government and Six Hundred Million People

Both India and China have over one billion people each in their nations. The Indian government announced a program to assign a sixteen-digit identification number to six hundred million of its people to help expedite national food and governmental services. They have estimated this system will save four billion dollars a year in just corruption costs. As of this writing, half of these numbers have been given out. The government is also using fingerprints and iris scans. Completion of this particular process is projected to be ready by the years 2017–2018. The idea of any government saving billions of dollars by using a chip, with encoded information, will become the selling point, even in America. This leads me to reveal a future part of the government-controlled health care that was forced on Americans without their approval.

The governments of the world desire to *mark their citizens*, not only so they can know the number of individuals in the nation, but also for economic and tracking purposes as well. Scholars have taught the "mark of the beast"—this number, name, and/or mark is introduced only to control buying and selling, which is the main purpose based on Revelation 13:18.

However, there is one thing every human needs, besides food—especially in contemporary nations—and that is their health care. It is imperative to have access to clinics, hospitals, and emergency rooms. What if the American government demanded each of its citizens to be implanted with a health care chip or tracking device? What if it were the law that any who resisted the chip, would lose their health benefits, be fined, or even jailed? Don't consider this impossible, as there are already financial penalties for not following certain parts of the new health law.

When I first heard from this former congressman, I realized one reason why President Obama underlined such urgency to sign the massive health care bill. With over two thousand detailed pages that would take a lawyer to interpret, I was uncertain of why such an important and yet expensive government program had to be signed in as soon as possible. Of course, everyone had an opinion as to why the president and the democratic leadership pushed it through.

> » The president was going to add millions of illegals, guaranteeing his political party votes, over time.

> » The longer it was delayed, the risk of Americans seeing what was in it increased, possibly rising up to stop it.

> » The bill had to be passed before the next election—as the opposing party could take the house and senate.

The Doctor's Information on the Chip

In the middle of the health care debate, a personal ministry friend was traveling by air from Pennsylvania to Orlando, Florida. Having ministered to the point of exhaustion, my friend hoped to rest the entire flight. He found himself sitting next to a colonel in the US military and seated on the other side was a doctor who also served on one of the nation's medical boards.

During the two-and a-half-hour flight, the doctor struck up a conversation with the minister and began asking him questions about the kind of work he did. In response, and to be a gentleman, the minister returned his questions. The doctor began explaining that he was on his way to a major meeting in Orlando to talk about the health care bill and the new medical implant device. My friend suddenly perked up! He began inquiring about this "implantable medical device." The doctor told him that one reason the administration was determined to pass this legislation as soon as possible was so the plans for implantable devices could advance to the next phase.

The doctor explained the government had been working for many years on this chip implant, but certain blood types had rejected the implant, causing slight complications. They had been working for years to ensure that all blood types could accept the implant. This particular doctor believed the challenges had now been met. This tiny device would hold, among other things, a person's medical records and other information and theoretically could save the government hundreds of millions of dollars. It would also cut expenses on the required forms and paperwork now required and reduce time spent in emergency rooms, which would be a major selling point for the public. As in Europe and Canada, the time spent in the emergency room can be as long as twenty-four to forty-eight hours before receiving help—depending upon the circumstances. Imagine the "relief" when a small device can save you time and money for health benefits.

My minister friend was astonished! The doctor also mentioned, that the implantation would be done in hospitals since people trust their local, personal doctors. Since this law is here to stay, it will take time to complete the implantation on millions of Americans (which was discussed behind closed doors). The projected time frame is around 2018. Only time will reveal if this will unfold and by that time technology will have advanced to a whole new level. If the information on the chip can be programmed with a number and specific data, it could also be expanded to be used at grocery stores, various checkout counters, and restaurants in a cashless government.

On the flight, after hearing of the implantation device, the colonel spoke up and said that he wasn't trying to listen in on the conversation, but he wanted to say that one reason he was headed for a meeting in Tampa, Florida, was because preparations were being made for *food riots* in the larger cities, soon. The military was preparing for some form of *internal civil war*, triggered by a major crisis coming to America. Later, other individuals linked to the military who said it was true confirmed this. Some of the huge underground bunkers, once used to store bombs and weapons, had been cleared out and were now being used to store huge amounts of food in these large underground bunkers on bases and at arsenals.[9]

Evidence of a Chip

Shortly after receiving this insight, I was ministering in Georgia and speaking on this possible "health care chip." I was unaware of two individuals in the congregation; one was a health care professional and the other, a well-informed state senator from Georgia. After the service the worker from the hospital relayed to one of my staff members that during the week he was in a special meeting with company representatives. These representatives would be the ones responsible for the medical implant device (chip). He was informed that money would be made from each person that is implanted with the chip. They will be charged ten dollars a month for its activation. When adding up the number of people required to have health care, at ten dollars a month, the income generated would eventually be into the billions of dollars. If the government can control health care, then the government agencies can "spread the wealth."[10]

During this same meeting, I was eating lunch and a distinguished man, who is a state senator, spoke with me. During our conversation he said he was aware of the coming health care device and as a Christian he would not justify placing something that both marked and numbered you under your right hand. He shared he was working on a bill for the state of Georgia, forbidding any type of tracking devices from being placed under the skin or in the bodies of any citizens from the state of Georgia.[11]

The Washington Post actually reported on a House of Delegates member who was commenting on the implantable devices:

> The House of Delegates is scheduled to vote Wednesday on a bill that would protect Virginians from attempts by employers or insurance companies to implant microchips in their bodies against their will....Del. Mark L. Cole (R-Fredericksburg), the bill's sponsor, said that privacy issues are the chief concern behind his attempt to criminalize the involuntary implantation of microchips. But he also said he shared concerns that the devices could someday be used as the "mark of the beast" described in the Book of Revelation.[12]

The report sadly pointed out some of his liberal colleagues were actually mocking him for his concerns and comments, even going as far as saying that voters were not concerned about such things. (I'm sure those would be voters who never pick up a Bible and read it!) Another report came from Pennsylvania in which a lawmaker was seeking to outlaw identification implants in humans, making it illegal to implant any form of device on or under a person's skin that would transmit personal information.[13]

Before Joe Biden was the vice president, he was a senator from Delaware. While speaking at the Supreme Court confirmation hearing for Chief Justice Roberts, Biden asked a very odd question. He asked future Chief Justice if he would rule against a mandatory implantable microchip, to track American citizens, warning Roberts he would have to address the issue during his tenure if approved for the Supreme Court.[14]

Various news sources have reported that debates have already occurred regarding airport workers receiving a tracking chip against their will. In Mexico some workers are being forced to take the chip or lose their jobs. In the US military plans are being made to use chip implants in soldiers to monitor their health on the battlefield.[15]

The use of chips now seems to be geared for tracking individuals, monitoring a person's location on a base or in a factory, tracking the whereabouts of a wealthy person, if abducted, or used for a worker to check in and out of a building. They are also used in intelligence facilities. A chip is essentially not needed at this point, as eye and right hand scanners and voice recognition devices serve the purpose of preventing an unwanted person from entering a facility. However, if the government was to force a bio-chip implant for health care, and make the program federally legislated then everyone would be forced to receive the chip.

More recently, I received a print out of one of the pages about the new computer program for health care. On the bottom of page twenty, there is a place to click if the person has the RFID chip.[16] Thus, this chip is already being prepared as part of the future of government controlled healthcare.

Was It in the Health Care Bill?

Was there any mention of such devices in the health care bill that was passed? I received a copy of the bill and also had several individuals who operate hospitals share some information with me. On pages 1,502–1,510 in the bill it alludes to medical devices that can be used for surveillance, including storing electronic records. On page 1,502, under line 10, there is mention of a National Medical Registry and further in the section it tells of a device that can be implantable. On pages 1,501–1,508 there is a paragraph that explains a medical device that contains a unique identifier for collecting information and for surveillance. The bill also mentions that these medical devices should be implemented within thirty-six months of enacting the bill! While this language is vague and could include numerous types of devices, it can also be read to approve the device we are speaking of.[17]

In the earlier days of America I am uncertain that such an implantable device would have received such praise from the legislators in Washington. In the past many of the men elected to the position of congress were raised in or around Christians or in a biblically literate family. They would have at least recognized the prophetic warnings of a global system marking individuals in the right hand as predicted in the Book of Revelation.

From all signs, we now have many leaders, who not only have never read the Bible, but also have never attended church; thus they know nothing about warnings in biblical prophecy of the "beast system." At the same time, since we are living in the time of the end, we know men must begin the process of initiating such scenarios to fulfill what has been predicted. There are a large percentage of liberals and social progressives in America who not only would gladly receive the mark, but would almost do so with an arrogant attitude. As if to say to a believer, "Look at me, you old fool. I don't believe your foolish prophecies in the Bible!"

National ID Cards

There are millions of Christians living in the United States, rooted and grounded in sound, biblical teaching, informed about future events as related to biblical prophecy. I believe if the government tried to force a chip implant on its citizens, there would be many groups who would immediately resist.

The first would be the older, evangelical community of believers, who would read such a law as the early stages of the system of the "mark of the beast." They would immediately reject forced implementation of such a device under their skin, in their hand or forehead.

A second group that has already resisted the health care bill is the Amish, who primarily live in Pennsylvania, Delaware, Ohio, Indiana, and

New York. The Amish are a pleasant group of individuals who live in their own communities, grow their own food, and reject the use of modern technology. They have their own doctors and take care of their families, often without any government assistance.

A third group would be the ultra-Orthodox Jews living in cities such as New York. A Jewish resistance would happen among those who are strict observers of the Torah (the five books of Moses). There are Scriptures, given by God through Moses, which specify a Jew should not place any marking upon their skin; thus, the Orthodox Jews would be against any type of tattoo. They would reject any type of cutting on their skin and would not take favorably to being forced to have an implanted device in their hands or foreheads.

Jews place a small black box called a phylactery on their heads that contain Scriptures. They believe their mind belongs to God and not to any government. Perhaps this explains why, when the Antichrist and False Prophet demand the worship of the image of the beast, and require everyone to take the mark, a huge remnant of Jews will flee Jerusalem to the mountains, where the Lord will supernaturally preserve them during part of the tribulation (Rev. 12).

One way to slip in an implantable device is to slowly bring in some form of national identification card first. By delaying this action, until those who would resist have been removed (the senior citizens), or supporters of the system outnumber us, we would have no power or voice to resist. The idea of a national ID card has been discussed by previous administrations and has been a method reconsidered to separate legal citizens from illegal aliens. As drug dealers and criminal elements sneak into America, causing more violent crimes on American soil, especially in states such as Texas and Arizona, there will be a call for a new form of identification card to mark legal individuals and to detect those who are not. A card can always be printed and forged, unless the card is using an embedded chip containing information that must be used with a national computer database.

While ministering in Elkins, West Virginia, I met a young man from Taiwan. I mentioned to him the possibility of a national ID card for America with a health care chip. He then produced his wallet and handed me a plastic card bearing his photo, name, and general information. Turning the card over, I saw a small, square, gold chip. He told me that every person in his home country must have and carry at all times even when working and traveling in the nation. If you are stopped by the police and do not have your card with you, you will be fined or possibly even sent to jail!

If you drive an automobile, you are required to have a driver's license card, which holds a photo ID and number. This helps the authorities to identify you, and if the vehicle is yours or stolen. It also lets them know if you have a criminal record or if you are someone on the run. If the nation of Mexico ever experiences a total economic collapse or a massive food shortage, there will be not just thousands, but possibly millions of people pouring across the border to find food or aid. This would overwhelm any farming community, as well as the major US cities near the Mexican border. At that point, issuing a National Identification Card would be both welcomed and accepted by the citizens, which would be the beginning of a more sinister type of control in the future!

Several years ago, a large company in Canada was requiring all of their employees to implant a small chip in their right hands that would track them. It would be used when employees were checking in and out, opening and closing doors and tracking their whereabouts. Three Pentecostal believers worked with this company and told the leadership they would not be implanted for religious reasons. After a court case, the three were permitted to be given a special card, instead of the embedded chip. The chips are certainly one possibility of how both a tracking device and an identifying mark can be used in an individual, with the national database computers systems.[18]

Password Vitamin—Google Gives You Superpowers

At the D11 conference, Google-owned Motorola had presenter Regina Dugan, the new senior vice president for advanced technology and projects at Motorola, introduce some advanced technology. A company called MC10 has developed a "stretchable circuitry" creating a wearable technology that has been used in the medical field in skullcaps for detecting concussions in sports, and for constant infant monitoring.[19] In a world where people are entering their passwords up to thirty-nine times a day,[20] they wanted to invent a new automated way of authenticating the user with each account they would access. See how innocently this new technology can be introduced?

As Dugan, the former *DARPA* (Pentagon) chief, talked about this new technology, she held out her wrist and showed off a very thin, clear "patch" stuck to her skin with a full circuitry board on it. It could have a design, like a tattoo, appealing to young people, complete with all circuitry, antennas, and RFDI to produce automatic user identification to the user's electronic devices. Dugan is also working with a company called Proteus Digital Health that already has FDA approval for an ingestible sensor as a medical device. She wants to use it for passwords, too.

She then took it a step further. "When you swallow it, the acids in your stomach serve as the electrolyte, and they power it up, and the switch goes on and off, and it creates an 18-bit ECG-like signal in your body. Essentially, your entire body becomes your authentication token." she explained. Dugan said that once the sensor has been swallowed, "it means that my arms are like wires, my hands are like alligator clips—when I touch my phone, my computer, my door, my car, I'm authenticated in. It's my first super power. I want that." The crowd went crazy with applause, ready to swallow the pill.[21]

The ultimate strategy has now been exposed; the goal is eventually to bankrupt the present insurance industry, forcing everyone onto government controlled health care. Only when the government is in total control can they forcibly demand every person to have some form of implant and tracking device. This device will not only hold all of your personal information, but will also track you anywhere on earth. It is about control and power over the common citizen.

This reveals the concern I have of men and women being in charge of the lives of multiple millions but knowing nothing about Bible prophecy or the "mark of the beast," which will control buying and selling. A name, number, or mark on the right hand will be enforced, and those who take the mark will be destined for destruction. Perhaps the health chip is not the actual mark, but with technology advancing at its current rate, a newer, more innovative system can emerge that may be a preview of what is to come.

The many sudden changes in America can be summed up by a statement made after a photo was released of President Obama talking to Israeli Prime Minister Benjamin Netanyahu. President Obama was flashing the bottom of his shoes, with his feet on his desk while on the phone with the

Prime Minister. Showing the bottom of your shoes is a terrible insult in the Middle East. It was reported in an Israeli paper:

> Israeli TV newscasters Tuesday night interpreted a photo taken Monday in the Oval Office of President Obama talking on the phone with Israeli Prime Minister Benjamin Netanyahu as an "insult" to Israel....Israel's Channel One TV reported that Netanyahu was told Tuesday by an "American official" in Jerusalem that, "We are going to change the world. Please, don't interfere." The report said Netanyahu's aides interpreted this as a "threat."[22]

Men who want to change the world must first begin by "fundamentally changing" their own country. A good beginning is forcing everyone to get government forced health care.

Chapter 12

AMERICA'S FINAL SPIRITUAL VISITATION AT THE TIME OF THE END

THE FUTURE OF America is not just in the hands of a sovereign God but may increasingly lie in the hands of the Christian population. To heal the land, God requires His people to humble themselves, pray, and turn from their wicked ways (2 Chron. 7:14). Consider how far our culture has fallen: from the pristine, mountain-peak, Christian experience to a hodge-podge of humanistic ideas. We've become master designers of our own mixed opinions, where few of us could recognize the truth, even if it slapped us in the face.

The Mottos of American Universities

Because America's early population centered in the Northeast, most of our initial universities were in the northeast corridor of the nation. The mottos of our universities speak volumes. Harvard's motto was "Glory in Christ." Brown University chose the motto "In God we hope." Rutgers selected the theme, "Sun of Righteousness Shine Upon the West Also," adapted from the motto of the University of Utrecht in the Netherlands, referencing Malachi 4:2. John Hopkins University's motto is "The Truth Shall Make You Free," based upon Christ's words in John 8:32. The theme "In thy light shall we see light" was the choice of Columbia University. Dartmouth selected as their motto "the voice of one crying in the wilderness," based on Isaiah 40:3, and verses in the Gospels. Amherst College uses the Latin motto, *Terras Irradient*, which is an allusion to the words of the prophet Isaiah: "The whole earth is full of His glory" (Isa. 6:3). Princeton selected the words, "Under the protection of God she flourishes."

Ministers founded many of America's colleges and universities, with an emphasis on teaching ministry, evangelism, and missions. Today those with religious departments are often chaired by liberal and even agnostic professors who have little or no faith in the integrity of the Scriptures. They teach it only as a historical book filled with errors and myths.

In America God has always had a faithful remnant who would pray in soul-winning revivals and times of refreshing. The Moody revivals in 1873 began at a YMCA in England and spread like wild fire to America. The outpouring of the Spirit that flowed in Armenia in 1880 eventually brought many Spirit-filled Armenians to the West Coast, where they joined in and helped initiate the noted Azusa Street Revival in Los Angeles, California. The Azusa Street outpouring occurred in one location, lasting several years, bearing fruit with thousands of converts and even more baptized in the Holy Spirit. Many major denominations eventually were birthed because of this explosive outpouring.

Years later a second revival, known as the Healing Revival, began after the restoration of Israel in 1948 and continued strong for about seven years until around 1955. Huge canvas tent-cathedrals were erected in towns and cities, accommodating crowds of often ten thousand to fifteen thousand seekers a night.

This was followed up in 1967 with a third outpouring wave that was a mix of the Jesus movement and the charismatic outpouring among Catholics and nominal church members. Some full-gospel scholars identify these numerous outpourings as the predicted "latter rain" outpouring of the Spirit (James 5:7).

Scripture indicates that God will visit the earth in a global downpour of His Spirit, impacting all flesh with a focus on the sons and daughters. Throughout church history, the hand of the Lord has moved on the younger generation, bringing forth shining lights during dark moments.

» William Booth, the founder of the Salvation Army, began preaching in the streets at age fifteen in the London slums.

» Charles Spurgeon, having been labeled as the greatest preacher of the nineteenth century, began preaching just after his sixteenth birthday, became a pastor at age eighteen, and within several years built a five-thousand-seat tabernacle in London, filling it every service.

» Jonathan Edwards entered Yale University at age thirteen in 1716. By the age of twenty-one, he was pastoring one of the great churches in America and led the nation into the Great Awakening.

» A young woman, Amy Carmichael, was twenty-eight years old when she departed to India as a missionary, serving fifty-six years without ever taking a furlough, living and ministering in dangerous areas.

» In 1844 George Williams was a young twenty-three-year-old businessman who started the YMCA as an outreach to businessmen.

» The famous minister, John Wesley, was twenty-six when he became the leader of the Holy Club started by his brother Charles at Oxford and experienced a revival that led him to evangelize throughout England and America.

» George Whitefield was a member of Wesley's Holy Club. In 1738, at age twenty-three, he took a journey to America. After preaching and witnessing, he received thirty thousand conversions to Christ.

» A young black slave girl, Phillis Wheatley, was seventeen years old when she wrote a poem about Whitefield and received national fame, becoming the first published African American woman and second published African American poet.

Christians in America often judge the spiritual movements of God based on what they are seeing or experiencing in their churches, conferences, or activities within the nation. However, America is only one out of hundreds of nations or regions, and at times more positive spiritual results are happening outside of America than within our boundaries.

In Indonesia, the world's largest Islamic nation, there are churches with one hundred and fifty thousand members and the majority of the attendees are under thirty years of age. The same is true in the growing churches in Asian nations, including the massive underground Christian population in China, Vietnam, and North Korea.

Years ago, when I was pondering on the direction our ministry would take for the future, I was petitioning the Lord to direct me in whatever assignments—known or unknown—that would facilitate His calling. I heard in my Spirit that God was moving toward the sons and the daughters, to fulfill His promise that, in the last days, He would pour out His Spirit upon them (Acts 2:17–18). After a series of unexpected circumstances, my heart was turned as I linked up with a local youth ministry. It has become our desire to not only to reach this generation but to also become a spiritual father to a generation of fatherless youth. The second emphasis is to bridge the generations, connecting the old with the new and seeing Joel's end-time army emerge on the earth.

The views concerning the condition and the future of America fall along the opinion lines of liberals, moderates, and conservatives. The liberals don't believe we have gone far enough to liberate this nation from the bondage of its traditional Christian heritage. The moderates believe we are about where we need to be and have gone just far enough, while many conservatives feel we have gone too far and are now on the path of no return.

Discerning the Times

People often ask me, "Is there any hope left for America?" to which I reply, "My hope is not in whom we elect or who is in charge, but in a promise that is being fulfilled, that one more revival is coming, a global outpouring, that will climax in the return of Christ (based on James 5)."

If there is hope, then what truly lies ahead? How can we discern the times in which we are living? Do prophetic patterns, such as those found in Jewish feasts, give us an idea of what is to come? I believe they do.

The Jewish feasts hold practical, spiritual, and prophetic applications. They are a preview of major events that will occur in the future, linked to the Messiah's appearing and His kingdom. I wrote more extensively about this in my book *Breaking the Code of the Feasts*, but I will give you a synopsis here.

During the first appearance of Christ, He fulfilled the three spring feasts. He was crucified at Passover, placed in the tomb during Unleavened Bread, and showed Himself to be alive to His disciples toward the conclusion of Firstfruits (John 20:26–27). Fifty days later on the Day of Pentecost, the Holy Spirit fell upon one hundred twenty believers and more than three thousand souls were converted to Christ (Acts 1:15, 2:1–4; 2:41). The gift of the Holy Spirit is promised to all believers until the very time that Christ returns (1 Corinthians 1:7). This means that, prophetically, the church has been living at the Feast of Pentecost for just under two thousand years.

On the Jewish calendar the next major feast that follows Pentecost is Rosh Hashanah, or the Feast of Trumpets. This feast is one that many prophetic scholars believe might coincide with the sounding of the trumpet when the dead in Christ will rise.

On the Hebrew calendar there is a four-month gap between Pentecost and the Feast of Trumpets. Those four months are the hot, dry summer season where there is almost no rain at all. In Israel rain comes in cycles that repeat yearly, not on the same day but in the same season under normal weather patterns called the early and latter rains.

From a prophetic perspective, the early rains are the outpouring recorded in Acts 2:1–4, which gave rise to the Christian church on the Day of Pentecost. The latter rain is an outpouring that has dropped spiritual rain from time to time in selected areas of the nation and the world. However, there is coming a global covering of the refreshing from heaven, that will impact all nations and all flesh.

This outpouring is a sign of the soon return of Christ. There will also be three indicators that when these occur, with the Spirit's visitation, you can be certain the time of the end has arrived and Christ will be returning.

1. When Men No Longer Repent

The Noah code indicates that the signs of Noah's day, prior to the flood, will be repeated before the return of the Lord (Matt. 24:37–39). Noah and his sons spent one hundred years preparing the Ark, with not one convert or one person repenting of their sins. Only eight souls, all related to Noah, escaped watery doom by believing the warning and preparing (2 Pet. 2:5). Christ predicted that the events in Lot's day would recycle and repeat themselves prior to His return (Luke 17:28).

After being warned by two angelic messengers that complete destruction was coming, Lot warned his daughters and sons-in-law to join him and get out of Sodom before the fire fell. We read where the information made them laugh (*mock*—KJV), not taking him seriously (Gen. 19:14). In both instances, neither Lot nor Noah won any converts.

In the future when God's judgments are unleashed during the tribulation, men will no longer repent. This fact is mentioned three times in the Apocalypse, where men "repented not" (Rev. 9:20; 16:9; 16:11).

In our present dispensation the church is preaching the gospel in "all of the world," but history must come full circle before the end comes (Matt. 24:14). If the gospel began in Jerusalem, scattering believers to reach the known world before Jerusalem was destroyed (a period of about forty years to spread the gospel), then it must again emerge from Jerusalem and somehow reach the world.

Jerusalem has three religious groups: Jews, Muslims, and Christians. The Orthodox Jews have in the past, resisted any form of Christian evangelism in the city. However, two major Christian television networks now have their headquarters in Jerusalem: Daystar and TBN. The Daystar network is reaching into countless homes in Israel through satellite. It was Christ who gave two interesting prophecies:

> For I say to you, you shall see Me no more till you say, "Blessed is He who comes in the name of the LORD!"
>
> —MATTHEW 23:39

Today at the Western Wall in Jerusalem, devout Jews and Holy Land pilgrims pray continually. One of the Jewish prayers is for the soon appearing of the Messiah. The phrase, "Blessed is he who comes in the name of the Lord," a prophetic psalm (Ps. 118:26), is part of certain prayers being prayed in Jerusalem, especially during certain festivals.

In a second prediction Christ said:

> For assuredly, I say to you, you will not have gone through the
> cities of Israel before the Son of Man comes.
>
> —MATTHEW 10:23

This verse cannot be applied to the first-century believers, as the Lord did not come in their day. It must refer to the gospel going through all the cities of Israel. While this has not yet occurred, we are seeing the early stages of technology creating the possibilities of such taking place.

The church is presently dispensing the message of grace, before the arrival of God's universal judgment. However, just as in Noah's and Lot's day, the sin and hardness of men's hearts built a wall of resistance against the spirit of conviction and repentance. It is becoming increasingly rare to see men and women genuinely repentant and turn to God. When our nation gets to the place where floods, hurricanes, and earthquakes do not humble us causing us to keep God's mercy, then the unrepentant generation will be marked for God's judgment, just as Christ's generation.

2. When the "Cup of Iniquity" Is Full

All men are born with sin nature. Sin is considered an offense against either God, man, or both. To God, sin is breaking the spiritual and moral laws of God. Sin has such a spreading effect that continual unrepentant sin will lead to new acts of sin, causing the higher level of perverseness called iniquity. Men move from viewing pornography to rape, incest, and pedophilia. From one glass of wine to abusive alcoholism and from smoking marijuana to smoking crack cocaine.

There is individual iniquity and national iniquity. America's national iniquities include abortion, same-sex marriage, and greed.

At times Americans live in a bubble of false security. Since we do not see major "judgments" hitting cities or states, we assume that we are getting by with legalizing iniquity and placing an approval on what God disapproves. However, this lack of response from the hand of heaven is actually God's restraint, since the nation's "cup of iniquity is not yet full."

God used this phrase when predicting to Abraham that his descendants would be taken to a nation (Egypt) for four hundred years, and after He would bring them back to the Promised Land. God was waiting for the cup of iniquity to become full among the Amorites, a pagan-like tribe that filled in the gap and took possession of Canaan Land, after the Hebrews departed and went to Egypt (Gen. 15:16). God's plan was to bring Israel out of Egypt at the end of the fourth generation. The law of God warns that iniquities of the fathers would be visited upon the third and fourth generation (Exod. 34:7–9). Thus, the release of Israel and the judgment on the Amorites was at the end of the fourth generation—a generation, in that time, being a cycle of one hundred years.

God uses the metaphor of a cup being full when describing how generations of sins eventually fill up a cup of iniquity. In Revelation 17:5 Mystery Babylon is destroyed in one hour because her cup of iniquity is full.

In the past Americans were a spiritually minded and motivated people. This spirituality was often mixed with patriotism, as we would sing "God Bless America," or "America the Beautiful." Liberal progressives have engaged in a war against God since the 1960s and sadly with silent believers sitting in comfortable pews, they have won the battles.

Today abominations are acceptable, and just as in Noah's day the earth is filled with violence and man's imaginations are evil continually (Gen. 6:5, 13). When iniquity becomes acceptable and righteousness is rejected, then we have entered the end of the end and the last days of the last days.

3. When Covenant Breakers Become Violent

The night that two angels in the form of men visited Lot, we read:

> Now before they lay down, the men of the city, the men of Sodom, both old and young, all the people from every quarter, surrounded the house. And they called to Lot and said to him, "Where are the men who came to you tonight? Bring them out to us that we may know them carnally."
>
> —GENESIS 19:4–5

When Lot refused to submit to the perverted demands of these sex-crazed men, there were two reactions. First, the mob of men attempted to crash through the door, dragging the two angels into the street to molest them. Second, they rebuked Lot for being "judgmental," threatening to do worse to him (implying raping him), if he did not bring the visiting strangers outside (Gen. 19:9). The city of Sodom had moved from perversion to violent perversion, a parallel three hundred years earlier with Noah's time, when the earth was covered with violence.

When the righteous are violently mistreated or threatened by perverse men and women, the "game changes" and God will eventually stand up and defend those in covenant with Him. One of the chief reasons the generation of Christ came under destructive judgment (in AD 70) was God's response to the Jews for shedding innocent blood, including slaying prophets and priests who were sent to them with divine earnings (Matt. 23:30–35). In the future God will permit the complete destruction of the city that was guilty of shedding the blood of the prophets and righteous men in one hour (Rev. 17:6; 18:24).

Living From Pentecost to Trumpets

For the last forty days of the four-month gap between Pentecost and Trumpets, Jews observe *Teshuvah*, a special season of repentance. They search their own hearts, write letters to each other, and recite Psalm 22 twice a day in preparation for the Day of Atonement. It's interesting to note that prior to the blowing of trumpets on Rosh Hashanah there is a major season of repenting in preparation of the fall feasts and the return of the rain.

I believe this gives us a prophetic picture of the time we are living in. As we prophetically move from Pentecost to the Rapture (Trumpets) two things will happen. First, there will be a major call to repentance to prepare people for the Rapture. As we come closer to the Rapture when the great trumpet sounds, I believe there will be a major emphasis on repenting and turning to God! Second, as the church moves closer to the Rapture, just as in the natural realm in Israel, the clouds will begin to form to prepare for the rain. The Holy Spirit will prepare for a final outpouring that will climax when the trumpet sounds. The dry spell of summer is breaking as today we are witnessing a global revival of souls and a fresh outpouring of the Spirit flowing from nation to nation!

These amazing prophetic patterns and cyclical repetitions of history that you have read that are now coming full circle in America, indicate that the nation is now the center of prophetic fulfillment by divine design. The world's past history reveals both the blessings and dangers of our future.

As the nation chooses its path, we too will choose our destiny, and perhaps find our place in the pages of once great empires.

That being said, if the only thing you take from this book is information, you have missed the point. More than information, we are in need of revelation. Christ needs to be revealed to the world as never before.

The things that are coming upon America and the rest of the world are coming because mankind has consistently turned a deaf ear to His plea to return to Him. This, and His unwillingness to relinquish His creation to destruction, made it necessary for God to provide a Redeemer: Himself. And so His Word came and healed our diseases; chief among them being our inherent inclination to sin. It only makes sense then that He would be the most consistent and most important "code" found in all of Scripture. He is the sum of it all.

Therefore, if you don't know Him or you don't know Him as you should, then I invite you to remedy that situation right now. Ask Christ to come into your life and change you so that your name will be inscribed in the most important book there is—the Lamb's Book of Life!

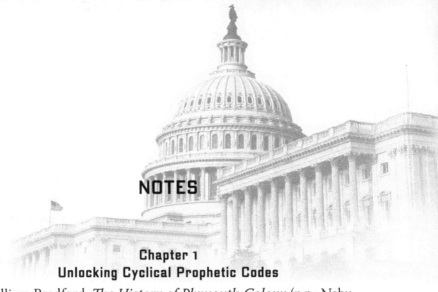

NOTES

Chapter 1
Unlocking Cyclical Prophetic Codes

1. William Bradford, *The History of Plymouth Colony* (n.p.: Nabu Press, 2011).

2. Abraham Katsh, *The Biblical Heritage of American Democracy* (New York: KTAV Publishing House, 1977), 70.

3. Aish.com, "Tisha B'Av - The Ninth of Av," http://www.aish.com/h/9av/oal/48944076.html?tab=y (accessed September 23, 2014).

Chapter 2
Three Ways of Counting Time in God's Cosmic Calendar

1. Aish.com, "Tisha B'Av - The Ninth of Av"; "America's Hebraic Heritage and Roots," http://www.threemacs.org/docs/Americas%20Hebraic%20Roots%20-%20Columbus%20and%20the%20Discovery.pdf (accessed September 24, 2014).

2. Slemen.com, "Beware the Ides of March," http://www.slemen.com/caesar.html (accessed September 24, 2014).

3. Justine Glass, *They Foresaw the Future* (New York: Putnam, 1969), 29.

4. Ibid.

5. Astronomy Today, "Augustus' Eclipse (14 CE)," http://www.astronomytoday.com/eclipses/ancient-part3.html (accessed October 9, 2014).

6. J. Stokley, *The Science News-letter*, 26, no. 716, 1934.

7. NASA Eclipse Web Site, "Eclipses of 2014," http://eclipse.gsfc.nasa.gov/eclipse.html (accessed September 25, 2014).

8. George H. Schodde trans., *The Book of Jubilees* (Muskogee, OK: Artisan Publishers, 1888).

9. Sacrednamebroadcaster.com, "Sabbatical and Possible Jubilee Years," http://sacrednamebroadcaster.com/pdf/sabbaticalchart.pdf (accessed November 6, 2014).

Chapter 3
When Prophetic Time Becomes "Crunched"

1. Christian Classics Ethereal Library, *Josephus: Antiquities of the Jews*, Book I, http://www.ccel.org/ccel/josephus/works/files/ant-1 .htm#EndNote_ANT_1.10a (accessed September 26, 2014).

2. *American Christian Heritage* (blog), "First New England History," October 5, 2011, http://acheritagegroup.org/blog/?p-692 (accessed September 26, 2014).

3. Nathaniel Morton, William Bradford, Thomas Prince, Edward Winslow, *New England's Memorial* (Massachusetts: Congregational Board of Publication, 1669), 5. Viewed online at Google Books.

Chapter 4
Prophecies Encoded in the Hebrew Alphabet and Numbers

1. Hebrew4Christians.com, "Birkat Kohanim—The Priestly Blessing," http://www.hebrew4christians.com/Blessings/Synagogue_Blessings/ Priestly_Blessing/priestly_blessing.html (accessed September 26, 2014).

2. Mount Ophel (2 Chron. 27:3), Mount Zion (Ps. 48:2), and Mount Moriah (2 Chron. 3:1) are three hills that join together to form the area from the southern to the northern slopes where the old city of Jerusalem with its walls now sits. Mount Moriah is the highest peak, where the first and second Jewish temples once sat.

3. Matityahu Glazerson, *Letters of Fire* (Jerusalem: The Kest-Lebovits Jewish Heritage and Roots Library, 1984).

4. E. W. Bullinger, *Number in Scripture*, Fourth Edition (London: Eyre & Spottiswoode (Bible Warehouse) Ltd., 1921), http://www.biblebelievers .org.au/number01.htm (accessed September 30, 2014).

5. Alexandra Twin, "Stocks Crushed," CNNMoney.com, September 29, 2008, http://money.cnn.com/2008/09/29/markets/markets_newyork/ (accessed October 9, 2014).

6. Vendyl Jones, "What are the Hidden Torah Codes? Part I," http:// howardrollin.com/judeochristiangap/Torah%20Codes%201.htm (accessed October 1, 2014); *The Researcher Magazine*, November 1996.

7. The author heard this story in a lecture given by the Institute of Judaic Christian Research in the 1980s.

8. BibleCodeDigest.com, "Isaac Newton, Bible Code Pioneer?", http:// www.biblecodedigest.com/page.php?PageID=74 (accessed October 1, 2014).

9. Wikipedia.org, "1990s Post-Soviet Aliyah," http://en.wikipedia.org/ wiki/1990s_Post-Soviet_aliyah#cite_note-demoscope-1 (accessed October 1, 2014).

10. Adolf Hitler, *Mein Kamf*, http://www.hitler.org/writings/Mein_ Kampf/mkv1cho2.html (accessed October 1, 2014).

11. National Right to Life, "Abortion Statistics" http://www.nrlc.org/uploads/factsheets/FS01AbortionintheUS.pdf (accessed October 1, 2014).

12. Glazerson, *Letters of Fire*, 233–234.

Chapter 5
Visions and Dreams Concerning America's Future Events

1. David Wilkerson, *Set the Trumpet to Thy Mouth* (New Kensington, PA: Whitaker House, 1985), 11.

2. Ibid., 29.

3. David Wilkerson, "Be Alert! David Wilkerson's "latest" prophecy," Sermonindex.com, http://www.sermonindex.net/modules/newbb/viewtopic.php?topic_id=27878&forum=36&40 (accessed October 1, 2014).

4. *David Wilkerson Today* (blog), "An Urgent Message," March 7, 2009, http://davidwilkersontoday.blogspot.com/2009/03/urgent-message.html (accessed October 1, 2014).

5. Bryan Walsh, "Beepocalypse Redux: Honeybees Are Still Dying—and We Still Don't Know Why," *Time*, May 07, 2013, http://science.time.com/2013/05/07/beepocalypse-redux-honey-bees-are-still-dying-and-we-still-dont-know-why/ (accessed October 1, 2014).

6. Remy Melina, "11 Wild Volcano Facts," LiveScience, April 16, 2010, http://www.livescience.com/11001-11-wild-volcano-facts.html (accessed October 1, 2014).

7. Robert Roy Britt, "Super Volcano Will Challenge Civilization, Geologists Warn," LiveScience, March 8, 2005, http://www.livescience.com/200-super-volcano-challenge-civilization-geologists-warn.html (accessed October 1, 2014).

8. Ker Than, "Huge Magma Pocket Lurks Beneath Yellowstone Supervolcano," *National Geographic*, http://news.nationalgeographic.com/news/2013/12/131218-yellowstone-supervolcano-eruption-magma-reservoir/ (accessed October 1, 2014).

9. Becky Oskin, "Yellowstone's Volcano Bigger Than Thought," LiveScience, April 17, 2013, http://www.livescience.com/28821-yellowstone-supervolcano-bigger-plume.html (accessed October 1, 2014).

10. Than, "Huge Magma Pocket Lurks Beneath Yellowstone Supervolcano."

11. The author heard these reports in personal conversations with pastor friends.

12. Williambranham.com, "1933 7 Visions of William Branham," http://www.williambranham.com/featured_stories/1933-7-visions-of-william-branham/ (accessed October 2, 2014).

13. Ibid.

14. Ibid.

15. Ibid.

16. Ibid.

17. Branham.it, "Prophecies of the End Time," http://www.branham.it/joomla/documenti/lingue/prophecies.html (accessed October 2, 2014).

18. Promised Restoration, "Broken Cisterns," July 26, 1964, http://www.en.branham.ru/messageedcc.html?sermonum=1061 (accessed October 15, 2014).

19. Williambranham.com, "1933 7 Visions of William Branham."

Chapter 6
Amazing Prophetic Patterns of American Presidents and World Leaders

1. Gordon Lindsay, *God's Plan of the Ages: As Revealed in the Wonders of Bible Chronology* (Dallas: Christ for the Nations, 1971).

2. Miller Center, "President Harrison Dies—April 4, 1841," University of Virginia, http://millercenter.org/academic/americanpresident/events/04_04 (accessed October 2, 2014).

3. Gordon Lindsay, *America's Presidents and Destiny* (Dallas: Voice of Healing, 1960); Viola Walden, comp., *Sword Scrapbook I* (n.p.: Sword of the Lord Publishers, 1969). Viewed online at Google Books.

4. Ronald C. White Jr., *The Eloquent President* (New York: Random House, 2006).

5. Dale Carnegie, *Lincoln the Unknown* (New York: Dale Carnegie and Associates, 1932).

6. Ward Hill Lamon, Dorothy Lamon Teillard, ed., *Recollections of Abraham Lincoln 1847–1865* (Washington DC: Published by the editor, 1911).

7. Wikipedia.com, "1880 Republican National Convention," http://en.wikipedia.org/wiki/1880_Republican_National_Convention (accessed October 2, 2014).

8. Wikipedia.com, "United States Presidential Election, 1960," http://en.wikipedia.org/wiki/United_States_presidential_election,_1960 (accessed October 2, 2014).

9. Art Toalston, "With JFK Jr.'S Death, Billy Graham Once Again Called Upon for Reflect," Baptist Press, July 23, 1999, http://www.bpnews.net/611/with-jfk-jr8217s-death-billy-graham-once-again-called-upon-for-reflect (accessed October 2, 2014).

10. BBC, "1971: Haitian dictator dies," http://news.bbc.co.uk/onthisday/hi/dates/stories/april/22/newsid_2525000/2525501.stm (accessed October 2, 2014).

11. "Burial At Sea: The Odyssey of JFK's Original Casket," http://deadpresidents.tumblr.com/post/6658190407/burial-at-sea-the-odyssey-of-jfks-original-casket (accessed October 2, 2014).

12. Bill Harris, *The Presidents* (New York: Portland House, 1990).

13. David McCullough, *Truman* (New York: Simon & Schuster, 1992), 730.

14. David McCullough, *Truman, vol. II* (Norwalk, CT: Easton Press, 1982), 595–597.

15. David McCullough, *American History* (New York: Simon & Schuster, 2011).

16. Michael T. Benson "Harry S. Truman as a Modern Cyrus," *BYU Studies* 34, no. 1 (1994).

17. McCullough, *Truman, vol. II*, 598–618.

18. David Jeremiah, *What in the World Is Going On?* (Nashville: Thomas Nelson, 2008), 22.

19. Michael T. Benson, *Harry S. Truman and the Founding of Israel* (Westport, CT: Praeger Publishers, 1997).

20. Bill Clinton, "Remarks to the Knesset in Jerusalem, Israel," October 27, 1994, http://www.gpo.gov/fdsys/pkg/PPP-1994-book2/pdf/PPP-1994-book2-doc-pg1890.pdf (accessed October 2, 2014).

21. Author's conversation with a personal friend of Bill Clinton. This is known among leading Pentecostal ministers.

22. Jonah Goldberg, "Shame on Tim Russert; The New York Times Wakes Up; Not That There's Anything Wrong With That," October 19, 1998, http://m.nationalreview.com/articles/204332/shame-tim-russert-new-york-times-wakes-not-theres-anything-wrong/jonah-goldberg (accessed October 2, 2014).

23. The author's conversations occurred in Israel the year following the election during his holy land tour at a dinner with six Jewish men who are involved in the travel industry. The author considers their observations as very unique.

24. Breitbart TV, "Obama: I'm Not a Socialist—My Favorite President Was a Republican," http://www.breitbart.com/Breitbart-TV/2014/07/09/Obama-Im-Not-A-Socialist-My-Favorite-President-Was-A-Republican (accessed October 2, 2014).

25. According to personal conversations the author had with a former government worker who now works in the private sector.

26. Barton Gellman and Ashkan Soltani, "NSA tracking cellphone locations worldwide, Snowden documents show," December 4, 2013, http://www.washingtonpost.com/world/national-security/nsa-tracking-cellphone-locations-worldwide-snowden-documents-show/2013/12/04/5492873a-5cf2-11e3-bc56-c6ca94801fac_story.html (accessed October 3, 2014).

27. Billy Graham Evangelical Association, "Billy Graham: Pastor to Presidents," http://billygraham.org/story/billy-graham-pastor-to-presidents-2/ (accessed October 3, 2014).

28. According to a private conversation with a friend and ministry colleague.

29. *Against All Odds: In Search of a Miracle*, DVD series, American Trademark Pictures, 2005.

30. Ibid.

31. Ibid.

32. Trevor N. Dupuy, *Elusive Victory: The Arab Israeli Wars, 1947–1974* (New York: Harper & Row, 1978).

33. "In all, it is estimated that some 15 to 20 million Christians were martyred under the Soviet regime", David Barrett, *World Christian Trends* (Pasadena: William Carey Library, 2001), cited by David Taylor, *21 Signs of His Coming: Major Biblical Prophecies Being Fulfilled in Our Generation* (Taylor Publishing Group, 2009), 220.

34. Bob Slosser, *Reagan, Inside Out* (New York: W Pub Group, 1984).

35. Ibid., as quoted in Bod Slosser, "The Prophecy," CBN.com, http://www.cbn.com/spirituallife/BibleStudyAndTheology/discipleship/Slosser_ReaganProphecy.aspx (accessed October 3, 2014).

36. Ibid.

37. Dr. and Mrs. Howard Taylor, *Hudson Taylor's Spiritual Secret* (Chicago: Moody Publishers, 2009).

38. From an original article titled "Spiritual Revival," published in Finland, 1945.

39. David Neff, "Gorbachev and God," *Christianity Today*, October 2000, http://www.ctlibrary.com/ct/2000/octoberweb-only/56.0b.html (accessed October 3, 2014).

40. Ronald Reagan, *An American Life: Ronald Reagan the Autobiography* (New York: Simon & Schuster, 1991).

41. Carl Bernstein, "The Holy Alliance," TIME, February 24, 1992, http://content.time.com/time/magazine/article/0,9171,974931,00.html and http://www.carlbernstein.com/magazine_holy_alliance.php (accessed October 3, 2014).

42. Slosser, *Reagan, Inside Out.*

43. Ibid.

44. Historyorb.com, "Historical Events for Year 1917," http://www.historyorb.com/events/date/1917 (accessed October 3, 2014).

45. *Israel Today Magazine*, no. 110, March 2008.

Chapter 7
Six Prophetic Warnings From General Booth

1. The Salvation Army, "Our History," http://www.salvationarmy.org.uk/uki/salvation_army_heritage (accessed October 3, 2014).

2. Catherine Le Feuvre, *William and Catherine* (England: Monarch Books, 2013).

3. Sermonindex.net, "General Booth in Jerusalem," http://www.sermonindex.net/modules/myalbum/photo.php?lid=38 (accessed October 3, 2014).

4. William Bramwell Booth, "His Life and Ministry," The Gospel Truth, http://www.gospeltruth.net/booth/boothbioshort.htm (accessed October 3, 2014).

5. Trevor Yaxley, *William and Catherine: The Life and Legacy of the Booths* (Ada, MI: Bethany House Publisher, 2003).

6. Goodreads.com, "William Booth Quotes," http://www.goodreads.com/author/quotes/151267.William_Booth (accessed October 3, 2014).

7. Catherine Booth, *Aggressive Christianity* (Philadelphia: National Publishing Association for the Promotion of Holiness, 1883), 171. Viewed online at Google Books.

8. *New York Times*, "Macaulay on Democracy: Curious Letter from Lord Macaulay on American Institutions and Prospects" March 24, 1860, http://www.nytimes.com/1860/03/24/news/macaulay-democracy-curious-letter-lord-macaulay-american-institutions-prospects.html (accessed October 3, 2014).

Chapter 8
Dangerous Soul Ties to Political Spirits

1. Gallup, "Congress and the Public," http://www.gallup.com/poll/1600/congress-public.aspx (accessed October 3, 2014).

2. Thinkexist.com, "Alfred Newman Quotes," http://thinkexist.com/quotation/crime-does-not-pay-as-well-as-politics/531524.html (accessed October 3, 2014).

3. Susan Ratcliffe, Oxford Treasury of Quotations and Sayings (New York: Oxford University Press, 2011).

4. William B. Whitman, ed., *The Quotable Politician* (Guilford, CT: The Lyons Press, 2003).

5. Thinkexist.com, "Larry Hardiman Quotes," http://thinkexist.com/quotation/politics-n-poly-many--tics-blood-sucking/213564.html (accessed October 3, 2014).

6. Thinkexist.com, "Ronald Reagan Quotes," http://thinkexist.com/quotation/politics_is_not_a_bad_profession-if_you_succeed/224781.html (accessed October 3, 2014).

7. Thinkexist.com, "Ronald Reagan Quotes," http://thinkexist.com/ quotation/politics_is_supposed_to_be_the_second_oldest/11926.html (accessed October 3, 2014).

8. Whitman, ed., *The Quotable Politician.*

9. Ibid.

10. Ibid.

11. Thinkexist.com, "Jay Leno Quotes," http://thinkexist.com/quotation/ if_god_had_wanted_us_to_vote-he_would_have_given/181927.html (accessed October 3, 2014).

12. The information was provide in private conversations with the author.

13. Flavius Josephus, *Antiquities of the Jews Book I*, Christian Classic Ethereal Library, http://www.ccel.org/ccel/josephus/works/files/ant-1.htm (accessed October 4, 2014).

14. Ibid.

15. Christimages.com, "The Tower of Babel," http://christimages.org/ biblestories/tower_of_babel.htm (accessed October 4, 2014).

16. Christimages.com, "European Union Poster," http://christimages.org/ Images_Genesis/european-union-poster-babel.jpg (accessed October 4, 2014).

17. Pittsburg Post-Gazette, "New coalition?: The World Must Brace for the BRICS," April 1, 2013, http://www.post-gazette.com/opinion/editorials/ 2013/04/01/New-coalition-The-world-must-brace-for-the-BRICS/stories/ 201304010180 (accessed October 4, 2014).

Chapter 9
America's Roman Road to the Bottom

1. As told to the author in a personal conversation with a pastor friend who was at the dinner.

2. New World Encyclopedia, "Mayflower Compact," http://www .newworldencyclopedia.org/entry/Mayflower_Compact (accessed October 4, 2014).

3. Maryland.gov, "Two Acts of Toleration: 1649 and 1826," http:// msa.maryland.gov/msa/speccol/sc2200/sc2221/000025/html/intro.html (accessed October 4, 2014); Yale Law School, "Maryland Toleration Act; September 21, 1649, An Act Concerning Religion," http://avalon.law.yale .edu/18th_century/maryland_toleration.asp (accessed October 4, 2014).

4. PennTreatyMuseum.org, "William Penn and His Pennsylvania Colony," http://penntreatymuseum.org/penn.php (accessed October 4, 2014).

5. Timothy Crater, *In God We Trust: Stories of Faith in American History* (Colorado Springs, CO: Chariot Victor Publishing, 1997).

6. The American Presidency Project, "Address Before the Attorney General's Conference on Law Enforcement Problems," February 15, 1950, http://www.presidency.ucsb.edu/ws/?pid=13707 (accessed October 4, 2014).

7. Harry S. Truman Library & Museum, "Address in New York City at the Convention of the Columbia Scholastic Press Association," http://trumanlibrary.org/publicpapers/index.php?pid=945&st=&st1= (accessed October 4, 2014).

8. John Dart, "Billy Graham Recalls Help From Hearst," *Los Angeles Times*, June 7, 1997, http://articles.latimes.com/1997-06-07/local/me-1034_1_billy-graham-recalls (accessed October 4, 2014).

9. *Los Angeles Times*, "Nixon: 'Go After' Jewish Contributors," http://articles.latimes.com/1996-12-08/news/mn-7124_1_jewish-contributors (accessed October 4, 2014).

10. Chris Gentilviso, "NSA Spied On Martin Luther King Jr., Declassified Documents Reveal," Huffington Post, http://www.huffingtonpost.com/2013/09/26/nsa-martin-luther-king-jr_n_3995150.html (accessed October 4, 2014); *Los Angeles Times*, "FBI Spied on Coretta Scott King, Files Show," http://articles.latimes.com/2007/aug/31/nation/na-king31 (accessed October 4, 2014).

11. Monticello.org, "Quotations on the Jefferson Memorial," http://www.monticello.org/site/jefferson/quotations-jefferson-memorial (accessed October 4, 2014).

12. Emma Lazarus, "The New Colossus," portion of Lazarus's poem engraved on the pedestal of the Statue of Liberty.

13. Americans United for the Separation of Church and State, "Prayer and the Public Schools Religion, Education & Your Rights," https://www.au.org/resources/publications/prayer-and-the-public-schools (accessed October 4, 2014).

14. Merrill Matthews, "We've Crossed the Tipping Point; Most Americans Now Receive Government Benefits," Forbes, July 2, 2014, http://www.forbes.com/sites/merrillmatthews/2014/07/02/weve-crossed-the-tipping-point-most-americans-now-receive-government-benefits/ (accessed October 4, 2014); Terence P. Jeffrey, "Census: 49% of Americans Get Gov't Benefits; 82M in Households on Medicaid," CNS News, October 23, 2013, http://cnsnews.com/news/article/terence-p-jeffrey/census-49-americans-get-gov-t-benefits-82m-households-medicaid (accessed October 4, 2014).

15. Terence P. Jeffrey, "Census Bureau: Means-Tested Gov't Benefit Recipients Outnumber Full-Time Year-Round Workers," CNS News, October 24, 2013, http://cnsnews.com/news/article/terence-p-jeffrey/census-bureau-means-tested-govt-benefit-recipients-outnumber-full (accessed October 4, 2014).

16. National Right to Life, "Abortion Statistics."

17. A. E. R. Boak, *Manpower Shortage and the Fall of the Roman Empire in the West* (Ann Arbor, MI: University of Michigan Press, 1955).

18. Lactantlus, *Divine Institutes, Book VII,* http://www.newadvent.org/fathers/07017.htm (accessed October 4, 2014).

19. Ibid.

20. A. H. M. Jones, *The Later Roman Empire 284–602* (n.p.: Basil Blackwell Ltd, 1964).

21. As stated in Trygve's Digital Diary, "How Long Is It?" March 12, 2006, http://www.trygve.com/taxcode.html (accessed October 5, 2014).

22. Cayman Net News, "Editorial: We Are Not the United States of America's Policeman," May 12, 2009, http://www.caymannetnews.com/article.php?news_id=15437 (accessed October 5, 2014).

Chapter 10
Is It 1933 All Over Again?

1. Jewishvirtuallibrary.org, "The Holocaust: Kristallnacht—'Night of Broken Glass,'" http://www.jewishvirtuallibrary.org/jsource/Holocaust/kristalltoc.html (accessed October 5, 2014).

2. United States Holocaust Memorial Museum, "The 'Night of Broken Glass,'" http://www.ushmm.org/outreach/en/article.php?ModuleId=10007697 (accessed October 5, 2014).

3. Franklin D. Roosevelt, "Inaugural Address, March 4, 1933," The American Presidency Project, http://www.presidency.ucsb.edu/ws/?pid=14473 (accessed October 5, 2014).

4. Kitty Werthmann, "America Truly Is the Greatest Country in the World," http://www.armsmart.com/includes/emails/2011/1938_Germany.html (accessed October 5, 2014).

5. As quoted in David Nichols, *Adolf Hitler* (Santa Barbara, CA: ABC-CLIO Inc., 2000).

6. Werthmann, "America Truly Is the Greatest Country in the World."

7. Ibid.

8. Charles W. Cooke, "The Great Ammunition Myths," National Review Online, March 5, 2013, http://www.nationalreview.com/articles/342161/great-ammunition-myth-charles-c-w-cooke (accessed October 5, 2014).

9. Study of Terrorism and Responses to Terrorism, "Hot Spots of Terrorism and Other Crimes in the United States, 1970 to 2008," January 31, 2012, http://www.start.umd.edu/sites/default/files/files/publications/research_briefs/LaFree_Bersani_HotSpotsOfUSTerrorism.pdf (accessed October 5, 2014); Public Intelligence, "DHS-University of Maryland Study: Hot Spots of Terrorism and Other Crimes in the United States 1970 to

2008," February 10, 2012, https://publicintelligence.net/dhs-umd-terrorism-hot-spots/ (accessed October 5, 2014).

10. This information was provided by an anonymous source.

11. As quoted in Erwin W. Lutzer, *Hitler's Cross* (Chicago: Moody Publishers, 2012).

12. Ibid.

13. From personal conversations with the author and Lester Sumrall.

14. As quoted in Andy Andrews, *How Do You Kill 11 Million People?* (Nashville: Thomas Nelson, 2011).

15. Ibid.

16. Corrie ten Boom Museum, "History," http://www.corrietenboom.com/history.htm (accessed October 5, 2014).

17. WW2History.com, "Tehran Conference Begins," http://ww2history.com/key_moments/Western/Tehran_Conference_begins (accessed October 5, 2014).

18. WW2History.com, "Yalta," http://ww2history.com/experts/Max_Hastings/Yalta (accessed October 5, 2014).

19. Louis Charbonneau, "Iran, Big Power Nuclear Talks Hit Snag on Centrifuge Research," Reuters.com, January 8, 2014, http://www.reuters.com/article/2014/01/08/us-iran-nuclear-idUSBREA0718V20140108 (accessed October 5, 2014).

20. Ibid.

21. Fred Lucas, "Iranian President: 'World Powers Surrendered to Iranian Nation's Will'," TheBlaze, January 14, 2014, http://www.theblaze.com/stories/2014/01/14/iranian-president-world-powers-surrendered-to-iranian-nations-will/ (accessed October 5, 2014).

Chapter 11
Behind the Scenes—The Unaffordable Care Act

1. Geffory Dickens, "What They Said Before the Train Wreck: The Top 10 Worst Quotes Pushing ObamaCare," November 18, 2013, http://newsbusters.org/blogs/geoffrey-dickens/2013/11/18/what-they-said-debacle-top-10-worst-quotes-pushing-obamacare#ixzz2sNDKgqp0 (accessed October 5, 2014).

2. Jonathan Capehart, "Pelosi defends her infamous health care remark," *Washington Post, Post Partisan* (blog), June 20, 2012, http://www.washingtonpost.com/blogs/post-partisan/post/pelosi-defends-her-infamous-health-care-remark/2012/06/20/gJQAqch6qV_blog.html (accessed October 5, 2014).

3. This was relayed to the author personally by a former U.S. Congressman during dinner together.

4. This was reported by an administration leader in Israel who was told this by someone in the Obama administration.

5. Bill O'Reilly, "TRANSCRIPT: Bill O'Reilly Interviews President Obama," Fox News, February 2, 2012, http://www.foxnews.com/politics/2014/02/02/transcript-bill-oreilly-interviews-president-obama/ (accessed October 5, 2014).

6. WND, "Schools Tag Kids With RFID Chips," September 15, 2010, http://www.wnd.com/2010/09/203529/ (accessed October 5, 2014).

7. Ibid.; David Kravets, "Tracking School Children With RFID Tags? It's All About the Benjamins," September 9, 2012, www.wired.com/threatlevel/2012/09/rfid-chip-student-monitoring/ (accessed October 5, 2014).

8. Beth Bacheldor, "Missouri School District Puts RFID on Buses," FRID Journal, http://www.rfidjournal.com/articles/view?2808 (accessed October 5, 2014).

9. Perry says this information was given directly to him by the minister who was on the plane and carried on the conversation with the doctor himself. He has requested that Perry not mention his name to prevent people from seeking him out for more information.

10. This information on the chip and the cost was given to one of my staff members while attending a regional conference in Atlanta, Georgia, where the chip and the process were discussed in detail.

11. In a personal conversation the author had with a state senator from Georgia.

12. Fredrick Kunkle and Rosalind S. Helderman "Human Microchips Seen by Some in Virginia House as Device of Antichrist," *Washington Post*, February 10, 2010, http://www.washingtonpost.com/wp-dyn/content/article/2010/02/09/AR2010020903796.html?hpid=newswell (accessed October 5, 2014).

13. State Rep. Babette Josephs, "Josephs Introduces Bill to Ban the Human Implantation of ID Devices," http://www.pahouse.com/pr/182092208.asp (accessed October 5, 2014).

14. YouTube.com, "Joe Biden Says There Is an Agenda to Get Everyone Microchipped and Brain Scanned," https://www.youtube.com/watch?v=FQw68jl7KXc (accessed October 6, 2014).

15. WND, "U.S. Military Developing Spychips for Soldiers," http://www.wnd.com/2012/05/u-s-military-developing-spychips-for-soldiers/ (accessed October 9, 2014).

16. A nurse at a major hospital showed the author a printout of the twenty pages under the new health care mandate. The author personally saw the place to identify if the patient had a chip implant.

17. GPO.org, "H. R. 3962," http://www.gpo.gov/fdsys/pkg/BILLS
-111hr3962eh/pdf/BILLS-111hr3962eh.pdf (accessed October 6, 2014).

18. The author recalls seeing this reported on Canadian news.

19. Liz Gannes, "Passwords on Your Skin and In Your Stomach....," June
3, 2013, http://allthingsd.com/20130603/passwords-on-your-skin-and-in
-your-stomach-inside-googles-wild-motorola-research-projects-video/
(accessed October 6, 2014).

20. Victoria Woollaston, "The Hi-Tech Tattoo That Could Replace ALL
Your Passwords....," Mail Online, May 30, 2013, http://www.dailymail
.co.uk/sciencetech/article-2333203/Moto-X-Motorola-reveals-plans-ink
-pills-replace-ALL-passwords.html (accessed October 6, 2014).

21. Gannes, "Passwords on Your Skin and In Your Stomach...."

22. CBS News, "Some Israelis Insulted By Obama Picture," http://www
.cbsnews.com/news/some-israelis-insulted-by-obama-picture/ (accessed
October 6, 2014); Gil Ronen and Hana Levi Julian, "The Great Obama
Shoe Photo Debate: What Was He Trying to Say?," June 12, 2009, http://
www.israelnationalnews.com/News/News.aspx/131837#.VDKDdGddVow
(accessed October 6, 2014).

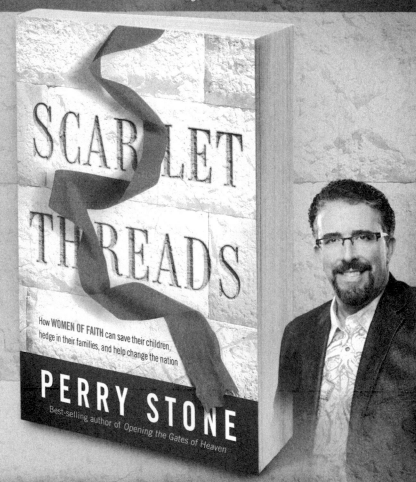